A L A S K A

NORTH TO THE FUTURE

Nancy Leichner
President, Wyndham Publications

ALASKA

NORTH TO THE FUTURE

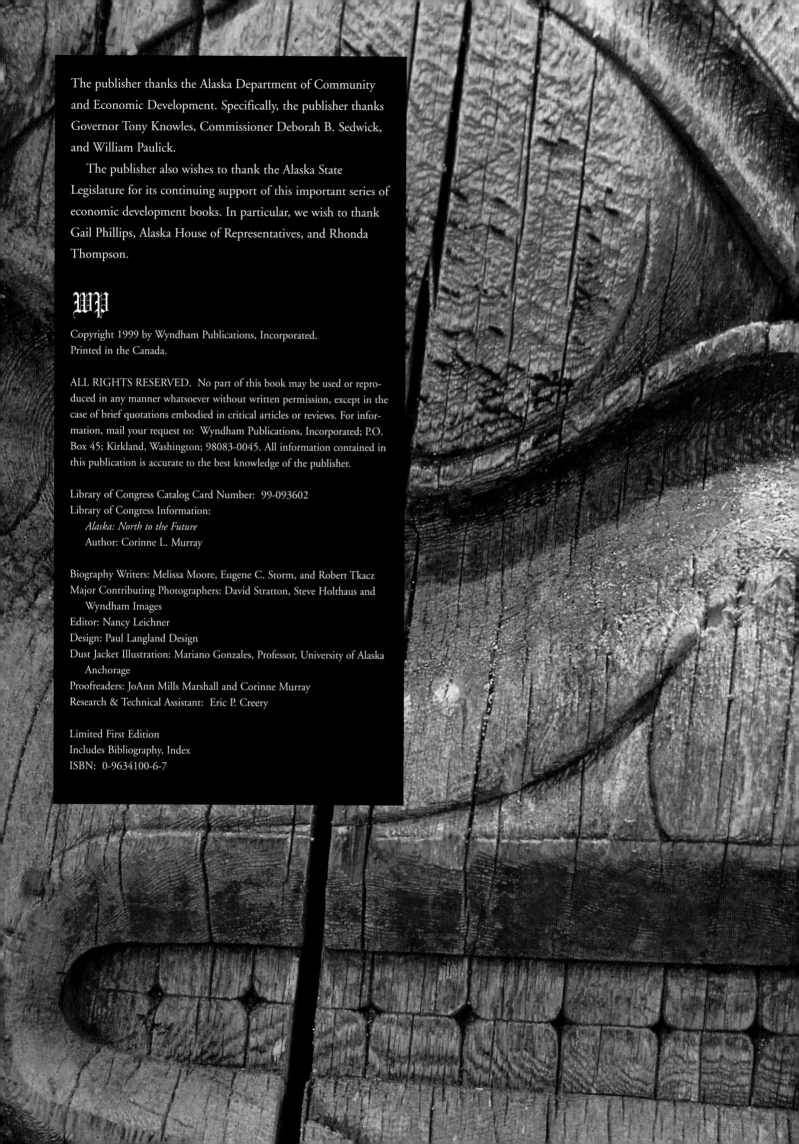

The publisher thanks the Alaska Department of Community and Economic Development. Specifically, the publisher thanks Governor Tony Knowles, Commissioner Deborah B. Sedwick, and William Paulick.

The publisher also wishes to thank the Alaska State Legislature for its continuing support of this important series of economic development books. In particular, we wish to thank Gail Phillips, Alaska House of Representatives, and Rhonda Thompson.

𝔚𝔓

Library of Congress Catalog Card Number: 99-093602
Library of Congress Information:
    Alaska: North to the Future
    Author: Corinne L. Murray

Biography Writers: Melissa Moore, Eugene C. Storm, and Robert Tkacz
Major Contributing Photographers: David Stratton, Steve Holthaus and
    Wyndham Images
Editor: Nancy Leichner
Design: Paul Langland Design
Dust Jacket Illustration: Mariano Gonzales, Professor, University of Alaska
    Anchorage
Proofreaders: JoAnn Mills Marshall and Corinne Murray
Research & Technical Assistant: Eric P. Creery

Limited First Edition
Includes Bibliography, Index
ISBN: 0-9634100-6-7

TABLE OF CONTENTS

Photo by Steve Holthaus

Courtesy of Fairbanks Convention and Visitors Bureau; Photo by Scott McLean

PART ONE

Chapter One
A Place Apart 8

Chapter Two
A Legendary Legacy 22

Chapter Three
Welcoming The World — The Visitor Industry 34

Chapter Four
Making Connections 50

Chapter Five
Global Communications Start At The Top 62

Chapter Six
A Resourceful Alliance 72

Chapter Seven
Bounty Of Land And Sea 90

Chapter Eight
The Outdoors Adventure 104

Chapter Nine
The Original Alaskans 130

Chapter Ten
The Human Ingredient 148

PART TWO: CITIES AND BOROUGHS 172

PART THREE: KEY PLAYERS
Government and Community Organizations 194
Networks 206
Raw Materials And Production 246
Seafood Industry 266
Business And Professional Services 274
Quality Of Life 294
Building Alaska 308
Marketplace, Accommodations, Tours And Journeys 322

Index Of Key Players 332
Bibliography 335
Index 336

INTRODUCTION

They call it The Great Land.

They say you have to see it to believe it. When you do see it, you still won't believe that a land so vast, so beautiful, so diverse, and so exciting can really be part of twenty-first century America.

Alaska is a vital, productive state, built on a rich and fascinating historical foundation. It's a cooperative place, where business, government, and the workforce form a dynamic and successful partnership to carry on the commerce of the coming millennium. A prosperous place, where 1997 saw a Gross State Product of nearly $26 billion. An adventuresome place, where "North to the Future" is more than a license-plate slogan.

Geographically and commercially, Alaska has been a global center since the birth of air travel. Technologically, it is rapidly becoming the newest frontier in space-age communications and scientific development. Philosophically, Alaska has maintained its grip on the human imagination for hundreds of years, and intrigued Americans for nearly a century and a half. This book offers an overview of the opportunities and challenges of the modern northland.

One element bridges the gap between the gold-rush Alaska of Jack London and the economic powerhouse of today. Something blends the many cultures, lifestyles, and viewpoints of this great country into a single vibrant whole. That unifying element is, of course, Alaska's people, and the spirit that drives them.

The spirit of Alaska is one of enterprise and adventure, of independence and pride, of respect for the land, and an enduring comradeship among the latter-day pioneers who live and work on what is still known as The Last Frontier.

This is Alaska. This is the future.

Welcome.

Chapter One

A PLACE APART

A PLACE APART

SIX WORLDS IN ONE

It's big — 586,412 square miles. Alaska is one-fifth the size of the contiguous U.S., the "Lower 48." It's more than twice the size of Texas, and larger than the three next-biggest states combined. It contains most of the continent's highest mountains, 45.5 percent of the nation's wetlands, and over 6,000 miles of coastline. Alaska is so diverse in topography, climate, and population that it can be naturally divided into six great regions. Each region is larger in itself than most states, and even many countries.

SOUTHEASTERN — This region, which includes the Alexander Archipelago, is an area of temperate rain forests with the state's greatest timber stands, and a comparatively mild climate. Known as the Alaska Panhandle, Southeastern contains about a thousand of the state's 1,800 named islands, more than a million acres of federally-designated wilderness (much of it in the Tongass National Forest, the country's largest), and the famed Inside Passage (beloved of cruise-ship passengers with its fjords, glaciers, and waterfalls), the state capital, and many picturesque communities.

Juneau — This was the first Alaska city established as a direct result of a gold strike in 1880. Proclaimed territorial capital in 1912, Juneau was retained as state capital. Government is still the primary employer for Juneau's nearly 31,000 residents, with tourism and commercial fishing and mining also bolstering the local economy.

Ketchikan — An ethnically and economically diverse community, Ketchikan is home to the world's largest collection of totem poles. The city has a population of approximately 9,000. It is located on the western coast of Revillagigedo Island, and has an economy based on fishing, timber, and tourism.

Anchorage.

Distant view of Wrangell from Nemo Point Campground and Overlook.

Photo by Steve Holthaus

Courtesy of Anchorage Convention and Visitors Bureau; Photo by Dennis Buller

Photo by Steve Holthaus

In every region of Alaska, Mother Nature has blessed the state with a wide range of fascinating and unique wildlife. In Alaska, it is still possible for the grizzlies, mountain goats and waterfowl to roam their natural habitat with a minimum of human intervention.

Petersburg — This bustling town of about 3,500 people is located on the north end of Mitkof Island. It grew from a Norwegian pioneer's homestead around the turn of the century. Several fish canneries and processing plants are located here (see Chapter 7).

Sitka — With more than 4,000 square miles in total geographic area, Sitka is the largest city in the United States. An old Tlingit settlement, the city's population of 9,000 is still 20 percent Native. Located on the west coast of Baranof Island and discovered by Vitus Bering in 1741, Sitka was once the second capital of Russian America, and was also the capital of U.S. Alaska until 1906.

Wrangell — This city of 2,500 is also an old Tlingit settlement. In the early 1800s, Russian fur traders established a trading post here, and by the end of the 1800s, Wrangell had become an important staging area for all three gold rushes. Today, the city's economic mainstays include timber and wood products, seafood, and tourism.

Skagway — Today a tourist-oriented town and important freight-shipping port of less than 1,000 people, Skagway was once the most famous city in Alaska, serving as the gateway to the Klondike gold fields via the White Pass and Chilkoot Trails.

SOUTHWESTERN — This region encompasses the vast Alaska Peninsula, and the lonely, far-scattered Aleutian Islands. It shares lush Kodiak Island with Southcentral/Gulf Coast Alaska. The Bristol Bay fishery is the nation's most productive, and its fleet is based in communities like King Salmon, Naknek, and Dillingham. Katmai National Park and Preserve, containing the Valley of 10,000 Smokes, is located in this region (see Chapter 8). One of the busiest, and prettiest, of Alaska's fishing and crabbing ports graces the area.

Wrangell's industrial waterfront and harbor.

Courtesy of the City of Wrangell; Photo by Ivan Simonek

Kodiak — This was the first capital of Russian America and was once the center of the fur trade. Today, with a population of 7,000 (nearly 13 percent of whom are Native), Kodiak is the hub of the region's commercial fishing industry. This beautiful green island is home to one of the earth's largest carnivores, the gigantic Kodiak Brown Bear.

The Aleutians — The Aleutian Islands make up one of the longest archipelagos on earth, a continuation of the Aleutian Range stretching about 1,100 miles from the Alaska Peninsula in Southwestern, westward toward Siberia's Kamchatka Peninsula; separating the Bering Sea from the Pacific.

The islands were visited and named by Vitus Bering in 1741. But, if current anthropological theory is valid, the Aleutians were discovered by Siberian hunters thousands of years ago. Their descendants gradually occupied the islands and migrated eastward to the mainland.

Around 150 small islands compose the chain, with a total land area of 6,912 square miles. Only two, Unalaska and Unmiak, are over 1,000 square miles in area; most are considerably smaller. Attu and Kiska, which were briefly occupied by the Japanese during World War II, are only 350 and 106 square miles, respectively.

The Aleutians have been described as barren, rugged, remote, and even desolate. The few trees that can survive are stunted, but grasses grow in abundance, which has helped a flourishing sheep-raising industry. Settlements are small. It is hard to imagine that anyone would *want* these isolated chunks of rock. But in 1942, the Japanese saw the Aleutians as stepping-stones toward the U.S. mainland. The establishment of a major U.S. military base on Adak, only recently closed and currently available for development, added to a regional economy primarily based on fishing, hunting, and sheep-raising.

The Native peoples of the islands have long been lumped together under the label "Aleuts," although they are actually divided into distinct tribes: Alutiiq, Unangan, and Yu'pik Eskimos. They are all shareholders in the Aleut Native Corporation (see Chapter 9).

The principal supply and trading center of the islands is Unalaska/Dutch Harbor (pop. approx. 4,000), located on Unalaska and Amaknak Islands. In 1768, Unalaska became an important center in the Russian fur-seal trade. In 1825, the Russian Orthodox Church of the Holy Ascension of Christ was built, and the founding priest composed the first written form of the Aleut language. The church is now the oldest Russian Orthodox cruciform-style church in North America. It was nearly destroyed in WWII — not, ironically, by the Japanese who bombed the island, but by evacuating U.S. troops. Most of the Native population was relocated to Southeastern for the duration of the war. Unalaska is also the site of the Jesse Lee Orphan's Home, established by the Methodist Church in 1880.

Commercial fishing is essential to the economy of the Aleutians. The cold waters, reaching depths of more than 25,000 feet in the nearby Aleutian Trench, create an ideal fish habitat for northern species of important food fish. The industry is especially important to Unalaska, as Dutch Harbor ranks as the nation's number-one port in fish volume and value. The city has also been developing a tourist trade, and is a frequent port-of-call for cruise ships.

The vast mountain ranges of Alaska are deeply carved by thousands of glaciers — rivers of ice that appear to be motionless, but are actually in constant, albeit incredibly slow, motion.

Courtesy of Wyndham Images

SOUTHCENTRAL/GULF COAST — This relatively temperate region surrounding Cook Inlet and Prince William Sound is home to Alaska's largest city, and is the state's economic, technological, and transportation hub.

Anchorage — Today a city for the 21st century, Anchorage was founded as a railroad tent-town at the head of Cook Inlet in 1915. Now a full-fledged metropolis with a population of about a quarter of a million, Anchorage is where many of Alaska's most important businesses and industries are headquartered, and where state and federal government also maintain a strong presence.

A comparatively mild climate makes Anchorage a favorite residential area for more than half the state's population. Temperatures rarely drop far below zero in winter, or climb much above 80 degrees in summer. Snowfall is usually moderate, and while daylight is indeed limited during part of the year, Anchorage enjoys close to 20 hours of light most summer days.

Because Anchorage is centrally located, via polar routes, among many major worldwide destinations, its airport serves as a midpoint stopover for air traffic, and the city itself provides convenient amenities for international business. As a result, residents of this "air crossroads of the world" enjoy a cosmopolitan lifestyle with a distinctive international flair. Musical and theatrical performances abound; museums and galleries of history and art entertain and enlighten; world-class restaurants and hotels offer the finest in cuisine and accommodations. Tourist-friendly neighborhood hangouts can still be found amid all the city glitter, and one of the world's great wilderness terrains is right in the backyard. With its hundred miles of trails for biking, hiking, and cross-country skiing, Anchorage is inviting territory for outdoor enthusiasts. The hundreds of thousands of acres of state and national parkland, located close at hand, offer relaxation and recreation to residents and visitors alike.

When a glacier calves, it is a most dramatic display. The ice thunderously cracks as a portion splashes into the water, revealing the other-worldly blue of the pressurized ice within.

Courtesy of Ketchikan Visitors Bureau

Courtesy of Wyndham Images

In many areas, it is easy to get a sense of the frontier atmosphere that is readily apparent in much of Alaska, since such structures as old and weathered docks and the ruins of abandoned mines, among other things, may be a short ride — or even walking distance — from downtown areas.

Native art from Alaska can be quite distinctive and dramatically beautiful. To the left is a carved face of a totem found on Chief Shakes Island, located in the City of Wrangell. To the lower right is a picture of interior carvings in Chief Shakes Tribal House.

Anchorage is not all streamlined modernism and big business. The annual Fur Rendezvous celebration each February harks back to the city's trading-post past, and reflects the adventurous spirit of its future. Competitors in the world-famous Iditarod Sled Dog Race also begin their 1,110 mile journey to Nome here each year.

Palmer and Wasilla — These two agriculturally-oriented towns of about 5,000 inhabitants each are in the heart of the Matanuska/Susitna Valleys farm country. The Alaska State Fair is held near Palmer each year, and the West Coast Tsunami Warning Center is also located here. Residents can enjoy a rural lifestyle within an easy driving distance of Anchorage's amenities.

Seward — This southern terminus of the Alaska Railroad has a population of about 3,000. Seward is located on Resurrection Bay on the southeast coast of the Kenai Peninsula.

Valdez — This beautiful ice-free deepwater port on Prince William Sound has a population of about 4,500. Valdez is the terminus of the TransAlaska Pipeline.

Kenai — First an Athabascan village, then a Russian trading post on the west coast of the Kenai Peninsula, today, with a population of 7,000, Kenai's economy is based on oil extraction and service and commercial fishing. The nearby Kenai River boasts the finest King and Silver Salmon runs in the world.

Homer — Built on a 4.5-mile spit extending into Kachemak Bay on southwestern Kenai Peninsula, this city of 4,200 is known as the "Halibut Capital of the World." Among its many positive attributes, Homer may list stunning scenery, small-town charm, and a notable artists' community.

Whittier — This tiny town of 300 is about to experience an overwhelming transformation. By land, Whittier is accessible only by train; however, this will change once road access is completed in 2000. When the road opens, Whittier's ice-free deepwater port on Prince William Sound will be easily accessible, and this isolated community will face a new millennium with endless opportunities.

INTERIOR — This region encompasses thousands of square miles of tundra and taiga. It is a land of great caribou herds, impressive natural wonders, and frontier-flavored settlements.

Fairbanks — The city was founded in 1902 on the banks of the Chena River after the discovery of gold nearby. With a population of over 30,000, it combines urban sophistication with honkytonk frontier charm. While the climate can be extreme, with temperatures ranging from minus 50 degrees Fahrenheit in winter, to the mid-90s in summer, Fairbanksians find plenty to enjoy year round in their unique hometown. Civic celebrations include the annual Midnight Sun Baseball Game and the Winter Carnival.

The main campus of the University of Alaska is located here, with its many research and experimental projects, programs, and facilities (see Chapter 10).

Fairbanks is the commercial center of Interior Alaska. While there are other towns in the area, few boast more than a couple of thousand inhabitants and many have fewer than 50. Still, places like Nenana, Chena Hot Springs, Eagle, and Tok have their own appeal to residents and visitors alike.

Winter scene in the Paxton Lake Area.

WESTERN/BERING SEA COAST — In this region, settlements are few and far between in tundra country. Mining and commercial fishing support the region's economy. Native inhabitants are primarily Athabascans and Yu'pik Eskimos. It is in the far western reaches of the Bering Sea that the United States makes its closest approach to Asia; just 2.5 miles of very cold water (and the International Date Line) separate American Little Diomede Island from Russian Big Diomede.

FAR NORTH/ARCTIC — This is the Land of the Midnight Sun, tundra, and permafrost. It is home to unique wildlife and the Native Alaskans (mainly Inupiat Eskimos) who have lived above the Arctic Circle for millennia. It is a key area for resource development. Major settlements are:

Nome — Located on the Seward Peninsula, on Norton Sound, in the western Arctic region, this is a city of 5,000 inhabitants, more than half of whom are Native. Nome has a rich and storied history and is today the finish line for the annual Iditarod Sled Dog Race.

Barrow — This is the Land of the Midnight Sun, the northernmost community in the United States. Located on the Chukchi Sea near Point Barrow, this site was inhabited as early as 500 AD. Today, Barrow has a population of approximately 4,400. About 70 percent of the residents are Inupiat.

Kotzebue — About 75 percent of the population of Kotzebue are Native, and mainly Inupiat; the total population is approximately 3,300. Located on Baldwin Peninsula, Kotzebue Sound, the city is the commercial and transportation center for the area's villages.

Photo by David Stratton

One may not generally associate riverboats with Alaska, but they have, in fact, played an important role in the growth of Fairbanks. This riverboat is on display at Alaskaland, a park in the City of Fairbanks.

Courtesy of Alaska Forest Association

Keeping Alaska beautiful is more than big business; for many, it is a moral imperative. Recognizing that the future of the environment and the future of the industry go hand-in-hand, the Alaska Forest Association, along with many other organizations, supports sound forest-management practices that protect fish habitat, water quality, and forest regeneration.

A LEGENDARY LEGACY

CHRONOLOGY OF ADVENTURE

From the early Russian fur trade, through the gold strike at Nome during the Gold Rush of '98, and on to the vigorous and diversified economy of today and tomorrow, Alaska's wealth has always been founded on the strengths of its people.

The precise dates and possible migration routes which led the first people to The Great Land are debated. However, the region's modern history certainly begins in 1741 with the voyage of Vitus Bering, a Danish explorer retained by the Tsar of Russia, for whom Bering promptly claimed the land.

What the Russians wanted was fur, and they found it in abundance. In fact, sea otters were hunted to the verge of extinction. In the hands of merchant-adventurers like Alexander Baranof and Grigorii Shelikof, the trade flourished, leading to the founding of such settlements as Sitka, Kodiak, and Kenai. Unfortunately, their prosperity was built by exploiting the Native population. Native peoples led an uprising at Sitka in 1804, but their rebellion sparked a massacre. Russian Orthodox missionaries and officials protested the abuses and excesses exhibited by some of their countrymen; but, given the general indifference of the imperial court, little change took place. However, they were able to establish their faith, and the Russian Orthodox religion is still practiced in many parts of the state today.

While the Russians were engaged in settling their new territory, Spanish, French, and English explorers were sailing the coastal waters, discovering and naming prominent features of the landscape. To look at a map of Alaska is to read the history of those early voyagers. Place names like Revillagigedo Island and Prince William Sound reflect the loyalties of the European adventurers who brought the western world north. Native names also still prevail across the state in places like Egigik, Anaktuvak, Hoonah, and Angoon. On his historic third and final voyage of discovery from 1776 to 1779, the great British explorer Captain James Cook charted the waters and mapped much of the

Gold fever gave rise to a bustling tent city called Nome.

Fishing boats crowd Ketchikan's harbor circa 1930.

coastline. He bestowed place names that still reflect his influence: Cape Farewell, Turnagain Arm, Mt. Redoubt, and of course, Cook Inlet. Agents of such far-flung business concerns as the Hudson's Bay Company and Northern Commercial Company were often as much explorers as traders.

But, when most people think of Alaskan history, it's GOLD that leaps to mind. Although the precious ore had been discovered by the Russians as early as 1848, and mines were established at Juneau in 1880, it was not until the Anvil Creek strike near Nome nearly 20 years later that Alaska felt the full impact of the infectious Gold Fever.

Probably the most famous episode in the northern history, the Klondike Gold Rush of 1898 brought both prosperity and attention to Alaska. Gold had been struck in the Yukon Territory, and getting there would be considerably less than half the fun. By the time the enormous flood of would-be treasure-hunters hit Seattle, the nearest major seaport for departure in the Lower 48, Jefferson "Soapy" Smith was already planning to swindle them in Skagway with the help of a roll of small bills wrapped around a bar of soap. Other entrepreneurs with similar plans lay in wait for the unsuspecting.

From Skagway and nearby Dyea, thousands of optimists struggled, mostly on foot, up to and over the treacherous Chilkoot and White Pass Trails, laboring to reach the mighty Yukon River, down which they could float to the Klondike goldfields once the ice melted. Many died from exhaustion, exposure, illness and mishap. Their pack animals dropped in their tracks by the hundreds, thereby giving the Pass and town of Deadhorse in the Yukon Territory their names.

For the sturdy treasure seekers came support industries such as saloons, inns, shops, laundries, and brothels. Gamblers, conmen, and even a few genuine entrepreneurs — everyone who wanted to strike gold in the miners' pockets instead of up the creeks and on the beaches — brought their businesses north. Thus, much of the early Alaskan economy, industry, and growth was literally built on gold.

Once they finally arrived at Dawson, where George Carmack had filed the discovery claim that triggered the rush, things only got worse for most. For every profitable gold strike, there were a hundred disappointments. Still, for several years, there was plenty of money circulating in Dawson. Some of that revenue inevitably found its way back across the border.

Meanwhile, gold was discovered near Nome, which then experienced its own boom. Local populations soared with the steady stream of these newest prospectors. Nome qualified as Alaska's largest city at one time, with 20,000 inhabitants; and the discovery of gold in the Tanana River Valley led to the founding of Fairbanks in 1902 (see Chapter 1).

After all the placer gold had been panned and rockered out, hardrock mining continued in some areas, and still does. The Rush of '98 indirectly led to the discovery of other mineral resources such as silver, copper, lead, zinc, and coal, which are still mined today (see Chapter 6). However, the real legacy of the Great Gold Rush is the adventurous, can-do, try-anything spirit of The Last Frontier.

Courtesy of The Anchorage Museum of History and Art, B65.18.344

Mining with Long Tom on Sub Marine Beach near Nome.

Customs House at the Summit of Chilkoot Pass.

WW2 soldiers loading onto a train at Whittier.

SEWARD WAS RIGHT

When Secretary of State William Seward urged the U.S. government to purchase Alaska from the Russians for $7.2 million in 1867, scoffers around the country sneered at "Seward's Folly." By the turn of the century, however, the value of the region's natural resources was being appreciated, and in 1912, the Territory of Alaska was formally organized.

Mining; fishing; logging; and starting in the 1930s, agriculture; were the mainstays of commerce and trade until World War II. A U.S. military presence had been established in Alaska since the Purchase in 1867. After the bombing of Pearl Harbor, the federal government saw invasion and occupation by Japanese forces as a very real threat; and it was. Dutch Harbor was bombed in 1942, and the Aleutian islands of Kiska and Attu were briefly occupied (see Chapter 1). During this period, the role of the military in Alaska was solidified by the establishment of Army and Air Force bases at Fort Wainwright (then Ladd Field) in Fairbanks, Elmendorf Air Force Base in Anchorage, and a major installation on Adak Island in the Aleutians which was closed in 1998. At the same time, the Territory's only direct land lifeline to the outside world, the Alaska/Canada Highway (a.k.a. the Alcan, now called the Alaska Highway), was constructed for the transport of military troops and equipment (see Chapter 4).

The Cold War, too, left its mark on the north, most notably in the construction of the Distant Early Warning (DEW) stations. These were America's listening posts on the very doorstep of the USSR and the Far East. Once again, the government and the military provided employment and modernization for many, and constructed the framework for the global communications nexus the state would eventually become (see Chapter 5).

The movement for statehood had been gathering momentum throughout most of the 20th century. Alaskans, tired of absentee rule, wanted a say in their government and their future. In January 1959, they got it. The 49th state was ushered into the Union to the accompaniment of celebratory festivities from Juneau to Nome.

Oil was discovered as early as 1903, but the Cook Inlet fields did not begin significant production until the 1950s. The tremendous commercial possibilities did not become fully evident until the massive North Slope strike of 1968 at Prudhoe Bay, and the subsequent $900 million oil-lease sale. Petroleum exploration, development, extraction, refinement, and marketing became the new state's primary industry (see Chapter 6). The question was, how would the oil industry get the Black Gold to markets in the Lower 48?

The concept of a pipeline from the North Slope to an ice-free seaport farther south was introduced as early as 1969, but it was not until 1974 that the mammoth Trans-Alaska Pipeline project was actually launched. By 1977, history's largest private construction project was completed. Alaska's population had exploded, and revenue was pouring into the state as oil poured out. In January of 1980, the one-billionth barrel of oil flowed through the line to the Valdez terminal. The pipeline boom led directly to the establishment of the state's

A damaged Japanese plane is hoisted onto a dock, Dutch Harbor.

Boy Scouts take a boat ride at Ketchikan, circa 1930.

Permanent Fund, the interest on which is paid out to Alaskan residents in the form of annual per-capita dividends (see Chapter 10).

Another form of revenue distribution was signed into law with the landmark Alaska Native Land Claims Settlement Act of 1971. This law ceded control of 40 million acres of land, and nearly a billion dollars, to Alaska Natives who formed corporations to administer their lands and funds (see Chapter 9).

The inevitable slackening of the economy following the pipeline years affected growth in the 1980s, but the 1990s have been a decade of energetic development and enterprise.

The history of Alaska is one of boom and bust, of prosperity and struggle. It has combined elements of the picturesque, the romantic, the adventurous, as well as the difficult and the dangerous. It is the foundation on which a rich present and glorious future have been built — and are still being built. It is a heritage of strength, diversity, and courage that lives on to this day throughout the 49th state.

RISING ABOVE

Not even the Natives of Alaska, the longest residents, have been able to live entirely at peace with this volatile, tumultuous land. Alaska is a young landscape, built on granite foundations ringed by fire. There are at least 80 potentially active volcanoes in the state, half of which have erupted since the 18th century. When Novarupta Volcano, on the Alaska Peninsula, blew itself apart in 1912, local residents were forced to evacuate in their kayaks as their villages were devastated. Smoke and ash darkened the northern hemisphere. The volcano created the Valley of 10,000 Smokes; and in 1918, Katmai National Monument, today known as Katmai National Park and Preserve, was dedicated (see Chapter 8). In the 1970s and 80s, both Mt. St. Augustine and Mt. Redoubt showered the Cook Inlet region with ash, as did Mt. Spurr in 1992. But, the Alaskans fought on.

Images from left to right:
Courtesy of The Anchorage Museum of History and Art, B72.67.4; Photo by LaRoche
Courtesy of Tongass Historical Society Incorporated; Photo by Fisher Studio
Courtesy of Tongass Historical Society Incorporated and Ed Elliott; Photo by Fisher Studio

The totems of Kasaan.

Alaska-Washington Airways Vega,
circa 1930.

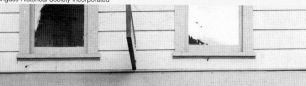

Ketchikan's position as Alaska's first port-of-call on the Inside Passage from the Lower 48, along with its base industries of timber and seafood, has maintained the city's active economy over the last century.

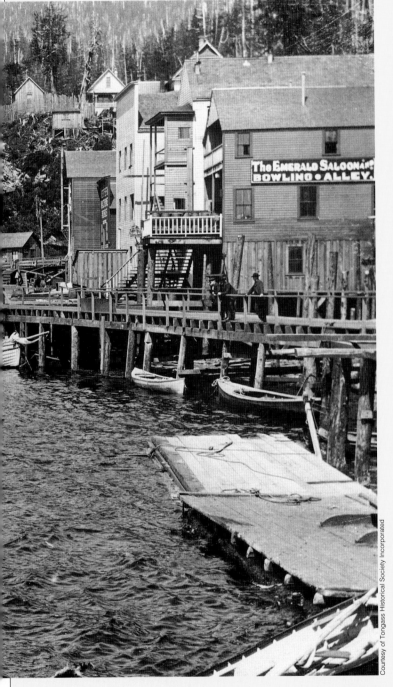

Courtesy of Tongass Historical Society Incorporated

One look at Alaska's mighty upthrust mountain ranges makes it clear that this is a land where the earth, when it moves, moves violently. Some 80 times in the past 100 years, the region has experienced earthquakes registering at least 7.0 on the Richter scale. The most infamous, of course, is the Good Friday quake of 1964. Estimated at 9.2, it is the strongest ever recorded in North America. Portions of suburban Anchorage toppled into Cook Inlet (an area now called Earthquake Park), while parts of downtown dropped 15 feet or more. Fortunately, the time of the event (early on a holiday morning), and the relatively sparse population of that time kept deaths to a minimum.

Tsunamis generated by the quake caused more death and destruction than the tremor itself. The city of Valdez, on Prince William Sound, was completely wiped out. Subsequently, it was rebuilt on a new and safer site. Even as assistance poured in from all over the world, Alaskans proudly continued to battle their sometimes-hostile environment. If any good can be said to have come out of the '64 Quake, it would unquestionably have to be the establishment and enforcement of more rigorous building codes statewide, coupled with scientific and technological advances in earthquake and tsunami forecasting and response programs. Today, the Alaska Tsunami Warning Center in Palmer shares information with other scientists around the Pacific.

Alaskans survive, overcome, and rise above catastrophes great and small: the diphtheria epidemic that decimated the Arctic villages in 1925; the Fairbanks flood of 1967; the environmental disaster of the EXXON *Valdez* oil spill in 1989; one of the state's greatest recorded wildfires (around Big Lake, near Anchorage) in 1995. Theirs is an epic display of that special spirit which is so much a part of The Great Land.

Chapter Three

WELCOMING THE WORLD —
THE VISITOR INDUSTRY

WELCOMING THE WORLD — THE VISITOR INDUSTRY

THEY COME

Yes, it's true. Alaskans *do* refer to the rest of the world, even the other 49 states, as "Outside." Yet it was only half a century ago that Alaskans seemed to be the outsiders — inhabitants of an enormous and distant land about which few non-residents had any direct knowledge. Only those with a strong sense of adventure, and the willingness to overlook inconvenience and sometimes discomfort, visited the northland for pleasure.

Today, they come from all over the globe, over 1,350,000 of them in 1997 alone. Tourism has grown into one of the state's predominant industries, and accounts for some $590 million in revenues annually. The Visitor Industry embraces transportation and accommodation providers; from bus lines, railroads, and planes to five-star hotels and remote fishing camps. It employs nearly 20,000 Alaskans who go out of their way to provide the kind of hospitality that comes naturally to people with frontier-style friendliness.

WHY THEY COME

Some people come to Alaska with a specific adventure in mind: a fly-in fishing or hunting trip; a tour of Native or Russian-American history and culture; winter sports or summer recreation.

Some just come to look. Alaska's breathtaking beauty is one of its hottest selling points. The glacier-carved, deeply forested, waterfall-laced fjords of Southeastern draw passengers to sail the Inside Passage on cruise ships or the ferries of the Alaska Marine Highway system (see Chapter 4). Rugged mountainscapes, studded with ice-fields, provide a dramatic backdrop to tree-dotted taiga and rolling tundra. The nation's only tidewater glaciers loom above comparatively tiny sight-seeing vessels.

When it comes to spectacular scenery, travelers on the Alaska Railroad (see Chapter 4) can see it all from the heights to the depths; from the 20,320-foot summit of awe-inspiring Mt. McKinley to the dizzying chasm of Hurricane Gulch spanned by its fragile-looking railroad bridge. Depending on the time of year, visitors may also see many animals. That is just exactly what a lot of folks come for.

Courtesy of Alaska Tourism Marketing Council;
Photo by Kristen Kemmerling

The traditional Eskimo kuspuk is a woman's parka. Here, Eskimo women of Barrow display the traditional garb. Kuspuks can be lined with fur for warmth, and are traditionally made of brightly colored or print fabric including velveteen, and trimmed with rickrack and fur.

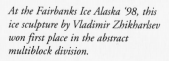

At the Fairbanks Ice Alaska '98, this ice sculpture by Vladimir Zhikharlsev won first place in the abstract multiblock division.

Photo by David Stratton

Denali National Park is a scenic, four-hour train ride south of Fairbanks on the Alaska Railroad.

Courtesy of Fairbanks Convention and Visitors Bureau

Photo by Steve Holthaus

A young moose peers cautiously from behind the foliage.

While eco-tourism is a relatively new concept in the rest of the world, people have been coming for decades to admire, observe, study, and capture images of Alaska's wildlife. In addition to the "Big Five" — moose, caribou, wolf, Alaskan Brown Bear, and Polar Bear — the 49th state is home to hundreds of other species of fish, birds, and land and marine mammals (see Chapter 8). Whale-watching cruises bring hordes of excited viewers to see the Humpbacks and Grays in migration. The huge mammals sometimes fling themselves clear of the water in exuberant breaching. They often follow the followers for miles. Such tours provide a welcome boost to tourism revenues, and offer additional seasonal employment to local guides and boat operators.

There are wildlife refuges throughout the state, and humans and animals live on very close terms almost everywhere. Natives in most regions are allowed subsistence hunting and fishing, and many other Alaskans also feed their families on the fish and game they bring in.

How They Come

There are, basically, three ways to visit Alaska: by air, by water, or overland. While an estimated 100,000-plus tourists do make the 1,520-mile journey up the Alaska Highway each year, the vast majority fly (more than half a million annually). International travelers, in particular, take advantage of Anchorage's position as "Air Crossroads of the World" (see Chapter 4).

Cruise-ship passengers have increased dramatically over the years (392,100 in 1997), and combination cruise/bus and cruise/rail tours have become very popular. But, tourists are not spontaneously generated. Potential visitors must be informed about, and invited to, Alaska. It is a job that takes a lot of people working together.

An excellent example of the kind of business climate that makes Alaska unique is the partnership between government and the private sector to promote and support tourism in the 49th state. The Alaska Visitors Association, a consortium of businesses, works with the state's Division of Tourism to maintain the Alaska Tourism Marketing Council. These entities cooperate to collect and disseminate information, sponsor and participate in promotional events up to the international level, and prepare and place advertising and public-relations materials all over the world. Most of the state's communities maintain their own Convention & Visitors Bureaus to provide specific information to both prospective and present guests.

When They Come

Most travelers prefer to visit Alaska between break-up (March or April) and freeze-up (usually October). However, there are many fantastic Alaska experiences that belong *only* to wintertime. Aside from such obvious activities as alpine and cross-country skiing, hockey, curling, ice fishing, dog mushing (see below), and snowmobiling, there is a whole world of cold-weather opportunity waiting. Aurora Borealis trackers can see the shifting, shimmering curtains of the Northern Lights as far south as Juneau, and scenery cloaked in snow, or diamond-dusted after ice fog, is stunningly beautiful.

Cruise ships have become an increasingly popular way to visit Alaska.

Off-season (April/May and September/early October) often offers discount prices on travel and accommodations, along with generally nice weather. Alaskans themselves frequently schedule their own Outside vacations to coincide with the muddy days of early spring.

Whatever the season, there are always memorable experiences in store for the adventurer with the vision, desire, and determination to seek them out.

MUSH, YOU HUSKIES!

...and Malemutes...and Samoyeds...and mutts!

In the world of mushing, if you're a smart, strong (and, preferably, furry) dog who was born to run and works well with others, you're in.

People just have to ask, "Do sled dogs really love to race as much as they seem to?"

They do! Any experienced musher will tell you that, when the dogs are in harness and ready to run, about all you can do is hang on tight. This eagerness to be on the trail tends to cause a lot of re-starts in races, and there are *many* races.

Mushing associations and clubs for both professional racers and hobbyists alike can be found throughout the state. Many excellent books and publications on the subject are available as well. Most communities sponsor some kind of event. Among the most notable are: the World Championships, held in Anchorage each February as the major highlight of Fur Rendezvous; and the North American Opens, held every March in Fairbanks. These are sprint races, held over several days, with best overall time winning.

The two longest dogsled races in the world both take place, wholly or in part, in Alaska. The Yukon Quest International is run from Whitehorse, in the Yukon Territory, to Fairbanks (about 1,000 miles). It was initiated in 1984 to help promote an international interest in the sport of dog-mushing.

One of the most exciting and highly anticipated events in Alaska is the Iditarod Sled Dog Race.

Fishing at Virginia Lake Forest Service Cabin near Wrangell.

Balloon sightseeing adventures are available out of Fairbanks.

Courtesy of Fairbanks Convention and Visitors Bureau;
Photo by Kathy Hedges

*An autumn scene in the
Donnely Dome area.*

Photo by David Stratton

But, the Great Grandaddy of them all is the Iditarod. Its 1,110-mile course is loosely based on the old mail routes that ran through the Interior and Arctic regions. It is a strictly-winter trail over boggy muskeg, through rugged passes, and across arctic ice. The course is roughly that which was followed by Leonhard Seppala and his famous lead dog, Balto, when they spearheaded the dramatic race to bring diphtheria serum to epidemic-threatened Nome in 1925.

The modern race, inaugurated in 1963 by noted Alaska musher Joe Redington, Sr., covered only 56 miles. The present distance, between approximately 1,135 and 1,165 miles, was established in 1973, and the race has been run every year since. The Iditarod was declared a National Historic Trail in 1976. In 1985, Libby Riddles became the first woman to win the Iditarod. Several competitors, like Rick Swenson and Susan Butcher, have won multiple races.

The Iditarod is a long hard road with river and bay crossings on ice, trails easily lost in drifting snow, hard labor, long days and black nights, biting winds, whiteouts, bitter cold, and blinding blizzards. It is easy for mushers and their dogs to get lost out there between checkpoints.

Nobody stays lost for long. Extensive and efficient search and rescue procedures are in place for both mushers and dogs. There are also stringent and rigidly-enforced regulations covering all aspects of the treatment of dogs: when and what they must be fed; when and for how long they must rest; and the minimum size of a team. Ill or injured animals are often airlifted out. Most mushers are much more interested in the team's welfare than in their own; their very lives depend on the dogs. A tired or slightly disabled dog can ride in a basket on the sled. Many mushers put little mukluks (boots) on their dogs to protect their feet from ice, rocks, sharp snow-crust, and other hazards.

Alaskans take special care to ensure that visitor services are widely available.

The mushers' typical lack of concern for themselves does not extend to each other. Whenever someone is lost or late, sick or hurt, exhausted or discouraged, fellow racers are there to help in any way they can, and they will sacrifice precious racing time to do so.

It's a partnership and a battle. People and dogs, united against the wilds and the weather, with a single goal in mind — the finish line on the main street of Nome.

THE BIGGEST CHILL

While alpine glaciers are fairly common in the northern mountains of the Lower 48, tidewater and sea-level valley glaciers are found only in the 49th state. In fact, an estimated 100,000 glaciers cover some 28,000 square miles of Alaska — 128 times the glaciated area in the rest of the U.S. combined. About three-fourths of all of Alaska's fresh water is frozen into glaciers.

Some, like Portage Glacier near Anchorage and Mendenhall outside Juneau, are conveniently close at hand for visiting. Others enhance the splendor of places like Glacier Bay National Park in Southeastern, and Prince William Sound near Valdez. A favorite tourist experience is cruising past these looming cliffs of ice, which may reach 200 feet, hoping to see one of them "calve" (dropping an enormous iceberg into the water). At one time, tour-boat operators would try to initiate calving with loud whistle-blasts, but this practice has been outlawed as too dangerous.

Tremendous pressure is required to turn centuries of piled-up snow into a glacier, so the ice is very thick and dense. Glacial ice can appear to be a deep, rich blue in color. The thickness of the ice absorbs the rest of the colors of the spectrum, reflecting back only the blue. This ancient ice is even considered fashionable for cooling drinks and seafoods at fancy parties and banquets around the world.

Most of Alaska's glaciers, like those elsewhere, are currently in the process of steadily receding. Scientists believe this phenomenon may be linked to global warming, but research continues.

GREAT LAND, GREAT FUN

Whatever the season or reason for visiting Alaska, there is always something fun or festive going on. In winter, there are ski races at Alyeska Resort near Anchorage, and in Juneau, Knik, and Skagway as well. Dog-sled racing takes place at Anchorage, Fairbanks, Tok, Bethel, Hatcher Pass, Nome, and Soldotna. Major snowmobile competitions are found in Haines, Homer, and Nome. Marathons and other foot races are held in Anchorage, Juneau, Kodiak, Sitka, Skagway, Seward, and elsewhere.

At Portage Lake around Portage Glacier just south of Anchorage, visitors are surrounded by floating icebergs that have floated toward the Begich Boggs Visitor Center. Portage Glacier is an active tidewater glacier, and the icebergs are formed when giant chucks fall from the glacier's face into the lake.

Many Alaskan celebrations have a historical or cultural basis, such as: Anchorage's Fur Rendezvous; the Fairbanks Festival of Native Arts; Skagway's Gold Rush Stampede; Copper Days in Cordova; Petersburg's Little Norway Festival; and Russian Orthodox ceremonies observed in Kodiak and Sitka.

Some events, including the various races, highlight sports. In Fairbanks, the Arctic Winter Games in January and the Midnight Sun Baseball Game in June display the opposite poles of life in the Interior. Softball tournaments, rafting competitions, winter swimming or golf challenges, and fishing derbies of all kinds (including ice fishing, naturally), take place across the state throughout the year.

Other festivities are purely artistic. Music events, like the famed Talkeetna Bluegrass Festiva each August, are always popular with Alaskans and their guests. Kodiak's yearly staging of the historical drama *Cry of the Wild Ram* is eagerly anticipated, and almost every town of any size hosts some sort of annual arts festival.

One of the most spectacular features of many winter events is ice-sculpture competition, which draws sculptors from around the world, and particularly from Japan. Ranging from the delicately intricate to the large and imposing, these impermanent works of art reflect and refract the moody, changeable light of an Alaskan winter day to the delight of all beholders.

Some Alaska events are just for fun. The Delta Junction Buffalo Wallow Square Dance Jamboree, the Talkeetna Bachelor's Festival, and the Midnight Sun Hot Air Balloon Classic in Anchorage are uniquely Alaskan in spirit.

Alaskans know how to have a good time, and everyone's welcome to join in.

Photo by Steve Holthaus

The setting sun glows through bare branches.

Ice fields and glaciers provide the perfect backdrop for early morning rides along the beaches of Kachemak Bay outside of Homer.

Courtesy of Alaska Tourism Marketing Council; Photo by Robin Hood

The hardy low bush cranberry grows on the tundra of Alaska, only inches from the ground. Naturally containing pectin, these berries are ideal for preserving as jelly.

Courtesy of Fairbanks Convention and Visitors Bureau; Photo by Dorothy Simpson

Courtesy of Alaska Tourism
Marketing Council; Photo by
Robin Hood

In gold rush days, transportation by sternwheeler was the quickest way to travel up and down Alaska's waterways.

Today, a sternwheeler trip along the Tanana River presents one of the best ways to see the sights.

Evidence of the pioneer spirit can be found throughout the Interior.

Courtesy of Fairbanks Convention and Visitors Bureau; Photo by Kathy Hedges

WHERE THEY GO

Popular destinations for visitors shift from year to year, but some are eternal favorites:

Portage Glacier — near Anchorage

Mendenhall Glacier, Juneau — Southeastern

Ketchikan Totems — Southeastern

Denali National Park & Preserve/Mt. McKinley — Southcentral/Interior

Skagway — Southeastern

Glacier Bay National Park — Southeastern

Russian and Native culture and performances, Sitka — Southeastern

*Rich marine life, Valdez, Columbia Glacier,
    Prince William Sound — Southcentral*

World's greatest salmon runs, Kenai River — Southcentral

OFFICIAL STATE STUFF

*Flag — eight gold stars, representing the Big Dipper and the North Star,
    on a blue field. Designed for a Territorial Flag contest in 1926
    by seventh-grader Benny Bensen.*

*Song — Alaska's Flag by Elinor Dusenbury (music) and
    Marie Drake (words).*

Flower — Forget-me not

Tree — Sitka Spruce

Bird — Willow Ptarmigan

Fish — King Salmon

Marine Mammal — Bowhead Whale

Mineral — Gold

Gem — Jade

Sport — Dog Mushing

Fossil (yes, really) — Woolly Mammoth

Motto — North to the Future

Chapter Four

MAKING CONNECTIONS

MAKING CONNECTIONS

BY AIR
It is not surprising that Alaska is so air-oriented. When you may have to travel several hundred miles to the nearest city, or more than a thousand to reach the rest of the country, aircraft offer the only practical solution. For most Alaskans, flight is a way of life, and they *really* take to it — in the Bush, in the cities, on the lakes and glaciers.

Alaska has more than 1,000 airports of all kinds and sizes, and boasts more small planes per capita than any other state. Thousands of residents hold private pilot's licenses. The float-plane base at Anchorage's Lake Hood hosts scores of these pontoon- and ski-equipped craft, with around 800 landings and takeoffs per day; making it the world's largest and busiest airport of its kind. There are only two designated international airports in the state, at Anchorage and Fairbanks, but Juneau also boasts a sophisticated facility. Many communities can accommodate the local commuter airlines which fly passengers between Alaska locations in Twin Otters, Pipers, and other small planes.

Commercial flights are vital strands in the transportation network. A host of different international, national, regional, and local airlines operate within, and in connection with, the state. Known as the "air crossroads of the world," Anchorage is almost equidistant, via polar routes, from London, New York, and Tokyo, and its importance as a transit center is evident. Carriers such as Alaska Airlines and Northwest Airlines consider Alaskan trade an extremely important part of their overall operations.

Air freight is also essential to life on the Last Frontier. Most fresh and frozen food must be flown in, particularly out-of-season fruits and vegetables. Both Anchorage and Fairbanks International Airports have experienced dramatic growth in international air-cargo traffic over the past decade. The business of business could not be carried on without the use of fast, efficient air service. Export trade is also heavily dependent on both air and water transport.

Courtesy of Cominco Alaska; Photo by Chris Arend

The 52-mile haul road from the Red Dog Mine to the Port.

The Great Land, *a Totem Ocean Trailer Express vessel, is ready to negotiate the ice-choked waters of Cook Inlet.*

Courtesy of Totem Ocean Trailer Express

Small aircraft play a vital role in the overall transportation network of Alaska. One out of every 58 Alaskans is a pilot.

The Alaska Railroad provides both a practical way to move people and cargo, and a comfortable way to see the sights of The Great Land.

BY WATER

While there are lots of ways to get to, from, and around in Alaskan waters, the Alaska Marine Highway ferry system, with more than 3,000 miles of routes, is the most heavily relied upon by residents and visitors. This fleet of nine car/passenger ferries brings travelers through the Inside Passage, to and from outside ports in Bellingham, Washington and Prince Rupert, British Colombia. But, the most vital function of the Marine Highway is to link the small, isolated communities of Southeastern — places like Hoonah, Kake, Pelican, Tenakee, and Petersburg — with passenger and delivery services. A separate set of ships operates in Southcentral/Southwestern. In 1997, the Alaska Marine Highway carried approximately 350,000 people and 98,000 vehicles.

The Marine Highway flagship, the largest and fastest vessel in the fleet, is the *M/V Columbia*. At 418 feet and a capacity of 625 passengers and 134 vehicles, it is the Columbia that links Alaska with the rest of the country from its base in Bellingham, Washington. During the summer months, deck space is often at a premium as seasonal workers camp out on their way north to jobs in fish canneries and processing plants. For more conventional travelers, there are cabins of various sizes and degrees of comfort. The ship boasts such amenities as a dining room, cafeteria, cocktail lounge, solarium, and enclosed observation lounge.

The other big boat in this unique fleet (382 feet and nine decks) is the brand-new *M/V Kennicott*. This ship fills a long-felt need, connecting ports in Southeastern with Valdez on Prince William Sound in Southcentral. The smaller ferries include the *M/Vs Matanuska, Malaspina, Tustumena, Bartlett, Taku, Aurora*, and *Le Conte*.

Not only are these ferries a favorite way to get around and see the sights in Alaska, they also provide a vital lifeline to dozens of remote communities. It is possibly the most unusual transportation network in the nation. It truly *is* a Marine Highway — a road across all the broadest waters of the 49th state.

Courtesy of Wyndham Images

There's no question about it, those dogs were born to run. Just watching them at any competition will convince the most skeptical that, in reality, sled dogs just can't wait to hit the trail.

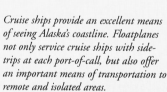

One of the most popular ways to see Alaska these days is from the deck of a cruise ship. These luxurious liners are operated by such companies as Princess, Holland America, Royal Caribbean, Royal Viking, Norwegian, and Carnival. While the Inside Passage trip through Southeastern is a favorite with visitors, cruise ships also call at Anchorage and other Southcentral ports; and even at Dutch Harbor in the Aleutians.

Container ships also play a key role as the only really practical means of shipping large cargoes nationally and internationally. Ships of the big companies may make more than 100 Alaska trips each year, carrying hundreds of containers and thousands of tons of commercial and personal freight.

BY LAND

One longstanding mode of land travel and shipping is the Alaska Railroad. Begun in 1915, it was completed in 1923 when President Warren G. Harding drove in the gold spike at Nenana. It is not only the nation's northernmost railroad, but was, for many years, the only railroad in the U.S. owned by the federal government. Today, it is owned and operated by the state. The ARR extends from Seward to Fairbanks, and is a familiar part of life in the wilderness between. Tourists in domed observation cars can revel in glorious scenery, and thousands do every year. Local residents, appearing out of the woods, hail the train the way New Yorkers grab a cab. For fishing, hiking, hunting, skiing, or just a ride to the nearest town, the trains of the Alaska Railroad go where the roads do not.

In Alaska, there are no freeways — not, at least, any recognizable as such by Outsiders. A "major highway" is a paved, four-lane, limited-access roadway like the Seward, Sterling, Glenn, and Parks Highways in Southcentral and the Interior. A "highway" is usually two-lanes, often meandering, and not always paved. In Southeastern, only Skagway and Haines have connections to Outside highways. The vast expanses of Southwest, Northwest, and Arctic Alaska are basically roadless.

Cruise ships provide an excellent means of seeing Alaska's coastline. Floatplanes not only service cruise ships with side-trips at each port-of-call, but also offer an important means of transportation to remote and isolated areas.

A Ketchikan entrepreneur sells newspapers to the passengers of the Jefferson, circa 1930s.

THE ROAD THROUGH NOWHERE

As is so often the case in Alaskan history, it took the U.S. military to plan, organize, and push through the immense project to connect the Territory with the rest of the country. After the attack on Pearl Harbor, the strategic importance of Alaska as the nearest U.S. possession to Japan made a land link to the Lower 48 imperative. Thus was born the Alaska/Canada Highway. Popularly known as the Alcan, it is now simply known as the Alaska Highway. This roadway is considered to be the northernmost section of the Pan-American Highway, which extends to just beyond Panama City in Central America.

It was a daunting prospect — fifteen hundred miles of road to be built across vast expanses of mostly-unmapped wilderness with few settlements, and through every extreme of climate. But the Army Corps of Engineers, working with civilian contractors, proved altogether equal to the challenge.

Negotiating the backroads during winter.

Photo by Steve Holthaus

Courtesy of The Anchorage Museum of History and Art, B62.X.15.8

*Spring break-up made traveling the
Alcan something of a challenge in 1942.*

Since they knew *where* they were going (to Fairbanks), but not exactly *how*, planning was difficult. Some 20,000 workers, about evenly divided between military and civilian, formed three groups. One crew began at Dawson Creek, British Colombia and worked northward; a second built south from Delta; the third, based in Whitehorse, went in both directions.

It was a primitive road indeed, unpaved and largely ungravelled. To build it, workers had to push through scrub and muskeg, across the tundra and the rivers, avoiding animals that might want to dispute the right-of-way. They wallowed in mud and choked on dust while battling wild weather and monster mosquitoes. But, it had to be done.

More to the point, it had to be done *fast.* Possibly the most amazing thing about the entire project is the fact that it was completed in just eight months. On November 21, 1942, the first truck arrived in Fairbanks, after driving the 1,523 miles from Dawson Creek, marking the start of a new transportation era in Alaska.

Russ Merrill on the park strip in Anchorage, 1928.

To help meet the growing needs of its Alaskan customers, Northern Air Cargo has expanded its fleet by purchasing three Boeing 727-100 freighters.

Over the ensuing decades, the Highway was gradually paved, bit by bit. Today, with the exception of whatever stretches may be undergoing construction or improvement, it is a comparatively easy drive. However, it is still a very long one, through a lot of lonely country. The wise traveler will always come completely prepared.

ROLLIN' ON THE RIVERS

From the Arctic coast to the southern tip of the Panhandle, Alaska is laced with rivers large and small — more than 3,000 of them. Principal navigable rivers include the Yukon, Kuskokwim, Tanana, Kobuk, Porcupine, Chilkat, Koyukuk, Naknek, and Stikine, among others. In the state, there are five rivers that are 500 miles or longer. Since such emphasis is placed on size in The Great Land, it is not too surprising that one 314-mile specimen is called Birch *Creek*. Waterways provide power, food, irrigation, sport, and, perhaps most important, transportation for thousands.

In the Arctic, one of the two major rivers is the Kuskokwim. It flows southwest across the state, roughly 600 miles, to its mouth on an inlet of the Bering Sea. Settlements range from good-sized towns like Bethel to smaller ones like McGrath, and downright tiny ones like Eek. Many Natives live along the Kuskokwim, pursuing a traditional lifestyle largely based around the river — hunting, trapping, and salmon fishing.

The Queen River of the north is, of course, the great Yukon. It flows nearly 2,000 miles from its source on the British Columbia/Yukon border north, and west to the Bering Sea with a drainage basin of some 330,000 square miles. Russian fur-traders knew as early as 1831 that the Yukon was navigable by shallow-draft vessels up to Whitehorse (capital of the present Yukon Territory), and local inhabitants had plied its waters for centuries. It was not until the Gold Rush that the river's value as a major transportation conduit was revealed. There are many settlements, mostly small, along the Yukon: Native villages like Anvik, Nulato*, and Kaltag*; former missionary-stations as Russian Mission, Holy Cross, and St. Mary's; and leftover mining centers like Ruby*, and Galena.

Today, a trip down the Yukon reveals the same long stretches of wilderness, punctuated by isolated outposts of humanity, that have characterized this mighty waterway throughout human history in the north.

The White Pass & Yukon Route Railroad, in Skagway, will celebrated its 100th birthday in 1998. Built in 1898 as a means of transporting gold rush stampeders to the Klondike gold fields, the railroad soon became famous for moving passengers throughout the north, a reputation maintained to this day.

* Checkpoints on the Iditarod Trail (see Chapter 3)

Chapter Five

GLOBAL COMMUNICATIONS START AT THE TOP

GLOBAL COMMUNICATIONS START AT THE TOP

AN WE TALK?

Starting with construction of the Distant Early Warning system (DEW), Alaska has led the way in high-tech communications. Since the days when direct-dial long-distance and live TV broadcasts were exotic rarities, the state has gone on to boast an impressive number of radio, television and cable systems; publishers and printers; telecommunications and satellite networks. Given the stupendous size of Alaska, and the vast distances separating its communities from each other and the outside world, quick and clear communications have always been vitally important to The Great Land.

The rest of the country had been using Samuel F. B. Morse's telegraph since 1844, and was joined to Europe by the first transAtlantic cable in 1866. However, it was not until 1898 that Congress appropriated funds for a telegraph link between Seattle and Alaska, another result of the great gold rush. In 1900, a land line was established between Nome and Port Safety, direct telegraph service was also established between Valdez and Fairbanks, and underwater cables were used in Southeastern. In 1905, submarine cable connected Seattle, Sitka and Valdez. A fragile statewide network was linked with stations in the Yukon, and thence to the rest of the United States.

Eventually, wireless radio-telegraphy replaced land lines. Virtually all of this was built courtesy of the U.S. Army Signal Corps, and was dubbed the Washington-Alaska Military Cable and Telegraph System. It would later be called the Alaska Communications System, when civilian usage overtook the military (but it would still be operated under the Department of Defense until 1971). Radio-telephone service began in Juneau, Ketchikan, and Nome in 1932. The Anchorage Telephone Utility (ATU) was founded in 1915 and is now the property of Public Technology, Inc. (PTI).

Photo by Linda Brucia

A grizzly goes fishing.

The Bald Mountain communications site.

Courtesy of Wyndham Images

Television in Alaska has come a long way since the days of two- to three-week delays of non-local broadcasts. Alaskans now enjoy live broadcasts from all over the world as a matter of course.

Courtesy of Alaska Film Office

Setting up a shot on the set of the critically acclaimed film Limbo.

For the greater part of the 20th century, the size and rugged, remote terrain of Alaska made communicating anything but simple. Although construction of the DEW line improved contact for military and government entities, ordinary citizens remained fairly isolated. The 49th state really came into its own as a communications center in the satellite age. In fact, direct-dial long-distance telephone calls were not possible before the early 1970s. At that time, RCA Alascom, then the state's only longlines carrier, fulfilled its mission of providing long-distance phone service to every Alaskan community of at least 25 people. That often meant, as it often still does, just one phone per village.

Not that the early days of satellite technology were easy. Yes, Alaskans were finally talking with the world, but they were often accompanied by an annoying echo effect due to multiple relays and synchronization problems. "All circuits are busy," calling overloads were expected, if resented, events at every holiday.

One of the biggest turning points in Alaska telecommunications history took place October 27, 1982, when Alascom (no longer an RCA property) launched its own satellite into orbit from Cape Canaveral. It was a major event in several ways. Not only was it the first completely solid-state satellite ever placed in orbit, the *Aurora* was also the first to be solely dedicated to the service of just one state. More recently, the successful inauguration in November 1998 of Alaska Aerospace Development Corporation's Kodiak Launch Complex, a commercial spaceport on Kodiak Island, demonstrated the immense potential of such a site for the deployment, maintenance, and monitoring of low-orbit telecommunications satellites, among other scientifically-important payloads.

Image Copyright © 1998 PhotoDisc, Inc.

The advancement of fiber-optic technology has helped to revolutionize the telecommunications industry in Alaska.

Such satellites have increased long-distance capability immeasurably. In the pre-fax days of telex and wire-photo machines, Alascom blazed the trail for type and image transmission to and from the state; established service in the areas of toll-free 800 numbers, WATS lines, telegrams and mailgrams; and pioneered the emerging field of computer data transmission.

Once communications got better, they continued to improve with amazing rapidity over the next two decades. Alascom's communications monopoly was broken in the 1980s, following court action by GCI. Soon GCI was conducting its own satellite program. The company built 56 remote earth stations, and joined with Hughes Communication in 1995 to secure sufficient C-band and Ku-band satellite coverage for the entire state.

GCI is still involved in serious research and development of fiber-optic possibilities. In Anchorage, the company completed phase one of its Metropolitan Area Network fiber-optic ring in 1996; phase one in Fairbanks was completed in 1997. Also in 1997, the company launched construction of the now completed Alaskan United Fiber Optic Cable System. In linking Alaska population centers with the Lower 48, this sophisticated system makes it as easy to do business in Anchorage as in Atlanta.

Following passage of the Federal Telecommunications Act of 1996 which mandated increased industry competition, firms like PTI entered the Alaska marketplace and Alascom was acquired by AT&T, broadening the competitive base still more.

From phone calls, to faxes, to surfing the Internet, doing business in Alaska is no different than doing business in Atlanta, thanks to a concert of technology and effort. Satellites have actually made Alaska a "telecommunications hub," due to the state's strategic geographic location. Companies like Alaska Fiber Star contribute to the fiber-optic networks linking Alaska's major metropolitan areas with the Lower 48, making communications fast, clear and easy. But ultimately, satellites and fiber optics notwithstanding, the familiar lineman still works hard to maintain Alaskans' contact with the rest of the world, and with each other.

Courtesy of Alaska Fiber Star. Photo by Chris Arend

WATCHING AND LISTENING

Competition has been good for Alaskans, who had not seen a live non-local television broadcast until the July 1969 moon landing, followed by that year's NFL playoffs. Where they once watched all network TV programming, including holiday specials, on a two- to three-week delay basis, Alaskans now receive live broadcasting from all over the world as a matter of course.

Today, there are dozens of commercial radio stations in the state, and the Alaska Public Radio Network alone has 29 stations. Radio has always played a vital role in far-north communication. The well-known "Bush Telegraph" ham radio messages still keep isolated residents in touch with each other, and with people, businesses, and support services in the cities. Many commercial radio stations also run programs featuring such messages. If someone needs to get in touch with friends, relatives, department stores, or medical facilities from the Bush, he or she is on the air.

Microwave tower.

Four of Alaska's 16 TV stations are PBS-affiliates, and a variety of cable, fiber-optic, microwave-broadcast, closed-circuit TV, and satellite services also accommodate residents, particularly in the Bush. Conventional cable television has always been a difficult proposition in much of Alaska. In the 1970s, the late Robert Uchitel, an Alaska broadcasting pioneer, founded Visions (later MultiVisions) in Anchorage. Visions was a pre-satellite-dish "cable" company which delivered programming via microwave, beaming a scrambled signal directly to subscriber receivers.

Publishing is another branch of the communications industry that thrives on the Last Frontier. The state can now claim at least 19 newspapers (dailies, weeklies, and special-interest papers), plus several magazines — perhaps the most venerable of which is *Alaska Magazine*, founded in 1935. There are book publishers as well.

The increasing influence of computers and the Internet on communications has not been lost on Alaskans. The Alaska Science & Technology Foundation (ASTF; see Chapter 10) has been spearheading a project to wire all the state's classrooms, including those in the most remote villages, for the Internet.

With the advent of the computer era, cable and satellite TV advances, fiber-optic development, and the coming-of-age of cellular telephone and digital technology, Alaska is poised to take advantage of its strategic geographical location and become a hub of the global communications network — now and in the future.

Image Copyright © 1996 PhotoDisc, Inc.

The Alaska Aerospace Development Corporation's Kodiak Launch Complex is a commercial spaceport on Kodiak Island.

Chapter Six

A RESOURCEFUL ALLIANCE

A Resourceful Alliance

WEALTH FROM THE EARTH
Resource development has been the principal mainstay of the Alaskan economy since gold, silver, and copper were first discovered here. It is still true in the present era of high-yield oil and gas exploitation. Secondary processing and manufacturing of Alaska's natural resources is also an area of industry into which the state and its business community are anxious to expand. Today, Alaska's well-developed infrastructure, technologically advanced communication systems, highly educated population, expansive and efficient shipping networks, and business-friendly tax structure all create a positive environment for such industries.

The extraction, transportation, and marketing of petroleum products and natural gas has always been a subject of controversy and debate in Alaska. It is hardly surprising that the future appears to hold more of the same. After all, Alaska accounts for 23 percent of total U.S. oil production; holds 31 percent of the nation's total oil reserves (7.5 billion barrels); and 18 percent of the total U.S. gas reserves (34.4 trillion cubic feet). As one result, Alaskans enjoy the lowest natural-gas rates in the nation.

The dynamic oil and gas industry, which generates nearly 80 percent of the state's annual revenue, brings in more than a quarter-billion dollars yearly and provides direct or indirect employment to 1,600 Alaskans throughout the state. The fact that environmentalists and developers have been able to reach workable compromises is what has made the modern era of oil, gas, and mineral recovery and processing possible. That, and the vision of forward-thinking enterprises from the old Treadwell Mines and Kennecott Copper to today's Alyeska Pipeline Service Company.

In the construction of the Alyeska Pipeline, great pains were taken to minimize the impact of the pipeline's presence on the environment. As shown at right, the pipeline is raised well above ground so that wildlife, such as the young moose above, may have unimpeded access to its natural habitat.

Alaska Interstate Construction blasts the frozen ground prior to excavation for gravel mining in the Tarn project.

A geologist studies the impact of an earthquake.

MINING

Mention mining in connection with Alaska and almost everyone automatically thinks "gold" (See Chapter 2). Gold is certainly still being extracted at such locations as Fort Knox, Nixon Fork, and the Alaska Gold Company mine at Nome. Future gold-mining operations are also planned for properties like Pogo and Donlin Creek.

But these days, gold is rarely mined alone. Polymetallic mines like Greens Creek, Illinois Creek, Niblack, and Kensington also yield silver, zinc, and/or lead. The Pebble Copper mine near Iliamna contains some 11 million ounces of gold, as well as several billion pounds of copper, an ore with a long history in Alaska mining. The Red Dog Mine, owned and operated by the NANA Regional Native Corporation, is the world's largest zinc mine. Red Dog shipped 373,000 tons of zinc and 70,000 tons of lead in 1997. Around the state, deposits of chromite, molybdenum, nickel, uranium, and even platinum have been located, and site development is being seriously studied. Semi-precious minerals like jade (the state gem) and hematite are mined as well.

Although the Usibelli mines near Healy, outside Denal National Park, are the state's only currently-operating coal mines, clean-coal technology is very important to the future. An existing 25-megawatt coal-fired power plant at Healy has been joined by an advanced 50-MW plant, at a cost of $270 million. A project is also underway to utilize Alaska's low-rank coal to produce an economical utility fuel for possible export. Clean-coal technology will continue to gain impact as potential reserves at Wishbone Hill, Beluga, and Northwest Arctic Coalfields are further explored and developed.

Mining of every kind is, and always has been, a major contributor to the economy of the Last Frontier. It will continue to be one into the next century and beyond.

Below right: The pit at the Red Dog Mine. Below left: Part of the gold-mining exhibit at Alaskaland in Fairbanks.

Courtesy of Cominco Alaska; Photo by Chris Arend

Courtesy of Wyndham Images

OIL AND GAS

The first exploratory oil well in Alaska was drilled in the Cook Inlet region in 1898. The initial commercial strike was made in 1902 at Katalla, east of Cordova. Between 1957 and 1962, oil and gas fields in Cook Inlet and on the Kenai Peninsula were discovered and developed by such concerns as Atlantic Richfield, Union Oil, and Amoco, which helped establish the region as one of the state's two major producing areas. Today, drilling platforms are scattered across the Inlet, and local residents benefit. A large fertilizer plant and Tesoro Alaska's petroleum refinery, at Nikiski near Kenai, help make it possible for Alaskans to enjoy the low-cost fruits of their state's abundant fossil fuels. Refining activities are also carried out in the city of North Pole near Fairbanks.

By the 1920s, the north slope of the Brooks Range, on the shores of the Arctic Ocean, was already being surveyed by both the oil companies and the government. In 1923, the latter created Naval Petroleum Reserve #4, comprising 23 million miles of North Slope land. The Navy conducted drilling operations on the Reserve (now called National Petroleum Reserve-Alaska) between 1944 and 1953 without significant results. Private enterprise was more successful. In 1968, the Prudhoe Bay oilfield, the largest in North America, was discovered by Atlantic Richfield (now ARCO) and EXXON.

The state is presently conducting a new Shallow Gas Leasing Program. This program allows the Division of Oil & Gas to issue non-competitive leases for the exploration and development of natural-gas reservoirs, including coalbed methane, within 3,000 feet of the surface. It is hoped that this program will help to develop local sources of fuel that can be economically delivered to remote villages. To encourage continuing private-sector participation, lease prices are being kept attractively low, and regulatory requirements as simple as possible.

Oil and gas and their byproducts are transported around, and out of, the state by a variety of means, including many standard-sized pipelines. But the biggest and most famous means is unquestionably the TransAlaska Pipeline.

Courtesy of Tesoro Alaska; Photo by Ken Graham Photography

Tesoro Alaska's oil and gas refinery in the town of Kenai.

Courtesy of Crowley Marine Services;
Photo by Patrick Bennett

Tug boats from Crowley Marine Services safely escort a tanker to Alyeska's Valdez terminal.

A crew from Alaska Interstate Construction is driving sheet piling in minus 35 degrees for the Endicott causeway breech project.

A technician turns valves in pipes at a Tesoro petroleum refinery.

Courtesy of Tesoro Alaska; Photo by Ken Graham Photography

BLACK GOLD AND HOW TO MOVE IT: THE TRANSALASKA PIPELINE

It would take three years of round-the-clock effort. It would cost $8 billion, and require the services of thousands of workers. It would be the biggest private construction project in human history. And when it was finished, it move billions of barrels of North Slope oil from Prudhoe Bay south to Valdez, across 800 miles of rugged, beautiful, yet fragile terrain that included mountains, rivers, and permafrost tundra. It was the TransAlaska Pipeline.

Following the massive 1968 Prudhoe Bay strike, a group of oil companies cast aside their usual competition and, for their mutual benefit, formed a consortium to construct and run the line. Out of this has evolved Alyeska Pipeline Service Company, which today handles all aspects of pipeline operation and maintenance.

Before the project was finally launched in 1974, planners had to contend with court actions brought by environmental groups. Activists all around the country, and the world, were worried about the Pipeline's possible impact on the land and its wildlife. Their concerns were valid. A tremendous amount of scientific planning and technological innovation would be required to complete the project while still protecting the delicate environment and its inhabitants.

For one thing, there was the permafrost problem. The huge pipe, 48 inches in diameter, could be conventionally buried in stable-soil areas. However, to avoid the possibility of thawing the ever-frozen tundra with hot oil, the line had to be elevated for more than half its length. Special refrigerator/ventilator units would be built into its supports. More than 800 streams and rivers were bridged; mountain passes were crossed; a haul road to the Slope was constructed (today called the Dalton Highway, open to the public as far as Deadhorse); pump stations and the Valdez Terminal were designed and built.

The line would pass through the natural ranges, and cross the migration routes, of many animals. People feared the effects of this large manmade obstacle on caribou, moose, wolf and bear populations. There was further concern that watercourse-crossings might affect fish species. Project engineers went to great lengths to design and build elaborate crossings for the animals over buried or under elevated lines. They also took great pains to leave streambeds as undisturbed as possible.

In the long run, none of the expected problems developed. The permafrost has stayed perma-frozen; and the wild creatures, by and large, have actually embraced the pipeline as part of their lives. Female caribou and moose, either pregnant or with very young calves, often deliberately seek out the pipeline right-of-way because this cleared area offers no cover for predators (a major consideration since the infant-mortality rate for caribou is nearly 50 percent). Bears, for reasons of their own, are known to amuse themselves by prowling beneath the elevated line and employing their long claws to rip apart the bands that hold the insulation around the pipe. The avian population gets into the act, too. Small birds sometimes build nests in the ventilators. In one case, an entire pump station was moved half a mile to avoid the habitat of a pair of rare peregrine falcons nesting at the original site. The birds promptly packed up too, and built a new nest closer to the station. They had discovered that the presence of humans meant more readily-accessible food for themselves and their fledglings.

Courtesy of Tongass Historical Society Incorporated

Men working a mine at New Town in 1900.

An old steam shovel once used for gold mining.

Gold nuggets are often found by novice panners. During the gold rush of 1898, nuggets like these made many a man and woman rich.

Courtesy of Alaska Tourism Marketing Council; Photo by Kristen Kemmerling

Courtesy of Wyndham Images

Image Copyright © 1996 PhotoDisc, Inc.

The Alaska Forest Association's mission is to take an active role in maintaining healthy forests for today and for the future.

Courtesy of Alaska Forest Association; Photo by Clark James Mishler

That's pretty much the way it's been ever since; intact ecosystem, undisturbed wildlife, oil flowing along to Valdez with its revenues landing in the pockets of Alaskans.

Pipeline owner/operator Alyeska takes good care of its investment. Scrapers called "pigs" are frequently sent through the line to clean it, and crews of "line walkers" are dispatched at regular intervals to cover literally every inch of the pipeline's exterior. A sophisticated alarm and shutoff system links pump stations and terminal, insuring prompt and effective response in the event of any emergency.

The result of such diligence is that there has never been a major land spill. The EXXON *Valdez* disaster of 1989 took place *after* the oil had made it all the way through the pipeline from Prudhoe. In the wake of that tragedy, more stringent marine-spill prevention regulations have been implimented and enforced. New escort procedures, extended radar coverage, and reduced speed limits have been imposed. Specialized recovery and cleanup equipement and response personnel are maintained close at hand, and in a state of constant readiness which is insured by frequent "spill drills."

Since that first barrel of oil made the big trip on July 28, 1977, followed by a billion more within the next three years and many more billions afterwards, the TransAlaska Pipeline has taken its place as an integral, and most profitable, feature of the northern scene.

Courtesy of the City of Wrangell; Photo by Olga Norris

A local mill transports logs from a Wrangell Island harvest area back to the mill for processing.

Wealth From The Woods

When one thinks of trees in Alaska, it is generally the dense, lush growth of Southeastern that comes to mind. The Tongass National Forest, the country's biggest, is the largest temperate-zone rain forest on earth. Here, massive cedar and hemlock prevail along with other evergreens. As one moves farther north, the softwoods predominate: birch, aspen, alder, willow, spruce, and fir. The permafrost regions above the Arctic Circle are entirely untimbered, with the exception of one lone tree, planted and pampered on the tundra by some wit, and dubbed "The Arctic National Forest."

It is easy to see why logging and the forest-products industry have always been essential elements of the Alaskan economy, particularly in Southeastern. Although round-log export to Japan continues, Alaska being the only state allowed to engage in such trade, the raw timber supply is dwindling. A number of pulp and lumber mills have had to shut down in the face of the increasing trend toward old-growth preservation. Nonetheless, this industry is still the mainstay of many small communities, and several larger ones. The Alaska Department of Natural Resources (DNR) is aided in its oversight of forestry and the timber trade by the Alaska Forest Association. This non-profit organization consists of some 300 private-sector companies active in the forest-products industry. It is another example of business and government working together to protect a great natural resource, preserve the economy and lifestyle of today's Alaskans, and encourage the growth and development so necessary to the future.

Ownership of a great deal of Alaska's forestland is in the hands of Native Corporations. They take their stewardship of this vital resource very seriously and are assisted by the federal Bureau of Land Management and the DNR. In the aftermath of the 1989 oil spill in Prince William Sound, several tribes have sold or are planning to sell some significant blocks of woodland back to the state, to avoid future clearcutting and prevent possible harmful soil erosion and runoff. Such varied examples of cooperation among all interested parties will surely help to ensure the prosperity of Alaska's forest industry.

Courtesy of Ketchikan Visitors Bureau

Alaskans strike a balance between the needs of the timber industry and the delicacy of the environment. For example, Alaska has more than 3,000 rivers and lakes, a number that rivals that of any other state in the union. With a backdrop of the Kenai Mountains, Kenai Lake is one of the spectacular. The state works to preserve such beauty and protect its waters, while still supporting an important segment of Alaska's economy.

Courtesy of Alaska Tourism Marketing Council;
Photo by Robin Hood

First called the Alaska Loggers Association, the Alaska Forest Association has represented the forest industry since 1957.

Courtesy of City of Ketchikan Museum Department, Tongass Historical Museum

Courtesy of Alaska Forest Association; Photo by Clark James Mishler

The forest regrowth on Betton Island, shown below right, is an example of the strong, sustainable forest-products industry advocated by the Alaska Forest Association. The AFA supports forest-management practices that protect wildlife, water quality and forest regeneration.

Courtesy of Alaska Tourism Marketing Council; Photo by Robin Hood

Courtesy of Alaska Forest Association; Photo by C. Keith Sturup

BUILDING THE FUTURE

When Alaskans build, they build fast and in quantity. Construction in The Great Land provides thousands of jobs and develops a lot of prime real estate. The industry accounts for 3.7 percent of the state's total employment.

But, nobody said it was going to be easy. Construction in Alaska presents enormous challenges not encountered in many places on the Outside. Contractors must cope with thaw-unstable soil, erratic weather, extremes of temperature, and a very brief construction season. They have had to develop innovative and effective methods, materials, and equipment to get the job done.

Get it done they will, regardless of circumstances or conditions. Building Alaska is a big assignment, after all, and it has been going on for almost 300 years. Contractors and construction and engineering firms of today show the same courage, determination, and competent efficiency displayed by their pioneering predecessors.

Chapter Seven

BOUNTY OF LAND AND SEA

BOUNTY OF LAND AND SEA

Courtesy of Alaska Seafood Marketing Institute;
Photo by Tony Lara

Crewmembers measure bairdi crab in the sea spray.

FISHING

Since Alaska has 6,640 miles of coastline, more than the rest of the U.S. combined and 38 percent of the nation's total, it is only natural that much of the state's prosperity has been closely connected with the sea. Nearly 60 percent of U.S. seafood production comes from Alaska, which is four times as great a yield as the next-most-productive fishing region.

Beginning with the Russian pursuit of sea otters, and the subsequent depletion of the fur seal population by American hunters, the frigid waters of Alaska have always contributed heavily to the success, and the coffers, of those who ply them for a living, especially the commercial fishers. In 1898, when Peter Buschmann built his homestead on the site of what would become Petersburg and opened the Icy Straits Packing Company, he was not breaking entirely new ground. The first Alaskan salmon canneries had been established in 1880.

Fishing is unquestionably the major harvesting endeavor of the 49th state and Alaska is indisputably the nation's number one when it comes to seafood production, studies show that fishing/processing is actually Alaska's largest private-sector employer, as well as its leading overall industry — employing 47 percent of the workforce, and producing more than 5.3 billion tons annually. This in turn earns processors some $2.5 billion. It is also the second-greatest contributor to the General Fund, after the oil and gas industry. In most of the state's coastal and island communities, significant percentages of the population own commercial fishing licenses. In fact, Alaskan fishers hold some 75 percent of the nation's active commercial entry permits. In 1998, there were as many as 765 seafood-processing permits issued to Alaskan companies.

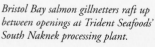

Bristol Bay salmon gillnetters raft up between openings at Trident Seafoods' South Naknek processing plant.

Courtesy of Trident Seafoods; Photo by Bart Eaton

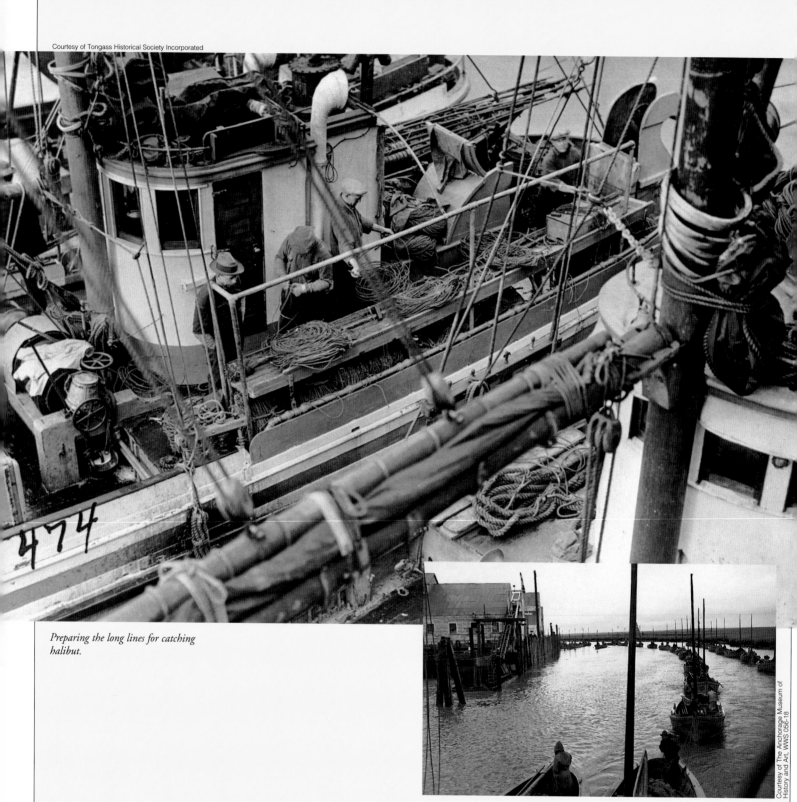

Preparing the long lines for catching halibut.

These fishing boats on Bristol Bay, dated before 1950, were commonly called "Bristol Bay Double-enders."

THE CATCH

When most people think of the finest Alaskan seafood, they think of the Kings — King crab and King salmon (also known as Chinook). These special treats do make up a certain percentage of the annual catch, but less rarefied species are in the vast majority: sockeye, coho, chum, and pink salmon; black cod, lingcod, rockfish, flounder, halibut and other bottomfish; Dungeness, Tanner, and Korean hair crab; scallops, abalone, and pink shrimp; herring, pollock, sablefish, and several kinds of sole. There is a variety of miscellaneous sea life for which new markets, mostly around the Pacific Rim, are being discovered: sea urchins, sea cucumbers, and some clam species, including the ugly giant of the Pacific Northwest, the geoduck. Plans are being made to increase management and production of these alternative fisheries, and intensify international promotion of the products. Sales efforts around the nation and the world are supported and assisted by the Alaska Seafood Marketing Institute, and the Salmon Council. These organizations were established by the state to assist government and industry in the marketing and distribution of the rich bounty of Alaska's icy waters.

Courtesy of Fairbanks Convention and Visitors Bureau; Photo by Steve Ulvei

The fishwheel is used by Native Alaskans in catching the salmon as they swim up stream.

THE FLEET

The Alaska fishing fleet is large and varied.

Purse seiners round up salmon and herring, and sell their catch whole to onshore processors to be canned, frozen, turned into bait, or stripped of their roe (salted herring eggs are a great delicacy in Japan).

Trollers catch salmon by trailing bait through the water. This method results in a low-volume, high-quality catch. Dressed on the spot at sea, troll-caught salmon are destined for public fish markets and upscale restaurants all over the world.

Longliners, as the name implies, lay lines on the seafloor up to a mile long, with thousands of baited hooks, to catch bottom fish. The catch is then ice-packed on board for later delivery to fresh and/or frozen markets.

Gillnetters catch salmon (primarily sockeye, chum, and coho) whose destination is usually canneries and freezing plants.

Trawlers drag their cone-shaped nets to collect pollock, pink shrimp, and bottomfish. While smaller vessels generally bring their catches to shore-based facilities, the enormous factory trawlers, which can reach up to 600 feet in length, generally feature onboard processing plants. In a two-hour tow, such a ship can net a catch of 100 tons. Much of the factory-trawler catch emerges as minced fish, to be used in fishsticks and surimi (imitation crabmeat), for which there is a large export market throughout the Pacific Rim.

Most of Alaska's marine mammal species are either endangered or protected, and harvesting is illegal. However, an exception to these restrictions is made for a certain level of subsistence hunting by Natives (see Chapter 9).

The cold waters off Alaska are prime crab-fishing grounds. Photos from left to right: crab traps; dungeness crabs on display; cleaning and packing king crab.

King crabbers aboard the F/V Oceanic work pot gear in the Bering Sea "lump."

FARMING

Alaska Natives have never been noted agriculturists. Their hunter/gatherer lifestyle provided subsistence for thousands of years; although some of the Eskimo tribes have herded reindeer for nearly as long.

While the acreage devoted to Alaskan agriculture falls far short of the boundless reaches of the oceans where seafood is gathered, various forms of farming and ranching are important to the state's economy as well.

Modern agriculture came north in the 1930s, when a group of farmers from the Outside formed a colony in the Matanuska Valley. It was part of an experiment by the federal government to relieve some of the hardships that weighed upon farmers by the Great Depression. Farming communities were soon established in the Tanana Valley around Fairbanks as well.

Not all of the colonists prospered, or even stayed. But, the project was successful enough that the descendants of many of the original settlers can still be found in the state's agricultural districts. Today, a broad range of vegetables are grown, processed, and marketed in-state including cabbage, lettuce, carrots, potatoes, and peas. However, most fruits, with the exception of berries, do not thrive in Alaska and must be imported.

Courtesy of Tongass Historical Society Incorporated

Oh no! This little girl looks troubled, but she's really covering her ears because the horn went off on her father's boat while he was making repairs in Southeast near Ketchikan. The tide would come in and the boat would be afloat once again.

While it is true that the intense, though brief, growing season can produce vegetables of mammoth size, these are mostly good only for exhibition at the State Fair (or, in the case of a 70-pound cabbage, coleslaw for the neighborhood). Barley, oats and feed grains are also important crops. Pigs and hogs, poultry, and cattle are ranched; sheep are raised in the Aleutians and elsewhere; musk oxen and reindeer are herded; and the state's 22 meat-processing plants include the only permitted reindeer-slaughter facility in the United States (foundation of the reindeer sausage industry).

Dairy farming has always been an important industry in the Valleys. Today, the dairy industry generates considerable annual revenue for the local and statewide economies, and provides fresh milk and other dairy products (yes, including ice cream) for area residents. This saves the prohibitive cost of flying these favorite items in from Outside.

Courtesy of Alaska Tourism Marketing Council; Photo by Kristen Kemmerling

There are at least 13 distinct caribou herds in Alaska. This one gathers on the tundra near Nome.

The growing season in Alaska is brief, but intense due to the extended hours of sunlight. As a result, vegetables can become huge.

Photo by Steve Holthaus

Courtesy of Wyndham Images

*The last brailer is brought aboard as the
sun sets on a long summer day.*

A typical day on the Bering Sea crab grounds means wind, rain and plenty of hard work.

Courtesy of Trident Seafoods; Photo by Bart Eaton

Look At The Size Of That Thing!

As should be obvious by now, "big" is the operative word where almost all things Alaskan are concerned. It is true of the land itself, of many of its animals, of the spirit and the plans of its people, and for the most part, of its products.

Take fish, for example. While the state's annual seafood harvest is, of course, enormous in itself, consisting of hundreds of millions of pounds each year, the most impressive individual specimens are often landed by sport fishers. A big king salmon may weigh as much as 60 or 70 pounds. While the all-time record halibut tipped the scales at some 500 pounds; 100 to 300 is the more usual range. The body of a really giant king crab can often measure a couple of feet across. Salmon derbies and other lively competitions for biggest and best are held across the state during the fishing season and the cash prizes awarded are usually secondary to the thrill of the catch.

Visitors and newcomers to The Great Land are also staggered by the sizes to which plants can grow in the long hours of summer daylight. This is as true of homegrown vegetables and flowers as it is of commercial produce. One-hundred-plus-pound cabbages and basketball-sized lettuces are not at all uncommon, while root vegetables thrive as well. The Alaska State Fair, held annually at Palmer in the Matanuska Valley, is a popular showcase for such monumental agricultural achievements, for both working farmers and enthusiastic home horticulturists.

THE OUTDOORS ADVENTURE

OME OUT AND PLAY

The Great Outdoors just doesn't get any greater. The biggest mountains, the wildest rivers, the densest forests, the grandest glaciers, the broadest waterways all await outdoor-minded Alaskans and visitors alike. Leisure and recreation related industry accounts for millions of dollars in annual revenues.

For those interested in preplanned activities, there are companies that organize fishing, hunting, and sightseeing trips; whitewater rafting voyages; ski tours and climbing excursions; or almost any other kind of outdoors expedition imaginable. Or you can wing it, all on your own — just you and the wilderness, face to face.

There are 15 national parks, preserves, and monuments in the state, comprising more than 54 million acres; and more than a dozen National Wildlife Refuges. More than half of the nation's 104 million acres of designated Wilderness (58,182,216 acres) is found within Alaska. The state holds 10 of the 15 National Preserves. Much of the federally administered land in Alaska is designated multiple-purpose, and one of the major purposes is recreation. The state, for its part, manages 130 parks, covering about three million acres.

Remote fishing and hunting camps, accessible only by light plane or riverboat, beckon to those who want to get as close to nature as possible. Clean and inviting camping areas provide comfortable havens for the less ambitious. Two world-class ski resorts, and several smaller ones, summon enthusiasts (see below). There are even extreme skiing facilities at Valdez. Mountain- and rock-climbing expeditions are also very popular.

Alaska is home to some of the most beautiful and productive fishing waters for both fly and spin fishermen. At the end of the day, there's nothing better than cooking the catch over a campfire.

Mountain goat.

*Game birds like this arctic ptarmigan
are popular with bird hunters.*

THE ANIMAL KINGDOM

In some places, the wildlife does indeed rule, and it is a wise human who bows to their authority. For instance, on Kodiak Island dwells the uncrowned monarch, the gargantuan Kodiak Brown Bear, which can weigh over 1600 pounds and stand 10 to 12 feet tall on its hind legs. The Kodiak "Brownie" likes to fish and will, if necessary, put up with adventurous human anglers who find themselves sharing the salmon run, almost side by side, with the great, preoccupied carnivores. The grizzly, with its characteristic shoulder hump, is found throughout the state, and there is a black bear population, primarily in Southeastern.

Then there is the polar bear. Competing with the Kodiak Brown for the title of Earth's largest land carnivore, it also weighs in at up to 1600 pounds, and measures as much as seven feet in length.

While bear attacks on humans are quite rare, many remote communities experience at least one such unfortunate encounter each year. In the wild, on their turf, it is always best to give the big boys plenty of space and warning of your presence.

The other major predator of The Great Land is, of course, the ever-controversial wolf. Although gray wolves are endangered throughout most of their indigenous North American habitat, the Alaska population is not only surviving but thriving. About 6,000 to 7,000 animals are scattered across the Interior and Arctic, in packs of various sizes. A big male may weigh up to 170 pounds, and measure 6'6" from nose to tail-tip. The wolf strain can be clearly seen in many Alaskan sled-dogs. Wolves are probably the animals that visitors to the state most want to see in the wild.

Courtesy of Alaska Seafood Marketing Institute

Polar bear.

Another creature with serious carnivore credentials is the shy and solitary wolverine, a scrappy animal with an aggressive attitude and an impressive natural armory of teeth and claws. Coyotes, relative new-comers, roam parts of the state, and that wily big cat, the lynx, is found in most areas.

A big bull moose, largest of the deer family, can stand up to 6-1/2 feet at the shoulder, and weigh 1,800 pounds. Cows are somewhat smaller, but not really enough to notice, especially if you happen to encounter one when you are driving a small car. Such encounters are quite likely, since moose are probably the most urbanized of Alaska's wildlife. They frequently stroll into and through towns, even the largest cities, especially in winter when forage is scarce. Long lines of stopped traffic, waiting for a cow and her calf to cross a major road, are common sights in springtime. Cows are generally nonaggressive, unless their calves are threatened; but a bull in rut will charge almost anything that moves, up to and including locomotives of the Alaska Railroad.

Caribou, and their largely domesticated relatives the reindeer, are Alaska's principal herbivores. Migrating caribou roll over the tundra in enormous numbers like the Porcupine Herd, currently numbering around 160,000. The major caribou predator is the wolf. Reindeer are herded and used for milk, meat, and as draft animals by many Native communities. A wild population is restricted to the Seward Peninsula and Nunavak Island. There is even a prosperous industry manufacturing reindeer sausage, a Polish-style delicacy that is a favorite tourist treat.

Mom?

The State of Alaska has 45.5 percent of the nation's wetlands.

Other members of the deer family include the Roosevelt Elk of Afognak and Raspberry Islands, which were imported from Washington State in the 1920s, and the small Black-Tailed Sitka Deer of Southeastern which is native to the region.

The biggest grazers on the tundra are the shaggy musk oxen. These longhaired bovines were once hunted to extinction in Alaska, mainly because it is about as difficult as hunting cattle. However, the population was re-stocked from Greenland in the 1930s. Today, their soft underwool (quiviut) is the basis of a considerable cottage industry. Quiviut is among the rarest, lightest, finest and most valuable natural fibers on earth. There are several farms and experimental stations where the domesticated animals can be seen, and quiviut garments purchased from Native crafters.

There are also a few hundred bison wandering about the Interior. Dall Sheep, the world's only wild white sheep, and mountain goats inhabit the highlands. Sure-footed climbers, they leap among the crags and canyons. Smaller animals abound in Alaska: beavers, river otters, porcupines, raccoons, martens, muskrats, arctic foxes, snowshoe and arctic hares, ermine, lemmings, pikas and a variety of marmots and other ground squirrels.

Hunting and/or trapping permits for most, though by no means all, Alaskan animals may be obtained through the Alaska's Department of Fish and Game, and about 100,000 hunters do so each year.

Humpback whales are a common sight in the waters of Alaska and kayakers often have the best vantage point — as long as they don't get too close!

Courtesy of Alaska Tourism Marketing Council; Photo by Robin Hood

A stranded starfish waits for the return of high tide.

Courtesy of City of Valdez

Sea lions on a rock in Prince William Sound.

Photo by Steve Holthaus

Horned puffins.

Courtesy of Alaska Department of Fish and Game

Courtesy of Anchorage Convention and Visitors Bureau

Ptarmigan.

Bird life is also extremely varied and includes many species rare and/or endangered elsewhere, such as bald eagles and peregrine falcons. Migratory species like the far-traveling Arctic tern (whose annual pole-to-pole round trip is the longest in the avian world) and the puffin contrast with such stay-at-homes as the enormous black raven (sacred to many Native clans), and the willow ptarmigan (the state bird), which changes the color of its plumage with the seasons. Waterfowl, including Canada and snow geese, inhabit lakes, rivers, and wetlands across the state.

Alaskan marine mammals are almost too numerous to detail, but include: porpoises, sea otters, fur seals, harbor seals, California sea lions (best known as performing seals), the extremely rare Steller's sea lion (with its characteristic mane), and the walrus, plus beluga, bowhead, gray, humpback, and killer whales (also known as orcas). Grays and humpbacks are both migratory, traveling between northern feeding grounds in summer and winter grounds in Mexico and Hawaii, respectively. Both species are classified as endangered. Some whales are still occasionally legally hunted by certain Native peoples to help sustain their ancient subsistence lifestyle (see Chapter 9).

There are no wild reptiles in Alaska, which is a matter of great relief to snake-hating residents and visitors. And, no matter what you have heard, Alaskan mosquitoes are *not* a separate and especially bloodthirsty breed; and no, they are not really the size of small birds, either. However, they do seem particularly large and vigorous, and it does require serious and intensive repellent to ward them off during their brief, but intense season. No Alaskan species carries disease, and they are generally a lot more trouble to the animal population than to most humans.

Courtesy of the City of Wrangell; Photo by Ivan Simonek

In spring, the Stikine River is host to the largest springtime congregation of bald eagles in the world.

Taking The Bait

Alaskans fish. People come to Alaska to fish.

Not just to make a living or fill the larder, but for fun. In fact, that is one of the main reasons people *do* come to Alaska, and why a lot live here. Sport fishing, for which over 400,000 licenses are issued each year, is a major contributor to the economy, supporting hundreds of companies and thousands of individuals. From day trips by road or river-raft, to fly-in lodges and fishcamps in the remote wilderness, to charter-boat expeditions for offshore angling, the Alaska fishing experience has something to offer everyone: king, silver, pink, red, and chum salmon; lake, rainbow, cutthroat, and Dolly Varden trout; northern pike, arctic char, arctic grayling, whitefish, shellfish, and halibut. Favorite fishing destinations are the Kenai, Copper, Kobuk, and Susitna Rivers; Kodiak Island; Kachemak and Resurrection Bays; Prince William Sound; the sheltered waters of the Inside Passage, and a wide variety of isolated streams and lakes reachable only by small plane.

This Alaskan fisherman knows that the only practical way to reach many parts of the state, including the best fishing spots, is by float plane.

Courtesy of Alaska Tourism Marketing Council; Photo by Robin Hood

Courtesy of Alaska's Fishing Unlimited Lodge

Off to the coast (Shelikof Strait and Kodiak Island area) to fish for the mighty Silver Salmon! One is definitely close to the pot of gold at the end of the rainbow at this beautiful location.

Fishing for silver salmon at Bird Creek, near Anchorage.

Photo by Gary Zimmerman

*Campers enjoy the evening and view in
a campsite at Nemo, near Wrangell.*

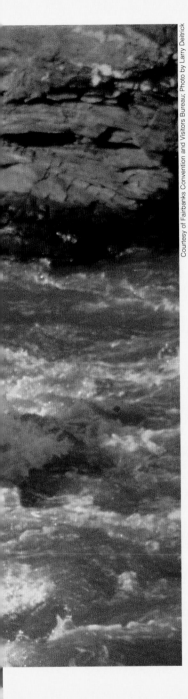

Fairbanks and the Denali area have some excellent rivers for rafting and kayaking thrills.

NUMBER ONE PARK PLACE

That is Alaska. Among the 54 million acres of national parks, preserves, and monuments in the state, are several of the world's most stupendous.

Denali is the Great One. That is the name given by Natives to North America's tallest peak. We know it now as Mt. McKinley. Denali is also the name of the vast national park and preserve that surrounds the mountain. Natives still prefer to call both peak and park Denali. The state passed a resolution to the same effect at one point, but it just did not seem to take with the rest of the world, especially the mountaineering community.

Every aspect of the climate and terrain of Southcentral and Interior Alaska is represented within the boundaries of the six-million-acre Denali National Park and Preserve: from thick forests of birch, alder, aspen, and evergreens; to rolling subarctic tundra dotted with lowbush berries and colorful ground cover.

For the most part, Denali belongs to the animals. Moose, caribou, Dall Sheep, mountain goats, wolves, and of course the mighty grizzly all roam the vast parkland. But, human presence is part of the place as well. The tiny mining settlement of Kantishna, deep within the park with its small Native-owned Roadhouse, is quite a contrast to the relative sophistication of the picturesque Park Station Hotel. Nearby towns like Healy and Cantwell offer more urban amenities. While the year-round population of the park is small, there will always be a few hardy souls who brave the isolation and extreme weather to prospect, raise their sled-dogs, conserve, create, work hard, and just plain survive.

There is, of course, the mountain itself. Soaring almost four miles into the sky, McKinley has long been rated as one of the most challenging, and sometimes deadliest, of the world's great climbing destinations. Since the initial attempt in 1903, and first successful ascent in 1913, thousands of climbers have achieved the summit. Today, over 1,000 make the effort annually, and in a good year, 50 percent will summit. Sadly, far too many have lost their lives in the attempt.

Weather conditions on and around the mountain during the brief May through July season can vary sharply, and prove extremely treacherous. Sudden blizzards, avalanches, ice fog, and spring thaws have all claimed their victims, and will probably continue to do so as long as there are those who are willing to challenge the continent's premiere peak.

Although Denali is undoubtedly Alaska's showcase park, there are many others. One of the most fascinating is Katmai National Park and Preserve on the Alaska Peninsula in Southwest. This park covers the area devastated by the 1912 explosion of Novarupta volcano (see Chapter 2), and includes the world-famous Valley of 10,000 Smokes and a portion of the Alagnak Wild River. First established in 1918 as a National Monument, Katmai was given Park and Preserve status in 1980. It is part of a National Wilderness as well.

About 55,000 people make the effort to visit Katmai annually. Since there is no direct road access to the park, it is only accessible by air or water. Backcountry hikers enthusiastically endorse the park, with its rugged terrain, still-steaming volcanic vents, and wide variety of wildlife. Air and boat tours out of the nearby town of King Salmon are popular ways to see the sights of Katmai.

Courtesy of Alaska Tourism Marketing Council; Photo by Robin Hood

Nearly every visitor to Alaska wants to see the famed Mount McKinley in Denali National Park. Mount McKinley, also know as Denali, is the highest peak in North America at 20,320 feet. Camping is available within the park boundaries and in nearby Denali State Park.

Courtesy of Fairbanks Convention and Visitors Bureau; Photo by Larry Deitrick

The dramatic flow of this glacier gives the impression of a frozen waterfall.

Courtesy of Alaska Tourism Marketing Council; Photo by Robin Hood

Sea kayakers are drawn to Alaska both to paddle its sheltered waterways and challenge its open coasts. Kayakers can visit tidewater glaciers such as this one in Glacier Bay National Park.

Courtesy of Wyndham Images

Another perennially popular destination is Glacier Bay National Park in the St. Elias Mountains of Southeastern. Tidewater glaciers up to 200 feet tall ring the bay, which is surrounded by great peaks such as Mt. Fairweather at 15,300 feet. This park is more than 5,000 square miles in area.

Wrangell-Saint Elias is the largest parcel in the National Park system, and extends from the Gulf of Alaska along the border with Canada's Yukon Territory. It contains the country's largest grouping of peaks over 16,000 feet, including Mt. Saint Elias, America's second-highest at 18,008 feet.

A National Park which has occasioned much controversy is Gates of the Arctic, which takes in 13,125 square miles of Arctic wilderness, including the Brooks Range. The fragile ecosystem and diverse wildlife of the area, which is also a Biosphere Reserve, makes this park unique in the national system.

Camping, hiking, fishing, kayaking and flightseeing are popular pursuits in Kenai Fjords National Park, southwest of Seward in Southcentral. This park contains the Harding Icefield, the nation's largest, as well as Exit Glacier.

The National Park Service also maintains parks, preserves, and monuments like Cape Krusenstern, Kobuk Valley, Noatak, and Aniakchak, as well as two National Historical Parks. The first, the National Historical Park at Sitka, was established in 1910 to commemorate the Battle of Sitka in 1804. It is Alaska's oldest federally-designated park (see Chapter 2 & Chapter 9). The 107-acre park also includes Sitka's striking totem-pole collection. Alaska's second National Historical Park (NHP), Klondike Gold Rush NHP, is unique in that it occupies two sites in two states — at Skagway and Seattle, Washington.

Courtesy of Southeast Alaska Tourism Marketing Council; Photo by John Hyde

The scenery along any cyclist's route is terrific. Mountains, glaciers, wildlife and gorgeous sunsets are all a part of the experience.

Ski jumping is not for the faint-of-heart, but facilities are available for those who have the skill — and the nerve.

Courtesy of Wyndham Images

Courtesy of Wyndham Images

Helicopter flightseeing is a great way to reach tops of glaciers, mountains and other places that might otherwise be inaccessible. In the winter, heli-skiing is a popular sport, while in the summer months, adventurers go heli-hiking.

State Parks include Denali, Chugach, Chilkat, Kachemak Bay, Shuyak Island, and Wood-Tikchik, among others. State Recreation Areas are found at Nancy Lake, Chena River, Caines Head, and Worthington Glacier. There are also Marine Parks at Surprise Cove and Shoup Bay. The state also maintains the Big Delta Historical Park on the Tanana River, Totem Bight Historical Park near Ketchikan, and the Chilkat Bald Eagle Reserve in Southeastern.

Not all of these areas are easily accessible, but each is well worth the effort of visiting. A visitor will never be closer to all the natural wonders of the world than he or she can be in Alaska.

Climbing The Peaks

Of the 20 tallest mountains in the United States, 17 are in Alaska. Mountaineering is another activity that draws people north. In addition to Mt. McKinley (see above), popular climbing destinations include: Mt. Saint Elias (18,008 feet); Mt. Foraker (17,400 feet); Mt. Fairweather (15,300 feet); Mt. Hunter (14,573 feet); and Mt. Wrangell (14,163 feet). Climbers find challenges in the Alaska, Brooks, Chugach, Kenai, and Wrangell Ranges. Much valuable information and support can be obtained from the Mountaineering Club of Alaska, Inc., a non-profit organization based in Anchorage.

*Winter back-country trekking on
Thompson Pass near Valdez.*

Courtesy of City of Valdez

Hitting The Slopes

*It may seem too obvious to say that lots of people come to Alaska to ski,
but it's a plain fact. Alaskans themselves spend a great deal of time, and
money, on the slopes as well, pointing with pride to such Olympic-caliber
competitors as medalists Tommy Moe and Hilary Lindh.*

*While almost every community of reasonable size and suitable terrain
has areas for alpine or cross-country skiing nearby, there are only four
facilities in the state that can really be considered ski resorts. Three are
located in the Anchorage area:*

*Alyeska Resort is well-established and the best-known ski resort in
Alaska with 470 acres in the Chugach Range and a 307-room
first-class hotel.*

Base elevation: 250 feet (lowest in U.S.)
Summit: 3,939 feet
Slopes: Beginners to double-black-diamond
Annual Snowfall: 580 inches
Trails: 62
Longest run: 10,560 feet; Vertical drop: 2,500 feet
*Lifts: 2 rope, 3 double chairs, 2 quad chairs, 1 high-speed quad,
     1 60-passenger aerial tram*
*Activities: alpine skiing, cross-country skiing, night skiing, glacier skiing,
     snowboarding, snowmobiling, kayaking/rafting, fishing, air tours,
     performing arts, llama pack trips, family entertainment, boating,
     sightseeing*

Ice climbing adds a unique twist for rock climbers interested in a new challenge.

Courtesy of Wyndham Images

Snowmobilers on Hogback Trail in Valdez.

Courtesy of City of Valdez

An avalanche in progress mars a fresh blanket of snow on this peak in the Chugach Mountains.

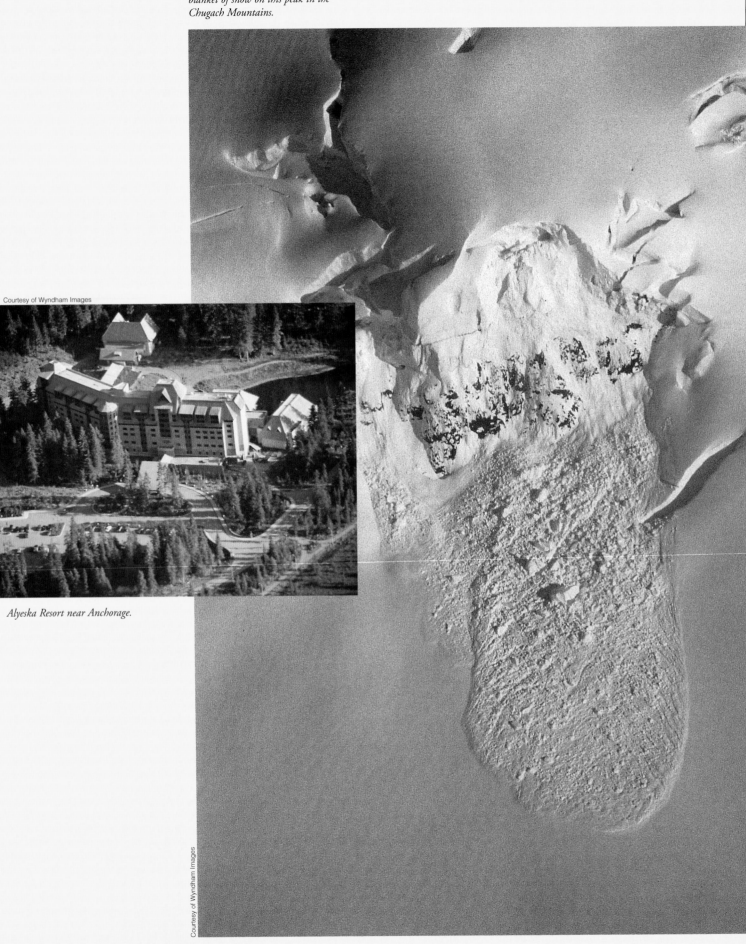

Courtesy of Wyndham Images

Alyeska Resort near Anchorage.

Courtesy of Wyndham Images

Alpenglow Resort

Base elevation: 2,500 feet

Summit: 3,900 feet

Slopes: Beginners to double-black-diamond

Annual snowfall: 250 inches

Longest run: 10,560 feet; Vertical drop: 1,400 feet

Lifts: 1 rope, 1 T-bar, 1 double chair

Activities: alpine skiing, snowboarding, night skiing

Hilltop

Base elevation: 600 feet

Summit: 894 feet

Slopes: Beginners to black diamond

Annual Snowfall: 100 inches (artificial)

Longest run: 2,090 feet; Vertical drop: 294 feet

Activities: alpine skiing, cross-country (75 km) skiing, snowboarding
(half or quarter-pipe), night skiing

Alaska's fourth sizable ski resort is Eaglecrest on Douglas Island in Juneau. It covers 640 acres, and is within 12 miles of the amenities of downtown.

Base elevation: 1,200 feet

Summit: 2,500 feet

Slopes: Beginners to double-black-diamond

Annual snowfall: 300 inches

Trails: 31

Longest run: 10,560 feet; Vertical drop: 1,400 feet

Lifts: 1 surface, 2 double chairs

Activities: alpine skiing, cross-country (5 k) skiing, snowboarding
(half or quarter-pipe), night skiing, heli-skiing.

Virtually all ski areas offer lessons at various levels and for all ages. Facilities like restaurants and lodging are found on-site or conveniently close.

Virtually all ski areas offer lessons and runs that are appropriate for beginners, as well as more difficult challenges for the experienced skier.

Courtesy of Wyndham Images

Chapter Nine

THE ORIGINAL ALASKANS

THE ORIGINAL ALASKANS

Muskox.

A LONG HISTORY IN THE LAND

Since the historic Native Land Claims Settlement Act of 1971, Alaska's Native peoples and their corporations have played a vital role in the modern economy, culture, and lifestyle of the north, matching their contributions throughout its history.

Alaska Natives can be loosely grouped according to geographic distribution, although there is a great deal of overlap statewide. For example, the Southeastern region is home primarily to the Tlingit, Haida, and Tsimshian tribes.

The Tlingit are the principal tribe of Southeastern. Scholars dispute whether or not the Tlingit arrived here after the hypothetical land-bridge migration from Asia, or came from the interior of North America more than 10,000 years ago. In any case, they established a wealthy and settled culture, fishing and trading throughout the Pacific Northwest. The Tlingit were famed for their cedar-plank longhouses, adorned with carved totems, and their elaborate potlatch celebrations. In 1804, the Tlingit attempted an uprising against the Russians at Sitka, in what would be the last armed conflict between Northwest American Natives and white settlers. The National Historical Park at Sitka (see Chapter 8) commemorates this event, which ended in a massacre.

The Haida and Tsimshian peoples, who share many cultural aspects with the Tlingits, arrived in Southeastern in the 1700s and 1800s, respectively. The Haida settled on Prince of Wales Island, and the Tsimshian on Annette Island. In the present-day Native communities of Southeastern, fishing and logging are the primary industries, with subsistence hunting and fishing helping to support life. The arts and artifacts of Southeastern Natives are rich and varied. In song, dance, and legend; carvings, paintings, basketry, and textiles; an old, prosperous, and fascinating culture is reflected.

A seal hunter stands on the Arctic ice in the spring.

Courtesy of Arctic Slope Regional Corporation; Photo by Chris Arend

*Eskimo children dance on the sealskin
blanket after a blanket toss.*

Southcentral and Interior Alaska are mostly Athabascan territory. The Athabascan presence in Alaska is very ancient, indeed, and their origins are mysterious. Anthropologists have discovered that the tribe's language is closely related to that of the Navajo of the American Southwest. The Athabascan people have historically dominated Interior, Southcentral, and much of western Alaska. Those historical boundaries now include Anchorage, Fairbanks, the Kenai Peninsula, Denali National Park and Preserve, and the vast Arctic National Wildlife Refuge.

Until early in the 20th century, the traditional lifestyle of this group was nomadic. They followed migrating game in birchbark canoes and on dogsleds. By hunting the caribou and moose, they derived food, clothing, and even shelter in the form of skins stretched over portable frameworks. Once having established permanent settlements, they spread their culture and art throughout northern Alaska and interior Canada. They are skilled basket-weavers, and are still renowned for their fine beadwork, a tradition dating back to the mid-1800s. It was at that time that the Hudson's Bay Company first introduced glass beads as trade goods to the Athabascans.

There are nine prominent tribes within Alaska's Athabascan population, each containing several major clans. Athabascans have also inhabited the Southwestern, Western Coastal, and Aleutian regions for millennia, together with the Alutiiqs, Unangan (also know as Aleuts), and the Yu'pik Eskimos. In the Aleutians these peoples, numbered about 16,000 at the time Vitus Bering showed up in 1741. They lived in large partially-buried communal houses and subsisted on fresh and dried fish (mainly salmon), seals, and sea otters, all of which they caught from their kayaks and umiaks, crafted from hides. They were famed for their beautiful fur and feather parkas and boots and their tall, elaborate wooden hats.

Courtesy of Alaska Seafood Marketing Institute

This Native is doing rather well as he fishes the freezing Arctic waters.

Courtesy of Alaska Tourism Marketing Council; Photo by Kristen Kemmerling

The fish-drying rack is a common sight in most Native villages. Summer is the time for harvesting and drying pink, silver and king salmon.

In Southeast Alaska, the Naa Kahidi Theater uses regalia and costume to tell stories.

The Unangan in particular were noted for their hospitality, which they freely extended to almost everyone. Including the Russians proved to be a tactical error for which they, like the Tlingit of Southeastern, paid heavily. For the most part, they lived in a spirit of peace and cooperation among neighboring villages.

The Arctic is largely the province of the Yu'pik and Inupiat tribes. While "Eskimo" is still used as a term of convenience in reference to all indigenous Arctic peoples, it must be remembered that this is *not* a Native word. Rather, it is a catchall description applied by early explorers to the inhabitants of Arctic North America, Europe, and Asia. Today's far-north Natives prefer to be called by their tribal designations, such as Inupiat, Inuit, and Yu'pik.

In their isolated communities, the Yu'pik had much less contact with white settlers than did other Natives, and therefore possess one of the least corrupted of Alaska's Native cultures. They still speak English as a second language, maintaining their own traditional dialects in everyday life, and are known for their beautiful and intricate basket-work.

Inupiat culture is venerable and multi-faceted. Prior to white contact, these people subsisted on migratory animals and birds, marine mammals and fish, and the greens and berries of the brief tundra summer. Barrow, for example, was a noted whaling community well into the 20th century. Even the great polar bear was fair, if challenging, game, and in some places, still is. Such a hunt was often an important rite of passage for the young men of the tribes.

Eskimo whalers in wooden whale boats at Point Barrow in 1920.

K'niuk, an Eskimo man of Northwest Alaska, circa 1920.

A Native Elder of Barrow.

Courtesy of Alaska Tourism Marketing Council; Photo by Kristen Kemmerling

*The totem pole is more than art.
The carvings tell family histories.*

Courtesy of Alaska Seafood Marketing Institute

While the precise origins of the first Alaskans are still being debated, they have certainly been a presence in the land for many thousands of years. In fact, evidence suggests that there has been a permanent settlement at the present site of Barrow for at least 1,500 years. Athabascan culture has been thriving here for some 8,000 to 10,000 years.

One of the most significant aspects of Native Alaskan history is purely contemporary. Passage of the landmark Alaska Native Land Claims Settlement Act in 1971 represented the first genuine effort by the U.S. government to compensate Native Americans for lands and livelihoods lost to later settlers. The Act was the culmination of an intensive multi-year international publicity campaign aimed at locating and registering all people of at least one-quarter Native ancestry (see sidebar). It ceded ownership and control of 40 million acres and nearly a billion dollars to Alaska Natives, who formed 12 Regional Corporations to administer their property, collect and distribute revenues, and handle investment. Another entity, The Thirteenth Corporation, was established to look after the interests of qualifying shareholders living outside the state. Although The Thirteenth received no lands, it did share in the financial settlement.

These Corporations play a major and vital role in the modern Alaskan economy and infrastructure. Companies owned and/or operated by bodies like Cook Inlet Region, Inc. (CIRI), Arctic Slope Regional Corporation (ASRC), and NANA Region Corporation are involved in almost every aspect of commerce and industry. Many have established partnerships with Outside interests to expand their influence into new markets.

An illustration by John Webber of the inside of a house in Oonalashka. It can be found in Atlas of Cooks Third Voyage, 1780.

Courtesy of The Anchorage Museum of History and Art, B86.94.10.58

Spring break-up on the Arctic Ocean.

LIVING OFF THE LAND AND SEA

Besides the reindeer and caribou which the Arctic inhabitants have hunted and/or herded throughout their history, many other species have been, and some still are, objects of subsistence trapping, hunting, and fishing by the Native population. The advent of modern fabrics has somewhat curtailed trapping and hunting of some fur-bearers, except for use in certain ceremonial garments.

The most important marine mammal species to many far-north dwellers is surely the walrus. Big bulls can measure 11 feet long and weigh as much as a ton and a half. Their tusks, which may reach more than a foot in length, are primarily used for digging up the clams, other bivalves, and crustaceans on which the massive animals live. The tusks are also used for help in ice-climbing and in occasional fights.

Historically, Native hunters have put every part of the animal to good use — bones, hides, tusks, and even whiskers. Today, Natives are the only individuals legally allowed to be in possession of unworked walrus ivory, a key component in many authentic Native arts and crafts (see sidebar). That is why Native craftspeople are as concerned as are the government and environmentalists about ivory-poaching activities, in the course of which walrus are often brutally decapitated for their tusks, and their headless carcasses left to rot.

Whale hunting is even more sensitive. Native peoples of the Pacific Northwest and Alaska maintained active whaling cultures up to, and even after, contact with white cultures. Bowhead and white beluga whales were a particularly important resource for Arctic dwellers. A chunk of blubber or piece of tail fluke (muktuk, or "Eskimo chewing gum") qualified as a prized delicacy.

In Barrow, the arched ribs of a whale stand on the beach of the Arctic Ocean as testament to the area's culture.

*Tundra in the summer on the
north slope.*

Tundra in the winter on the north slope.

As modern thought tends increasingly toward preservation of Earth's largest creatures, whales are hunted somewhat less in the north. Native hunters traditionally pursued whales in small boats, using hand-held harpoons. Due to the great size and wandering ways of the migrating grays and humpbacks it would be difficult to exterminate these whales systematically using such methods. However, the introduction of western technology, beginning with the invention of the harpoon gun in the 1860s, increased the efficiency of the kill and changed everything. From that point on, populations of both species declined sharply.

Whale hunting by Native peoples is generally still carried out in traditional fashion, and tends to be more ritualistic than practical, except in those few cases where whale is still a significant element in a subsistence diet. Humpback, gray, and killer whales are represented with great reverence in the totems of a number of Southeast clans.

Old Mary, a basket weaver of Orca, Alaska, 1907.

CALLING ALL NATIVES

It was a massive, worldwide campaign that began in 1968 and continues to this day. It is the Alaska Native Enrollment Program, aimed at locating, identifying, and educating individuals of full or partial Native extraction.

The project was launched as soon as it became evident that Alaska Natives would indeed receive official compensation of lands and money. It was administered by the Bureau of Indian Affairs (BIA) under the auspices of the federal government. Through a series of public-service materials (none were taxpayer-funded), the Bureau sought to locate and register everyone of one-fourth or more Native ancestry. Prominent spokespeople of Native American heritage, such as Jay Silverheels and Cher, were recruited for TV and radio spots. Overseas military publications and broadcasters helped to inform potential beneficiaries abroad. Eventually, eligibles were found in almost every country on earth.

While the original program featured a tight deadline for registration, this was extended several times. Some Native Corporations, especially the Thirteenth Corporation, are still accepting new members. A few of the more prosperous corporations have expanded their criteria to include members with one-eighth, or even one-sixteenth, Native blood.

Native Alaskans have dried salmon for centuries and many still use the traditional methods.

Eskimo blanket toss.

Courtesy of Arctic Slope Regional Corporation; Photo by Chris Arend

Courtesy of Fairbanks Convention and Visitors Bureau

The Athabascan culture is shared with locals and visitors in many ways: tours, art festivals and dance.

ACCEPT NO SUBSTITUTES

Many of those who visit The Great Land come home with beautiful craft items or works of art created by Alaska Natives: jewelry, ivory or wood carvings, paintings, sculpture, and bead or quill embroidery. Artists and craftspeople work in a wide variety of media, like soapstone and jade; gold, silver, and hematite; furs and fabrics and fibers. Crafts are the basis for cottage industries of considerable importance to the Native community.

That is the reason for Alaska Native Arts & Crafts (ANAC), a state-sponsored program designed to certify the authenticity of Native-produced articles of art and culture. The oval black ANAC seal, with its silver hand, is a familiar symbol to Alaskans. It is the buyer's guarantee that purchases are the genuine, real Alaska deal.

THE HUMAN INGREDIENT

The University of Alaska Museum, one of the state's top 10 attractions, offers exhibits on Alaska's natural and cultural history. These Eskimo drummer sculptures are located on the University of Alaska Fairbanks campus.

THE BIG QUESTION

What makes an Alaskan?

Of course, there are as many answers as there are Alaskans. But there is an overall spirit that knits them together, a special attitude and outlook which sets Alaskans apart from everyone else on earth.

They're tough. It took strong people to settle this wilderness, and others just as strong maintain their foothold in the face of climatic extremes, changing fortunes, and a variety of natural disasters.

They're young. Alaska's median age is just 30.5. While this number fluctuates with the years and Alaska's economy, it is *always* low. Aside from those born and raised here, bright young people from all over the world seem to find an irresistible challenge on the Last Frontier.

They're educated. Statistically, well over 80 percent of adult Alaskans have completed high school, much higher than the national average, and many have had some college. Primary- and secondary-school students consistently score above the national average on the standardized tests mandated by the state. Alaska's public-school system is widely acknowledged to be one of the best in the United States. There was a time, not too long ago, when Alaskan youths who wanted to complete a four-year degree in-state had no option but to head to Fairbanks and the main campus of the University of Alaska. Today, with a number of community and junior colleges (including Sheldon Jackson Junior College in Sitka, the state's oldest institution of higher learning) and distance-learning programs, the University of Alaska continues to meet the post-secondary needs of thousands of residents. A variety of technical, vocational, and professional institutions and training programs offer many continuing-education options to ambitious residents.

This ice sculpture entitled Fire Starter *by Peter Slavin and Scot Rella was an entrant in Ice Alaska '97 in Fairbanks.*

Photo by David Stratton

These patriots are ready to celebrate Independence Day.

Summertime brings summer sports. Devoted fans root for their favorite semi-pro teams.

They're clever, creative, and ingenious. The great size and harsh conditions of the land can often render conventional tactics and solutions impractical, or even impossible. Decisions on methods and materials can be affected by climate and weather, distance, time-differences, and labor-availability, among other factors. So, Alaskans have to be able to think fast on their feet to achieve their goals. Many innovative techniques and products have been developed by Alaskans in response to their unique environment, and then put to work around the world for the benefit of others.

They're politically aware, and *very* active. The structure of their state and local governments make such involvement easy. Like most states, Alaska has a bicameral legislature, consisting of a 20-person Senate (with four-year terms and elections staggered every two years) and a 40-seat House of Representatives (with two-year terms). At the local level, boroughs (rather than counties), and the municipalities and communities they contain, enjoy a considerable degree of autonomy. The Governor and Lieutenant Governor serve four-year terms. Because of its small population, the state has only one Representative in the U.S. House, and its two Senators. Alaskan politics tends to be at its most intense at the grassroots level. Initiative and Referendum procedures are frequently employed by a citizenry with a strong sense of civic responsibility and self-determination.

They're friendly. While it's not exactly *Northern Exposure,* there *is* a sprit of neighborly small-town camaraderie that binds Alaskans together, and holds out a hearty welcome to all those "Cheechakos" (newcomers) who wish to embrace the northern lifestyle. Indeed, there are always lots of offbeat and colorful characters around. Alaskans are also intensely individualistic.

Courtesy of University of Alaska Anchorage; Photo by Michael Dinneen

The UAA Seawolves face perennial powers in Division I Western Collegiate Hockey Association action.

They've got the Alaskan Attitude. It is a generally casual, relaxed, and open-minded approach to life, coupled with a fierce determination to achieve and excel.

They're enterprising. It is no accident that the population boasts such a high percentage of entrepreneurs. The same drive, ingenuity, initiative, and sense of humor that make living in the north possible are put to work in business in new and unusual ways. These imaginative explorers often find that the Alaska experience offers a fresh perspective on all their ongoing endeavors.

The value of Alaska's potential workforce is virtually unlimited. The state enthusiastically supports employers and workers in every area of business and industry by providing a wide variety of resources and assistance.

THE RESEARCH RESOURCE

The Alaska Agricultural College and School of Mines opened in Fairbanks in 1915, became the University of Alaska in 1935, and evolved into the future state's only public institution of higher learning. Today the University is a statewide system with additional full universities in Anchorage and Juneau, satellite campuses throughout Alaska, distance-learning programs in 113 communities, and more than a hundred different research sites and facilities. The University of Alaska Anchorage is the state's largest and most comprehensive university and includes three academic schools, four colleges, and a wide range of centers and institutes focusing on various cultural and scientific fields. The University of Alaska system is a source of information and enlightenment for business, industry, and governments, as well as scientists and scholars, around the world.

Students cross the UAA Quad to reach their next classes.

Courtesy of University of Alaska Anchorage; Photo by Michael Dinneen

Courtesy of University of Alaska Anchorage; Photo by Michael Dinneen

*Students find the perfect place to work
at the UAA Campus Center.*

Inland boaters will find hundreds of river and lake systems suitable for travel by canoe.

Courtesy of Alaska Tourism Marketing Council; Photo by Robin Hood

Nothing brightens the day like a round of golf on a crisp fall morning in the Interior.

Courtesy of Fairbanks Convention and Visitors Bureau

But, in the end, it all comes back to the original main campus in Fairbanks. That is where some of the most important research in the scientific world is taking place. It is where new and exciting discoveries are being made in the fields of computing, geophysics, geology, ecology, astronomy, climatology, biology, agronomy, agriculture, and aquaculture. It is where Arctic experts study everything from reindeer herds, to high-latitude food crops, to the composition of the northern atmosphere. As the nation's only Arctic university, UAF offers unparalleled opportunities for research into conditions and changes in northern climate, and their effects on the rest of the world. The International Arctic Research Center, now underway, is being funded by Japanese investors, and demonstrates the principle of partnership that is at the heart of most successful UAF programs.

UAF is the site of the Arctic Region Supercomputing Center, which boasts a high-speed, mega-memory 450 MHz Cray T3E computer system. The ARSC, with its enormous computing capacity, acts as a resource for researchers in science and engineering, and supports the activities of the University's many programs, including the Institute of Arctic Biology; the Institute of Northern Engineering; the Agricultural and Forestry Experiment Station (AFES); the Water and Environmental Research Center; the Mineral and Petroleum-Development Laboratories; the School of Fisheries and Ocean Sciences and the world-renowned Geophysical Institute. All are engaged in studies having direct impact and lasting effects on the businesses, industries, and ordinary citizens of Alaska.

Courtesy of Fairbanks Convention and Visitors Bureau; Photo by Christopher Batin

This hiker has found that the tundra turns bright red in the fall with the abundance of fireweed.

Photo by Steve Holthaus

The Geophysical Institute's Poker Flat Rocket Range is the site of many experimental and research programs, including the study of atmospheric phenomena. It was the nation's only such non-governmental establishment until the inauguration of Alaska Aerospace Development Corporation's Kodiak Launch Complex, a commercial spaceport on Kodiak Island, in November 1998. The success of both these facilities in the launching and tracking of low-orbit telecommunications, remote sensing, and space-science payloads demonstrates the immense potential of the Alaskan aerospace industry.

But the University of Alaska System has a higher purpose than just collecting and disseminating information, however valuable. It is a working school, with a main campus hosting some 10,000 students, which may confer graduate and post-graduate degrees up to the doctoral level. The innovators, builders, businesspeople, scientists, and leaders of tomorrow are receiving the training and knowledge they will need to sustain Alaska into and through the 21st century.

The Learning Experience

Alaskans have always placed a premium on education, possibly because choices were so very limited for so many years. Native children past the elementary level were generally sent to boarding schools in larger towns and cities. Many in the remote villages of the Arctic still are.

When Alaskans set out to do something, it gets done thoroughly. In order to build the public educational system that would teach and nurture the state's future leaders, the government and the public have had to work together. It is not always an easy partnership, but the results have justified the effort. Alaska spends more money per student than almost any other state, and administers 53 school districts and 20 Regional Attendance Areas, covering almost 700,000 square miles.

The Geophysical Institute has earned an international reputation for its high-latitude research. Scientists study a whole spectrum of geophysical processes ranging from atmospheric phenomenon such as the Aurora Borealis to the creation and structure of the earth.

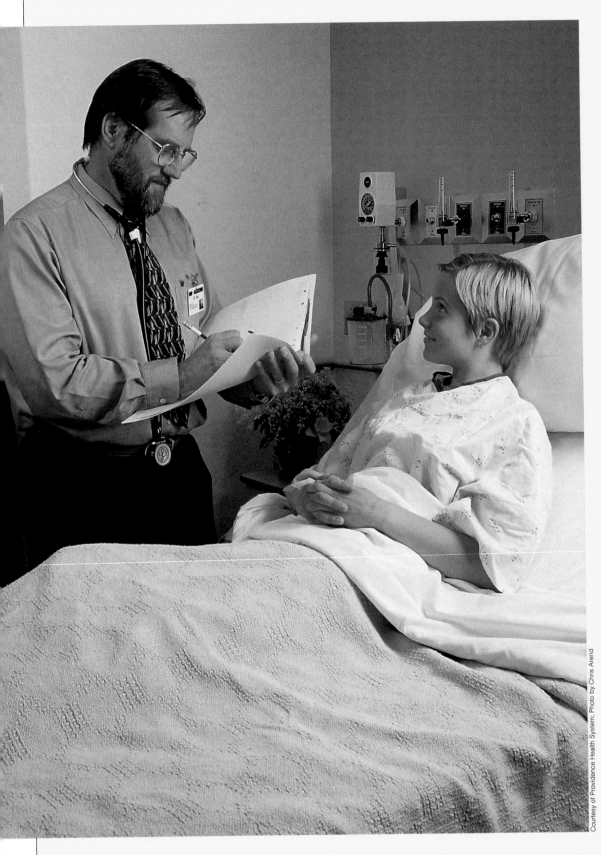

Providence Health System professionals believe the healing process involves more than miracle drugs and treatment; it also involves treating patients with compassion, respect and caring hearts.

Courtesy of Providence Health System; Photo by Chris Arend

Although nearly 125,000 students, from kindergarten through grade twelve, pass through the Alaska school system on an average day, class sizes, unlike those in most other states, are comfortably small, with a ratio of 16.9 students to every teacher, and those teachers are special. They are highly trained and qualified professionals, receiving a considerably higher-than-national-average salary, and they are much in demand. Modest class sizes give these educators the opportunity to work closely with individual students. Most schools are provided with the latest in specialized equipment and modern high-tech learning tools. Currently, a program is underway to wire all Alaska classrooms for the Internet. All of this, plus a number of alternative schools for challenged or otherwise nontraditional students, may help to explain a public secondary-school dropout rate of only 4.1 percent. Private school and home schooling options are also available in most areas. In recent years, home schooling, in particular, has made great strides in the Bush.

Parents in Alaska are extremely involved in the educational process, and most are proud to entrust their children to the superior school system of the State of Alaska.

T L C, ALASKA STYLE

In an environment as remote and potentially hazardous as Alaska, health care, especially acute and emergency care, is obviously vital. There are 17 acute-care hospitals in the state (one or more in every major city, and some in much smaller towns), and virtually every community has at least one emergency facility. Most of the major urban hospitals can provide air-ambulance service to remote patients who are in need of serious medical attention.

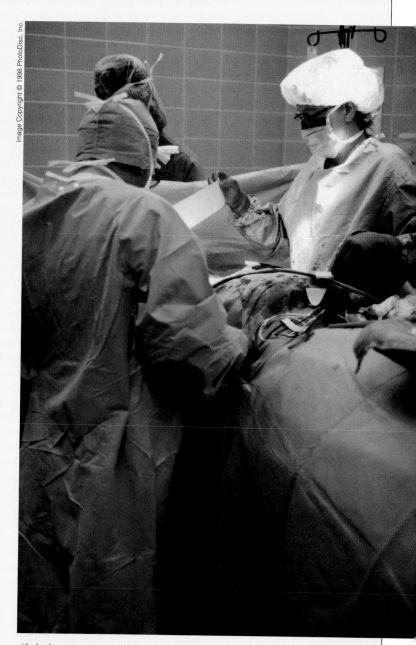

Alaska has 17 acute-care hospitals throughout the state and most major hospitals can provide air-ambulance service to remote patients in need of serious medical attention.

Up-to-date hospitals committed to providing excellent health care are located throughout Alaska. The not-for-profit Providence Alaska Foundation, started by the Sisters of Providence as a hospital in Nome in 1902, and Ketchikan General Hospital, established by the Sisters of St. Joseph of Peace and now a part of PeaceHealth, have a special commitment to financially disadvantaged Alaskans. The state also has a number of HMOs and health insurance companies, the largest being Blue Cross Blue Shield of Alaska. There are also walk-in clinics and non-acute-care clinics as well as recovery and extended care facilities. Specialists in almost every field can be found practicing in the 49th state; in fact, facilities like Bartlett Regional in Juneau and Alaska Regional in Anchorage have reported a significant increase in the number of patients electing to remain in Alaska for major medical procedures. Alternative treatment options are also widely available, including pain-management, stress-control, chiropractic, and naturo-pathic therapies. Across the Great Land, these facilities and their pro-fessionals are working together, every day, to take the best possible care of Alaskans.

BUSINESS CLIMATE: FAIR AND WARM

Now that Alaska has built the communications and networking infra-structure necessary to support and sustain modern commerce at the national and international levels, both the government of the State of Alaska and the northern business community are anxious to promote, encourage, and support the establishment and growth of new business and industry within Alaska. The state is particularly interested in attracting high-technology and clean-air industries, as well as those engaged in value-added activities that will enhance Alaskan products

The State of Alaska and the northern business community are quick to point out the many advantages of doing business in The Great Land.

Image Copyright © 1998 PhotoDisc, Inc.

With the infrastructure and state-of-the-art communications, a unique geographic location that places Alaska in a "global crossroads," a well-educated workforce, and numerous tax incentives and assistance programs, Alaska has a great deal to offer.

Image Copyright © 1998 PhotoDisc, Inc.

Courtesy of Alaska Interstate Construction; Photo by Judy Patrick

Sheet piling raised by AIC for bridge construction on the Tarn project.

Although commercial fishing is usually a full-time job, some charter operators take on visitors willing to work the nets for a period of time.

It may be a cold, wet day for fishing, but that does not deter these anglers from having a good time!

and exports. One of the best ways to bring such enterprises north is, of course, to make the process as simple, positive, and mutually profitable as possible. So the state offers employers a number of incentives and assistance programs including several kinds of grants, as well as tax credits for participation in various work-aid programs designed to benefit potential employees. The state's tax structure favors both companies and their workers. There is no personal state income tax, no statewide sales tax, and a modest corporate income tax levied only on revenues above a certain level. Another business/manufacturing advantage lies in accessible and affordable energy (the nation's lowest natural-gas costs, for instance).

The state's banking industry also stands ready to help. Alaska currently has three state-chartered and five national-chartered banks; one state-chartered mutual savings bank, one federal savings bank, five small loan companies, 17 premium finance companies, two state-chartered and 13 federal credit unions, two trust companies, and one BIDCO. Total assets for all banks with home offices in Alaska were $5,099,523,000 in 1997. More than $775 million of those assets were in state-chartered banks, while assets in all the state's credit unions totaled $2,476,317,501.

In order to fulfill its mission of helping the state to expand its high-tech-based private economy, the Alaska Science & Technology Foundation (ASTF) is currently managing more than 100 projects. ASTF offers Alaskan technological companies and entrepreneurs financing and other services.

There is one Alaska resident benefit about which everyone is always curious: the Permanent Fund Dividend. Derived from the interest on Alaska's share of oil-industry revenues, this unprecedented share-the-wealth program, initiated in 1982, takes the form of annual checks for every man, woman, and child of at least six months

This musher takes a break with her team.

Courtesy of Fairbanks Convention and Visitors Bureau; Photo by Sheila Romero residency in the state. This yearly windfall is an integral part of the modern Alaskan economy. Since dividends are issued at a fixed time each fall, and the amount (though varying with oil-industry fortunes and population figures) is always known in advance. Most retail establishments, service industries, and even many airlines and travel agencies are able to offer "Buy Now, Pay When Checks Come" arrangements to their customers.

LIVING ALASKAN

"Quality of life" is a slippery concept. Alaskans know what *they* mean by it, and they are always willing to share it with the world.

It is a collection of contrasts: the thrill of modern pioneering and discovery and the peace that can come from personal communion with one of the world's greatest wildernesses; a deep reverence for the past coupled with a boundless enthusiasm for the new and different, and the challenges of the future. It is dogsled races and symphony concerts; snowshoe-trekking and renting a limo for the prom. The Alaskan way of life is indoor/outdoor and all-weather; it is rambunctious or elegant; exciting or enlightening, and sometimes all of these at once. Most of all, to Alaskans, it's fun.

Alaskans point with pride to their outstanding library system, the gem of which is the Z. J. Loussac Regional Library in Anchorage. Libraries and bookstores thrive in Alaska, especially in wintertime; while public and private recreational facilities such as golf courses and tennis courts help residents while away the long summer days. There are no professional sports franchises in the state, but semi-pro baseball

Alaskans value their children's future and place a premium on education. Alaska spends more money per student than almost any other state.

The UAA Sinfonia in dress rehearsal.

and hockey teams draw many ardent fans. The State High School Basketball Championship in Sitka is an annual attention-getter for hoops-lovers, as is The Great Alaska Shootout competition for college teams from around the country.

Just about every community, big or small, boasts at least one organization devoted to some facet of culture or the arts, everything from Gilbert & Sullivan to traditional Native dancing. The range of special events includes midwinter carnivals and Renaissance Faires, midnight baseball games and Russian plays. A variety of musical ensembles, festivals, theaters, galleries, museums, and exhibitions offer experiences in every aspect of music, dance, drama, and the visual arts.

The spiritual life is rich as well. Members of almost every imaginable religion, formal and otherwise, practice their faiths across the state. In fact, at one time, Anchorage had more churches per capita than any other American city.

Once the ideal quality of life has been achieved, a lot of effort is required to maintain it. That is why, from the very beginning, Alaskans have tried their hardest to fill their lives with the educational, inspirational, interesting, and entertaining. Quality of life — in Alaska, it is not such an elusive idea after all.

THE BIG ANSWER

Getting back to our original question, what makes an Alaskan? It is clear that it takes many attributes to make an Alaskan — brains and talent, strength of character and will, intense determination, enthusiasm and optimism, a keen sense of humor, a strong work ethic, and a deep appreciation for both their beautiful state and all their fellow Alaskans. It takes special people with special ideas.

Like you?

The onion-domed churches of the Russian Orthodox faith are found in many communities throughout Alaska.

Courtesy of Alaska Tourism Marketing Council; Photo by Kristen Kemmerling

A horned puffin just caught his supper!

Alaska Department of Fish and Game

MYTHS OF THE NORTH COUNTRY

Anyone who's going to live and/or work in or with Alaska should be pre-
pared to answer some very odd questions. Some may seem unbelievable,
but they are heard all the time:

Q: Do you take American money/checks/credit cards/postage?
A: Certainly. Alaska is as much a part of the United States as Kansas.

Q: Do foreign shipping and communications rates apply?
A: See question 1.

Q: Can I phone Alaska directly from my home or office?
A: Of course. Direct-dial long-distance phone and fax service to and from
Alaska has been available for some 30 years. Computer-related services
for both business and personal applications are as accessible in Alaska as
in Manhattan, Cleveland, or Dallas (or, for that matter, London or
Rome). For more information, see Chapter 5.

Q: Is it true that it stays completely dark for six months of the year?
A: Only well above the Arctic Circle (66"30' north). The major metro-
politan areas (Fairbanks, Anchorage, Juneau) are far enough south to
enjoy a reasonable balance of night and day throughout the year. Shorter
winter days are more than offset by the long, lingering hours of light in
the summer months.

Q: Do people actually live in igloos? (Yes, it is hard to credit in this day
and age, but folks really do still ask.)
A: No. Igloos are temporary snow-block shelters, mainly built by Native
hunters in the Arctic. Some people build backyard or schoolyard igloos
just for fun and/or instruction, so you can usually see a few around.

Q: Will we have to shoo the polar bears off?
A: Highly unlikely, even if you move to the high Arctic. Like most bears,
they are basically shy of people, and will stay away unless tempted by
trash or wantonly provoked.

"You Are Here." This moose just needed to check out the park bulletin board for directions.

Courtesy of Wyndham Images

Courtesy of Wyndham Images

Just what's this Halloween stuff all about, anyway?

Part Two

CITIES AND BOROUGHS OF ALASKA

Anchorage

A City Ready For A New Century

By Rick Mystrom, Mayor

Anchorage, Alaska, one of America's most livable cities, prospers and thrives in one of the world's most spectacular settings. Located in the middle of a magnificent wilderness, Anchorage prides itself on being an all-season gateway to adventure and natural beauty. But the city's greatness comes from within. It's found in its quality of life, from clean streets to beautiful facilities to a remarkable "anything-is-possible" attitude among its people.

We who live in Alaska enjoy a reputation as pioneers. This image, earned during the Gold Rush of the late 1890s, still rings true one hundred years later – but in a different sense. We no longer think of ourselves as the last frontier but eagerly look forward to the adventure of crossing the threshold to a new century to the frontier of the future.

A clue to that new frontier is our unique location. As every international pilot knows, Anchorage lies at the hub of the world population centers, closer to Europe, Asia and Russia than any other North American city. That explains why our international airport is number one in North America for air cargo. And that explains why we are becoming the international logistics center for Asia, North America and Europe and the gateway to the Russian Far East.

Welcoming business innovations

Today's Anchorage inspires those with adventure in their blood. For those ready to make business investments, we present opportunities for real financial reward. To those ready to face new challenges, Anchorage offers good wages. Sophisticated satellite and fiber optic telecommunications link us instantly to all corners of the world, and the wealth of natural resources untapped in Alaska, combined with the unrivaled beauty of the natural environment, promise a strong economy for the future.

Exceptional public assets

No other city our size in America has the combination of outstanding, modern facilities that Anchorage has. Nights and weekends are filled with cultural and sporting events in our sports arena, convention center, library, museum and performing arts center. A city of participants, Anchorage has over 30,000 residents who compete in local sports leagues.

Lowest taxes in the nation

We constructed these public buildings in the 1980's with oil revenues from Alaska's North Slope and paid for them with cash, limiting our community tax burden. Even today, we pay neither city sales tax nor state income tax. Not surprisingly, we were ranked in a 1996 survey as the city with the lowest taxes in the US.

Anchorage Museum of History and Art

ZJ Loussac Public Library

Egan Convention Center

The Sullivan Sports Arena

*S*ome people dream of flying halfway round the world to catch a once-in-a-lifetime rainbow trout, king or silver salmon. In Anchorage, that dream can be fulfilled on the way home from work.

Taking pride, taking part

Anchorage is a winning city, receiving national awards for its first class trail system and the best tasting water in America. It is a place where daily life is enriched by a wealth of year-round recreation set in a majestic landscape, and the residents are determined to keep it that way. As Mayor, I admire the pride I find in the people. Literally thousands of individuals, week-in, week-out, plant and tend pocket parks, pick up litter, coach and officiate kids' sports, promote culture and the arts, serve food to the needy, and voluntarily care for the ill and elderly.

"The City of Lights and Flowers"

I see that pride in how the city looks, highlighted in the summer with private and public gardens filled with flowers, and accented in the winter by millions of miniature, white lights, decorating public buildings and private homes throughout the city.

Creating a community of friends

To celebrate the harmony in our community, leaders from twenty-five cultural traditions joined me recently to inaugurate a citywide effort called Bridge Builders. Nearly two hundred members are building "a community of friends" among people of all races, religions and national backgrounds. These new connections among diverse people with multiple talents and perspectives help make Anchorage a friendly, caring and exciting place to live and do business.

A great place to raise a family

Anchorage's outstanding quality of life fills the community with optimism. We're proud of our dramatic drop in crime in all categories, partly the result of community policing and innovative programs such as Parent Networks, which we started here and are now being adopted nationwide.

We applaud our many outstanding teachers with the Mayor's Community Recognition of Educational And Teaching Excellence (CREATE) Awards in which top students pick their most inspirational teachers. Alternative, private and charter schools add to our fine public school system, all reasons why Anchorage was named by *Readers Digest* as one of the best places in America to raise a family.

As you can tell, I am proud of Anchorage, a healthy northern city built in harmony with resource-rich Alaska. We welcome solid investment, creative ideas and those infused with the unlimited potential of the frontier spirit. With that combination, we have not only prospered, we are becoming a model for other cities our size the world around.

With Anchorage's skyline and the Alaska Range beyond, students at the new Tyson Elementary enjoy a break. Ninety percent of our adults have high school diplomas. Sixty-five percent have attended college.

Valdez

Valdez has excellent facilities for all those who ply the waters of Prince William Sound for the bounty of the deep.

Welcome to Valdez, the northern most ice-free port in North America. Home to the Terminus of the Trans Alaska Pipeline, and the Petro Star Refinery, Valdez is well equipped to handle all sizes of inbound cargo. The community boasts the largest concrete floating dock in the world: 700 feet long and 100 feet wide. Add to that a 21-acre marshaling yard; 3000 acres of adjacent industrial land; Foreign Trade Zone #108; and a 20,000-square-foot Convention & Civic Center, and Valdez becomes the perfect port of entry for goods ready for shipment into Interior Alaska and North Slope oil fields. Support needs are well taken care of by the healthy array of local businesses. With a population base of 4,700 year-round residents, the community supports amenities that rival those of cities twice the size. Prince William Sound Community College provides the necessary venue and staff to handle any educational, technical, or industrial training need. Excellent infrastructure combined with one of the grandest land-and-sea-scapes on earth make Valdez a sound choice for business or pleasure.

Beauty is not all that Valdez has to offer. The community is committed to making it easier to do business by providing both the facilities and the infrastructure necessary to business and industry, including the 20,000-square-foot Convention and Civic Center, pictured to the left, and the largest concrete floating dock in the world, pictured below.

Year-round, if fun is what you seek, outdoor activities abound in Valdez. The surrounding Chugach Mountain Range and Prince William Sound provide unmatched possibilities for activities ranging from sea kayaking to heli-skiing. They include fishing, flightseeing, hiking, glacier and marine wildlife tours, kayaking and rafting. When the weather turns wintry, it's time for skiing, snowboarding, snowmobiling, dog mushing, and ice climbing.

As both a home and a destination for business and leisure travel, Valdez is an Alaskan dream come true. Access to Valdez is as easy as a 35-minute plane ride from Anchorage. Other transportation alternatives include driving the Glenn and Richardson Highways or cruising across Prince William Sound from several different ports.

Whether for business or pleasure, come discover the "Little Switzerland of Alaska!"

Valdez is in the enviable position of being nestled between the Chugach Mountains and Prince William Sound. Sportsmen and athletes alike can enjoy activities ranging from salmon fishing to extreme skiing.

Activities in the Valdez area may run from the expected, such as a hike near Bridal Veil Falls in Keystone Canyon, to the unexpected, as in a mid-winter sail (in Alaska?) in ice-free waters by the Alyeska Marine Terminal.

Ketchikan Gateway Borough is the first Alaskan northbound port-of-call on the Inside Passage from the Lower 48. It is a lovely place, favored with dramatic mountain-to-sea vistas.

Ketchikan Gateway Borough

Tucked away between prominent Deer Mountain and the cool waters along the Tongass Narrows lies the Ketchikan Gateway Borough of the 49th state. While walking the streets of Ketchikan, one discovers a small-town charm tinged with a unique Alaskan flavor. One also appreciates the history that Alaska's First City embraces. A single excursion reveals Ketchikan's appeal as a great place to live, work and do business.

Ketchikan is open for business! While the residents of Ketchikan Gateway Borough do hold dear their heritage, they do not live in the past. Since the city itself was founded in 1900, its economy has been supported by a pragmatic pioneer vision and plain hard work. The fact that Ketchikan is Alaska's first northbound port-of-call along the much-traveled Inside Passage is a major contributing factor to Ketchikan's economic stability. Upon its completion, a highly anticipated industrial area will further stimulate the borough's healthy economy. A coalition of civic leaders from both the public and private sectors is also working to develop new economic opportunities for future development.

One such opportunity will allow Ketchikan, in connection with developers in the Lower 48, to help expand the world's understanding of oceans and marine life. An exciting, state-of-the-art aquarium built on nearby George Inlet will allow researchers, educators and the general public to gain valuable knowledge about Alaska's sealife and the ecosystems of the region's waters.

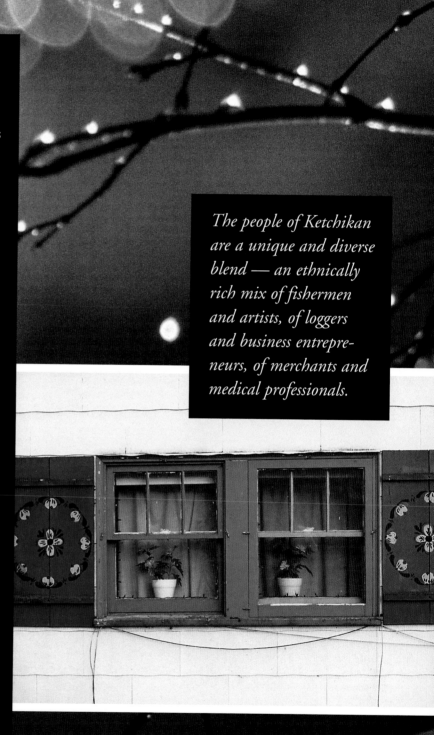

The people of Ketchikan are a unique and diverse blend — an ethnically rich mix of fishermen and artists, of loggers and business entrepreneurs, of merchants and medical professionals.

Ketchikan is a modern community with a deep sense of its historic and ethnic roots.

Inset photos from left to right:
Courtesy of Wyndham Images
Courtesy of Tongass Historical Society Incorporated
Courtesy of Ketchikan Visitors Bureau
Courtesy of Wyndham Images
Courtesy of Ketchikan Visitors Bureau

Background photo: Courtesy of Wyndham Images

Ketchikan's shipyard and drydock are also expanding to meet the growing needs of the busy shipping and ferry traffic along the Alaska Marine Highway System. The Ketchikan shipyard, which serves both state and local vessels as well as the nearby U.S. Coast Guard cutters, will gain a new ship lift, a pier crane, fabrication facilities and additional floating piers.

No roads lead into the city. Ketchikan is, however, served by the extensive state ferry system and a full-sized jet airport. Being just two hours from Seattle and one hour from Juneau by air makes Ketchikan readily accessible — while still preserving the city's sense of privacy and peace.

There is a great deal that Ketchikan offers its residents. Educational opportunities from the University of Alaska, an accredited hospital, a public library, a full range of public utilities — most of which are generated locally — and a host of recreational and educational experiences are just a few of the amenities available.

Ketchikan Gateway Borough has a pleasantly unexpected cultural side. Since its earliest days of existence, Ketchikan has drawn artists to its extraordinary community, earning it the tongue-in-cheek nickname of the Paris of Alaska. This small city boasts two museums that primarily exhibit local and Alaska Native art, and several local art galleries. The community also hosts plays and theater workshops.

Ketchikan is also a great place to retire. Senior citizens find the moderate year-round temperatures pleasing and, as an added bonus, they are not charged sales or property taxes.

These are just a few of the reasons to visit, live, and do business in Ketchikan — a special community of remarkable Alaskan charm and economic opportunity.

Perhaps there are no land-based roads that lead into Ketchikan Gateway Borough, but the waterways and the airways serve the community well. The region is well-connected via the state's extensive ferry system and through its full-sized jet airport. There are also the float planes that come and go throughout the day, providing an essential link for the residents of Ketchikan.

WRANGELL

Located amid the stands of evergreens of the Tongass National Forest in the heart of Alaska's Southeastern panhandle is Wrangell — a true Alaskan town. Wrangell is a place where one can take a step back into history to a time when life was, in many ways, simpler. It is a place with a sense of community values that sets it apart from larger urban areas.

It is also a place that is rich in cultural and ethnic diversity. About 20 percent of Wrangell's 2,600 residents are Tlingit-Haida natives. Many Tlingits are among a group of local artists who contribute an uncommon cultural wealth to the city, including ethnic art and magnificent hand-carved totems.

The Wrangell area attracts nearly 60,000 visitors each year, visitors who truly enjoy the area's unique natural beauty. The trip to Wrangell, located just 700 miles from both Anchorage and Seattle and only 150 miles from Juneau, is among the most lovely ventures on the Last Frontier. Visitors heading to the panhandle can take the Alaska Marine Highway ferry system up the scenic Inside Passage and relax while watching the passing mountains and fjords. Travelers can also take a jet on one of several destination routes that serve Wrangell daily.

Once arriving in Wrangell, visitors have the opportunity to enjoy the many attractions in the area. Tour excursions to Anan Bear and Wildlife Observatory, a unique facility in which people can safely view bears in their natural habitat, or to Shakes Glacier on the Stikine River, offer spectacular scenic and wildlife viewing. Local "must see" attractions include Petroglyph Beach, which is full of mysterious carved stones believed to be thousands of years old, and Chief Shakes Island, with its clan house and totems.

The City of Wrangell, which is nearly equidistant from Anchorage and Seattle, is a popular port-of-call along the Inside Passage. Visitors have an unique opportunity to see samples of ethnic art and culture in this diverse community, such as the carved corner post with abalone eyes in Chief Shakes Tribal House.

Everyone can get in on the catch in the rich fishing waters near Wrangell. For the land-lubbers, young entrepreneurs are ready to sell beautiful garnets obtained from nearby Garnet Ledge.

Upon arrival, visitors become immediately aware that Wrangell is a port with personality. Cruise ship travelers are greeted not only by the charming community itself, but also by the charming "Shady Ladies," the city's colorful promotional group.

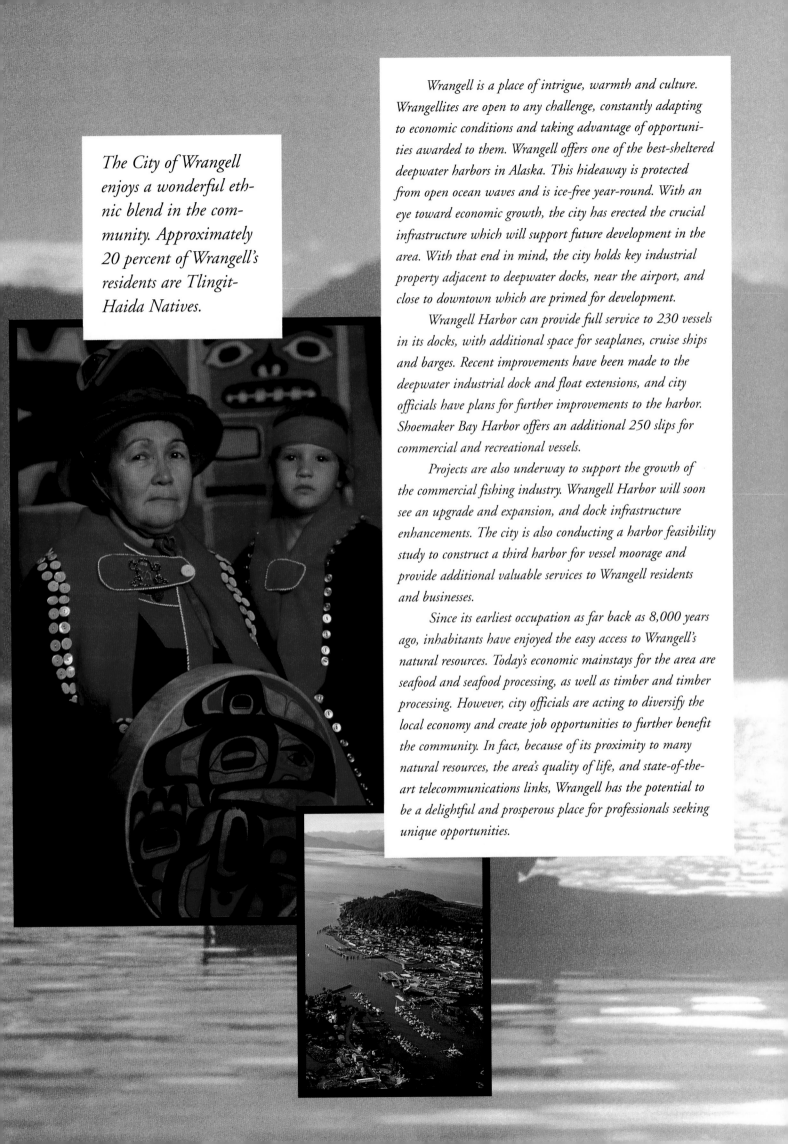

The City of Wrangell enjoys a wonderful ethnic blend in the community. Approximately 20 percent of Wrangell's residents are Tlingit-Haida Natives.

Wrangell is a place of intrigue, warmth and culture. Wrangellites are open to any challenge, constantly adapting to economic conditions and taking advantage of opportunities awarded to them. Wrangell offers one of the best-sheltered deepwater harbors in Alaska. This hideaway is protected from open ocean waves and is ice-free year-round. With an eye toward economic growth, the city has erected the crucial infrastructure which will support future development in the area. With that end in mind, the city holds key industrial property adjacent to deepwater docks, near the airport, and close to downtown which are primed for development.

Wrangell Harbor can provide full service to 230 vessels in its docks, with additional space for seaplanes, cruise ships and barges. Recent improvements have been made to the deepwater industrial dock and float extensions, and city officials have plans for further improvements to the harbor. Shoemaker Bay Harbor offers an additional 250 slips for commercial and recreational vessels.

Projects are also underway to support the growth of the commercial fishing industry. Wrangell Harbor will soon see an upgrade and expansion, and dock infrastructure enhancements. The city is also conducting a harbor feasibility study to construct a third harbor for vessel moorage and provide additional valuable services to Wrangell residents and businesses.

Since its earliest occupation as far back as 8,000 years ago, inhabitants have enjoyed the easy access to Wrangell's natural resources. Today's economic mainstays for the area are seafood and seafood processing, as well as timber and timber processing. However, city officials are acting to diversify the local economy and create job opportunities to further benefit the community. In fact, because of its proximity to many natural resources, the area's quality of life, and state-of-the-art telecommunications links, Wrangell has the potential to be a delightful and prosperous place for professionals seeking unique opportunities.

The area surrounding Whittier is a veritable wonderland filled with outdoor adventure opportunities.

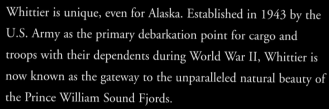

Whittier

There is a level for every would-be adventurer, from the sedate to the extreme. The fun ranges from whale watching to kayaking and sailing, from hiking to fishing and crabbing.

Whittier is unique, even for Alaska. Established in 1943 by the U.S. Army as the primary debarkation point for cargo and troops with their dependents during World War II, Whittier is now known as the gateway to the unparalleled natural beauty of the Prince William Sound Fjords.

Whales, eagles, seals and other sea life are a common sight in this wondrous small town. Hike the Portage Pass or Salmon Run Trails to go berrypicking or birdwatching. Or visit the many waterfalls — including Horse Tail Falls, reputed to flow upward, toward the sky. The adventurous may go sea-kayaking along the numerous coves and bays to capture a close view of the glorious glaciers nearby.

Perhaps the most popular Whittier pastime is boating. Summer visitors and residents alike dock their vessels at Whittier's 332-slip Small Boat Harbor for weekend fishing trips or during breaks in commercial fishing.

The bountiful sea lures sports fishermen to the waters off Whittier's coast. Halibut, red snapper, salmon and sea bass are all waiting to be caught during the summer months. Hunters can fill their freezers for the winter with prizes from the range of wildlife that roams the nearby wilderness. Regional game includes black and grizzly bear and the delectable Sitka blacktail deer.

Whittier's fewer than 350 residents maintain a range of services for themselves and visitors as well. Amenities such as restaurants, gift shops, hotels and camper parks are readily available. Seafarers are supported by a harbor office, boat launch and lift, marine fuel and marine service shop.

Access to Whittier may be limited — but getting there is half the fun. The 12-mile, 35-minute train ride from Portage takes visitors through some of the state's most breathtaking regions, past glaciers and mountains, and through two mysterious tunnels to enter Whittier. The first sight after emerging from one long, dark tunnel is Passage Canal, one of Prince William Sound's many majestic fjords.

Visitors can also fly over Alaska's spectacular Chugach Mountains, which overlook snow-capped peaks and blue-tinted glaciers.

Another marvelous option is to travel on the Alaska State Ferry System to experience Prince William Sound and all its wonders. Numerous tour options are available through local vendors or nationwide travel agencies.

The quaint town of Whittier is about to undergo a tremendous boost that will dramatically ease access to the community and provide opportunity for economic expansion. After much discussion and fanfare, construction of road access to Whittier is scheduled for completion in May 2000. The road will follow along the current railway route from Portage, allowing visitors and residents vehicle passage between the tiny town and the outside world.

This development is expected to bring extraordinary changes to Whittier and town officials have vowed to be ready for them. By acquiring land for parking lots, boat ramps, camp grounds and working on a much-needed harbor expansion to allow for an additional 900 boat slips, Whittier will be prepared to welcome the onslaught of visitors expected after the roadway is opened. The boon to the visitor industry will be huge for Whittier. Currently, the number of travelers visiting Whittier is about 200,000 a year. When the road is completed, that number is expected to rise to 900,000 visitors during the first year of road access. The visitations by the year 2015 is expected to be in excess of 1.5 million trips per year.

The next challenge to the citizens of Whittier will be the defining of a robust, diverse and non-seasonal economy. New development has been slight since the United States government lost interest in Whittier back in the fifties. However, entrepreneurs and soothsayers alike predict that the coming decade will quickly put Whittier on a par with other emerging coastal communities. New proposals for development of a broad range of recreational and commercial ventures are being put forth daily. The face of Whittier will be changed forever by these developments.

So how does Whittier find a comfort zone between life as it has always been and the world of 2000 and beyond? City officials plan to pursue the establishment of amenities that will enable permanent residents and visitors alike to increase their pride and presence in a year-round social and recreational setting that other small towns can only envy.

The future is full of promise for this enchanting hamlet. The combined efforts of city officials and residents will keep Whittier the incomparable place of beauty it is today, while preparing it for its exciting tomorrow.

Visitors are often overwhelmed by how much there is to see and do in the Whittier area. The region is blessed with both stunning mountain vistas and sweeping views of Prince William Sound.

One can take a boat or ferry ride, or perhaps camp along a glacier or beside a shining lake to wonder at Mother Nature and her many beauties.

Inset photos from left to right:

Courtesy of the City of Whittier; Photo by Douglas Latta
Courtesy of Alaska Tourism Marketing Council;
   Photo by Robin Hood
Courtesy of Alaska Tourism Marketing Council;
   Photo by Robin Hood
Courtesy of Alaska Tourism Marketing Council;
   Photo by Robin Hood
Courtesy of Alaska Tourism Marketing Council;
   Photo by Paul Souders/Tourism North

Background photo: Courtesy of Wyndham Images

Part Three

GOVERNMENT AND COMMUNITY ORGANIZATIONS

ALASKA DEPARTMENT OF MILITARY & VETERANS AFFAIRS—ALASKA NATIONAL GUARD

They are called the busiest rescue unit in the entire military. Besides helping aircrews in trouble, members of the 210th Rescue Squadron save more than 50 Alaskans annually. If you have fallen down the mountain, gotten lost, or crashed your plane, chances are high that you will be seeing them.

For more than 60 years, members of the Alaska Air and Army National Guard have been dedicated to protecting and serving Alaska and our nation. About 4,000 Alaskans voluntarily serve with the Guard. An additional 500 people work alongside them as either full or part-time employees or volunteers of the Department of Military & Veterans Affairs. The divisions or programs they represent include the Alaska State Defense Force, the Alaska Naval Militia, the Division of Emergency Services, Youth Corps, Counter Drug Program, Veterans Affairs, Administration, and so forth.

Like Army and Air Guard units across the country, the Alaska National Guard brings together citizen soldiers and airmen who blend their civilian knowledge and experiences to benefit America's military. When they go back to their civilian lives, they take with them new leadership skills and insights with which they build solid families, better businesses, and stronger communities.

There are daunting challenges for Alaska's National Guard. Rural areas of the state are comparable to many third-world countries in that they have no running water or sewage systems. Most rural residents live off the land — often an unyielding, treeless, barren terrain.

It is in this spartan setting that members of the Guard thrive and succeed. In addition to plying their soldierly skills, they are also good neighbors. Each year, elements of the Alaska National Guard join with other National Guard and Reserve troops from the lower-48 states to take part in a training exercise known as *Arctic Care*. Working with the Public and Indian Health Services, they serve over 4,500 medical and dental patients during a two-week stint in a dozen remote villages.

During the Christmas holidays, the Guard steps up to haul Santa and Mrs. Claus to see an average of 3,000 children in

Governor Tony Knowles, center, flanked by Brigadier General Tom Westall, right, inspects members of the Alaska State Defense Force. This volunteer force of some 250 Alaskans provide emergency assistance and communications support throughout the state.

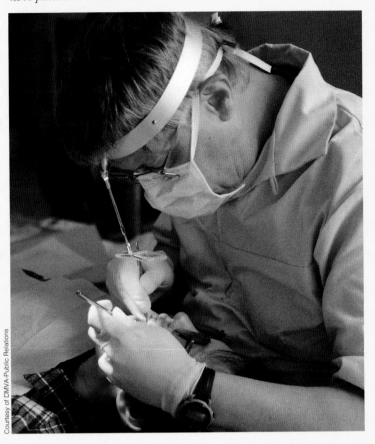

The annual "Arctic Care" 15 day medical exercise brings military care-givers to selected Rural Alaskan villages. Over 4,500 patients are treated.

Courtesy of DMVA-Public Relations

Alaska National Guard soldiers and airmen embrace their federal and state missions. They strive to be the most ready reserve in the world by setting high standards for leadership, training, and resourcing to accomplish national security and global military objectives. To that end, Alaska National Guard members have been deployed to several "hotspots" to take part in America's national security missions, including *Operation Allied Force*, Bosnia, Haiti, Rwanda, Somalia, Turkey, Korea, and the deserts of Kuwait, Saudi Arabia and Iraq for *Operation Desert Storm*. Likewise, Alaska National Guard units have trained in some 60 nations in the past three years alone.

At home, it is the Guard that gets the call to help search for and rescue their neighbors. In 1997 and 1998, the Guard rescued over 150 people from life-threatening situations. It simply did not matter whether it was from crashed airplanes, off of mountains, out of rivers, or from dead-end tundra trails. They each got a hand-up from the Guard.

The men and women of the Department of Military & Veterans Affairs are committed to mirroring the values of the people of Alaska. The world is a restless place, and the Alaska National Guard will continue to respond to the needs of the state while being part of the foundation of the nation's defense.

12 villages each year. Clothing, books, videos, and toys are the order of the day, just as Santa's surprises have always been since the program began back in the mid-1950s.

The Guard is also about hopes and dreams for another generation. High-school dropouts can have an opportunity to start a new, more disciplined life when they choose to join the Alaska National Guards' Youth Corps ChalleNGe Program. At-risk 16-to-18 year-olds volunteer for this 22-week life-changing event (to date,

over 750 have graduated). They complete it with an Alaska State High School Diploma (through the University of Alaska) and job skills and confidence to succeed in life. Each graduate enters into a one-year mentorship program working with adult volunteers to prepare for work or higher education.

The Guard reaches out in another way, too. Through partnerships with educators and law enforcement agencies, each year the Guard's Counter-Drug program visits with some 53,000 youth and adults across the state. The anti-drug education impact is powerful and the reinforcement of positive values are strongly emphasized to youth and adults alike.

Courtesy of DMVA-Public Relations

Each Christmas season, Santa and Mrs. Claus, with a little help from their friends in the Department of Military & Veterans Affairs, provide gifts of clothing, books, videos and toys to some 3,000 youngsters in a dozen rural Alaska villages. The program is 44-years old.

THE ALASKA STATE LEGISLATURE

20th Alaska State Legislature   April 28, 1998

*Members of the 1997-1998 Alaska
Legislature and staff on the steps of the
Alaska State Capitol in Juneau. Senate
President Mike Miller and House
Speaker Gail Phillips are in the center
of the front row.*

The Alaska Legislature, since its territorial beginnings in 1912, has represented the men and women of the last frontier who have dared to dream the impossible.

Alaska became the 49th state in 1959. In the forty years since statehood, Alaska legislators have built an infrastructure of laws to secure, and transmit to succeeding generations, a heritage of political, civil, and religious liberty within the Union of States.

This success did not come easily. In early statehood, amidst worldwide turmoil including the Cold War and Vietnam, challenges were faced on the home front. Vast distances between remote villages and towns, a harsh arctic environment covering much of the state, limited communications and transportation infrastructure, and a lack of basic services hindered the development of government and

our land. Perhaps the greatest challenge for lawmakers in 1959, however, was creating a state constitution and drawing up a new code of laws to govern a brand-new state.

Over the years, laws were developed within a unique political environment that included complex land distribution-challenges, Alaska Native claims, and the sudden prosperity following the discovery of oil.

Success followed the efforts of our pioneers. Since statehood, Alaskans have engineered many initiatives that now serve as

models for other states and nations. These initiatives include the Alaska Permanent Fund and the long distance delivery of medicine and education. Alaska is also at the forefront of arctic resource development technology.

The search for furs, gold, oil and a sense of adventure brought people to this great land. Challenges and opportunities kept them here. Mirroring the independence and diversity of all Alaskans are the legislators who carry the people's voice each year to the state capital in Juneau.

*The first Territorial House of
Representatives.*

JOINT HOUSE & SENATE OFFICE OF INTERNATIONAL TRADE POLICY

The 20th Alaska State Legislature, led by House Speaker Gail Philips and Senate President Mike Miller, has been very involved in international issues, welcoming 13 delegations in 1998 from regions of Canada; Ecuador; Venezuela; New Zealand; western and eastern Russia; Eastern Europe; Bulgaria; Taiwan, ROC; and the Peoples Republic of China. Many of these foreign delegations came to Alaska for the first time, exploring the establishment of formal relations with Alaska — both government and the private sector.

The Alaska State Legislature has an official protocol with the Yukon Territory, coordinated by Senator Randy Phillips in 1983. In 1996, the 19th Alaska State Legislature signed a protocol with the Khabarovsk Krai Duma in Russia. Alaska has a sister-state relationship with Khabarovsk, which borders China in the Russian Far East.

In 1996, Senate President Drue Pearce and House Speaker Gail Phillips signed a protocol with the 2nd Sakhalin Oblast Duma. Following two years of delegation exchanges, most recently in September 29, 1998, Representatives Brian Porter and

John Cowdery presented a civics/legislative workshop for Sakhalin Duma deputies and district and city representatives in Sakhalin Island, Russia.

Additional protocols are currently under development that will tie into transportation links, environmental policies on oil and gas spill responses, and clean air agreements. Representative Ramona Barnes, Chair, House Special Committe on World Trade and State/Federal Relations, has coordinated formal delegations to Moscow and Krasnagorsk, Russia; Korea; and Taiwan, ROC for the past six years.

The Joint House/Senate Office of International Trade Policy was created in 1995 to provide a liaison and protocol

Protocol signing ceremony, April 1996 (left to right): Tania Tolkachova, International Affairs Councelor for Khabarovsk Krai Duma; Viktor Ozerov, Chairman, Khabarovsk Krai Duma, Deputy N. Kostiouchenko; then Senate President Drue Pearce; and House Speaker Gail Phillips in the Speakers Chambers in Juneau.

point of contact for the Alaska State Legislature. The office is the main contact for the Gore/Primakov US West Coast & Russian Far East Working Group, the Alaska-Arctic Council, and numerous federal and state trade organizations and international education and training groups.

Work session between Sakhalin Regional Duma and Alaska State Legislature in Yuzhno-Sakhalinsk in September, 1997 (left to right): First Deputy Chair Lyubov Shubina; Alex Ponomarev;

Whisper Communications, AKRA Consultant Paul Fuhs; House Majority Leader Brian Porter; Senate President Mike Miller; and House Speaker Gail Phillips.

TANANA CHIEFS CONFERENCE

While each village in Interior Alaska have elected and traditional chiefs of their own, the Tanana Chiefs Conference region has a regional "traditional" chief, and a "second" chief. Currently, the First Traditional Chief is Peter John, Minto (right) and the Second Traditional Chief is David Salmon, Chalkyitsik. Former chiefs include Chief Andrew Isaac, Dot Lake, and Chief Walter Northway, Northway.

The Tanana Chiefs Conference, Inc. fills that role.

TCC works towards meeting the health, economic development, and social service challenges for more than 10,000 clients spread across a region of 235,000 square miles in the interior of Alaska. TCC has taken the lead in providing those services under an annual budget that exceeded $54 million in 1997. Over half the budget is under a contract from the Alaska Area Health Service, and employs health care professionals to meet the health needs of rural Alaskans.

Other programs and services in the Tanana Chiefs region include a new Temporary Assistance for Needy Families Program, Indian Child Welfare Act, energy assistance, economic development, wildlife and parks, tribal government services, and a village public safety officer program.

For thousands of years, Athabascan leaders have gathered at a place called Nu-cha-la-woy-ya — "where the two rivers meet" — to discuss tribal matters through the voice of the people. The confluence of the Yukon and Tanana Rivers is now the home of Tanana.

In June 1962, in an effort to protect Native land rights in Interior Alaska, an array of young, educated Native leaders began pushing the land claims issue toward a suitable goal. Out of this meeting, the Tanana Chiefs Conference was incorporated.

The Alaska Native Claims Settlement Act of December 1971 set up 13 regional for-profit corporations for Alaska

Natives. TCC incorporated Doyon, Limited as the regional corporation for the specific purpose of making a profit for their stockholders. The Act left a place for non-profit corporations to administer health and welfare programs for the people.

Interior Alaska is home to the Athabascan Indians. Prior to the colonization by western civilization, clothing was made of animal skins including moose, wolverine, bear,

beaver, wolves, and caribou. When non-Natives settled the area, cloth, beads and yarn were introduced and Natives mastered various creations of the new material.

AFL/CIO

Courtesy of Alaska State AFL-CIO

Mano Frey, Executive President, Alaska State AFL-CIO.

As the single largest representative group in Alaska, members of the local American Federation of Labor and Congress of Industrial Organizations (AFL/CIO) have touched virtually every resident and visitor of Alaska.

With more than 60,000 workers represented throughout the state, it is easy to see why. From retail to tourism, and from construction to public employment, members of the AFL/CIO are committed to the improvement of the quality of life for residents of Alaska, and ultimately play a key role in the state's economy and well-being.

Established on December 5, 1955, the AFL/CIO is a union of unions. Housing a federation of about 100 international labor unions in the United States and Canada, the AFL/CIO holds about 44,000 local unions under its roof. The Alaska chapter of the AFL/CIO holds more than 60 local unions.

Members of Alaska's AFL/CIO have been called to contribute their vast array of skills to such projects as the transAlaska Pipeline construction and Alaska's highway system. Members helped rebuild after the 1964 earthquake which was the most destructive force ever to hit modern Alaska. They were also called upon to work with people from across the globe during the cleanup of the devastating Exxon Valdez oil spill in 1989.

But since its founding, the AFL/CIO has known that its existence serves a much greater purpose than just putting people to work. Day-to-day issues, such as safety in the workplace, are of paramount importance to the lives of working Alaskans — and are vigorously fought for by the AFL/CIO.

AFL/CIO officers have a list of goals to achieve when they represent their members. The list includes improving wages and working conditions, promoting opportunity for all union workers, and offering the necessary political support in the legislature to help meet these goals.

Representation of Alaska's union members has ensured the safety and security of an important work force throughout much of the state. This, in turn, has given the represented a sense of pride and accomplishment in the work which they have contributed, and has offered residents and visitors alike a sense of pride in the community.

Alaska Department of Community and Economic Development

Kodiak Launch Complex at Narrow Cape on Kodiak Island.

The Department of Community and Economic Development works to encourage investment and sound economic development throughout Alaska. The efforts of the Department are part of the State of Alaska's overall economic development strategy. At the core of this strategy is working closely with our private sector partners who are doing business, or thinking of doing business, in the 49th state. In these rapidly changing times, it is an approach that works. Alaska also offers a highly skilled, educated and motivated workforce. Alaska is open and ready for business but the cornerstone for this policy is doing development right. This means protecting Alaska's air, water, fish and wildlife habitat, and scenic beauty — the assets that make Alaska a wonderful place to live and visit.

Since the gold rush, the development and marketing of natural resources, including recreation and tourism, have been the backbone of Alaska's economy. While these industries continue to be important, the 1990s have seen significant changes in this traditional picture. Pacific Rim trade and international transportation and shipping are sectors experiencing major growth and expansion. The modern communications and high-technology industries are making great strides in Alaska. For example, the only commercial rocket-launch range in the United States, not co-located with a federal facility, is under development and experienced its first rocket launch in Kodiak. Completion of this complex is spawning an entirely new sector for Alaska's economy, with new jobs ranging from construction workers to aerospace engineers and operating technicians for the ground stations.

Alaska has long been known as the land of opportunity. The Department of Community and Economic Development's mission, as part of an ongoing partnership for progress, is to encourage investment opportunities for Alaska's future. Working together, with an emphasis on innovation and flexibility, individuals, business, and government can meet the challenges and achieve the goals of sound economic development, productive jobs and high quality of life well into the 21st century. The Department of Community and Economic Development welcomes the chance to work with you in exploring business and investment opportunities in Alaska.

Commissioner Deborah B. Sedwick, State of Alaska Department of Community and Economic Development.

WORLD TRADE CENTER ALASKA

One of the many ways that the Alaska World Trade Center promotes international trade is through trade missions.

tion companies, financial-service providers, construction companies, professional international trade advisors, and translators. No business is too big or too small to take advantage of the international trade services provided by the World Trade Center Alaska.

The mission of the World Trade Center Alaska is to promote and facilitate profitable trade for Alaskans. This mission is accomplished in several ways: educational programs, networking opportunities, trade leads and information, trade missions, and member services. WTCAK is dedicated to increasing the bottom line of its companies and thereby expanding the economy of Alaska. Improving the business environment for Alaskan companies with an expanded market and network of business contacts is essential to continued success in international markets.

World Trade Center Alaska is part of a worldwide network of World Trade Centers which combine trade information, communication services, trade education programs, and trade mission assistance with private businesses operating in international markets — all under one roof. Membership is reciprocal and international business leaders may take advantage of the network of over 370 member cities.

Creating successful international trade can be quite a challenge. For Alaskan companies, the first step to expanding into new markets is utilizing the resources of World Trade Center

Alaska. With over 10 years of experience assisting exporters, the WTCAK staff is able to expertly advise its member companies and help them grow internationally.

World Trade Center Alaska brings together many types of Alaskan business including Native corporations, communications companies, transporta-

Awards are given out at an annual conference at the Alaska World Trade Center.

ALASKA FILM OFFICE

A television commercial is being filmed for Fisherman's Friend (Bristol Meyers).

Courtesy of Alaska Film Office

From the Arctic Circle to the shores of Southeast Alaska, the State of Alaska Film Office has provided directors, producers, and film crews with professional and technical assistance to help them successfully film in the Great Land. Location scouts, equipment rentals, caterers, grips, and gaffers are all part of the Film Office rolodex that industry professionals rely on when they come here to complete big-budget TV commercials, still-photo shoots, award-winning documentaries, and feature films, all with Alaska as the scenic backdrop.

Since its inception over 15 years ago, the Alaska Film Office has grown into a multi-million-dollar production assistance office that routinely receives calls from some of the film industry's biggest names. The first full-length movie filmed in Alaska was *Runaway Train* in 1985. Since then, the roster has included *White Fang, On Deadly Ground, Alaska: Spirit of the Wild,* and other well-known productions, including the most recent John Sayles film *Limbo.* Besides enticing visitors to Alaska from all over the world, these films have pumped millions of dollars into the economy, resulting from the purchase of goods and services in communities statewide.

Filming on the set of Star Trek VI.

Courtesy of Alaska Film Office

Courtesy of Alaska Film Office and Alaska Division of Trade & Development

Alaska's dramatic and unique landscapes, such as McBride Glacier, make the state an excellent choice for filming.

ALASKA STATE CHAMBER OF COMMERCE

Governor Tony Knowles congratulates ASCC President Pamela La Bolle and Chairman David Marquez on passage of Tort Reform by the State Legislature.

In 1953, a few years before Alaska was granted statehood, the "All Alaska" Chamber of Commerce was formed for the purpose of promoting commerce in Alaska. The construction boom, brought about by World War II, was winding down, and Alaska's business leaders recognized the need for an organized effort to develop a new, stronger economic base for Alaska. The first leaders of the Alaska Chamber discussed tax incentive legislation, development of the state's forest and mineral resources, promotion of the tourism industry, and increasing agricultural production. With statehood, the name was changed to the Alaska State Chamber of Commerce, and the organization represented the first unified effort to have the voice of business heard in the state legislature.

A few Alaska State Chamber leaders have gone on to become state and national leaders. Walter Hickel, once chairman of economic development for the State Chamber, became Governor of Alaska, twice, as well as U.S. Secretary of the Interior. Former board chairman and prominent hotelier Bill Sheffield later became Governor of Alaska, and U.S. Senator Frank Murkowski also once served as chairman of the board.

The Alaska State Chamber still serves as the voice of business. Today, the Alaska State Chamber of Commerce has approximately 700 business members, represented by a 78-person board of directors which includes representatives of thirty-five local Alaskan chambers and the chambers of Seattle, Tacoma, Bellingham, Portland, and the Yukon. Members annually select the priority issues they want addressed by the legislature. These become the focus of the State Chamber's active lobbying program and range from issues that are ongoing, like fiscal planning and regulatory reform, to specific economic-development issues in resource development and land access. Among its many achievements to date, the Alaska State Chamber successfully lobbied for paving of the Alaska Highway, launched the first Alaskan trade mission to Japan, and was instrumental in passage of major tort-reform legislation.

ASCC members with the Senate President and Speaker of the House in the Speaker's Chamber at the Capital Building.

Part Three
———
NETWORKS

ALASKA RAILROAD

Courtesy of Alaska Railroad

The Alaska Railroad carries locals and tourists through some of the state's most breathtaking scenery.

The Alaska Railroad runs more than 500 miles from the Gulf of Alaska to the heart of Alaska's Interior. For the past 75 years it has provided full freight, passenger and real estate services in one of North America's most beautiful settings.

The publicly owned Railroad provides essential transportation services to Alaska businesses and communities, is geared toward service and growth and, through its revenues, is self-supporting. It is the only railroad in North America still providing both passenger and freight service. The Railroad is operated as a public corporation, is run by professional railroaders, and is governed by a seven-member Board of Directors appointed by the Governor of Alaska.

The Alaska Railroad is one of the state's most historical institutions. It was built by the U.S. government between 1914 and 1923, and played a central role in the founding of Anchorage. It was also essential to settlement and development from the coast deep into the Interior, to national defense before and after World War II, and as a supply route for the construction of the Trans-Alaska Pipeline System.

Today the Alaska Railroad is one of the most important elements of the state's transporta-

Visitors to Alaska have found riding the Railroad to be a destination in itself.

No matter what season of the year, the Alaska Railroad hauls freight and carries passengers.

tion system. The Railroad carries more than 400 million gallons of refined petroleum products distilled from Alaska crude oil. In addition, it links Alaska to export markets by hauling Interior coal bound for Korea. It also connects Alaska to the freight network of the rest of the continent via weekly barge service to the Lower 48 states and Canada. Tidewater ports at Seward and Whittier serve as gateways for export, freight service and the visitor industry.

More than 600,000 visitors ride Alaska's rails from Prince William Sound and Resurrection Bay, through Anchorage, and on to Denali National Park and Preserve and the Interior city of Fairbanks. Much of the route departs from the road system and passes through wilderness terrain in the Chugach Mountains and the Alaska Range — within sight of Mount McKinley, North America's highest peak.

The Alaska Railroad operates year-round. While much of the passenger service is seasonal, Alaskans can count on weekly service from Anchorage to Fairbanks, as well as shuttles from Portage, on Cook Inlet, through the mountains to Whittier, on Prince William Sound. On the northern route, passengers can ride the train on a "flag stop" basis, hailing the locomotive from remote points all along the line. It is the last "flag stop" service in North America.

Today the Alaska railroad is preparing to enter the 21st century with an ambitious expansion program aimed at providing even better service to Alaska. Among planned improvements are upgrades to the Seward and Whittier ports, major intermodal transportation centers at Anchorage International Airport and in Fairbanks, new, more comfortable depots at key locations such as Denali National Park, and commuter rail service serving Anchorage from northern and southern points on the line.

For a uniquely Alaska experience, local groups and organizations charter the Alaska Railroad to bring them into territory inaccessible by automobile.

The Alaska Railroad transports coal for export to Korea from Healy to the Port of Seward.

The 20-year MAPCO Alaska fuel-hauling contract is the backbone of the Alaska Railroad's freight operations.

From mid-May to mid-September, the passenger services division runs daily coaches between Seward and Fairbanks, and year-round service to Whittier and Fairbanks.

The Alaska Railroad offers year-round barge service between Seattle and Canada, and the deep-water port of Whittier.

GCI

GCI provides cable television service to 109,000 subscribers, passing 75 percent of Alaskan households.

The story of GCI, the company that brought long-distance competition to Alaska, serves as a model of what is happening in the telecommunications industry.

The Telecommunications Act of 1996 is reshaping the way the world communicates. Technology and regulatory environments are changing rapidly. These changes have broken the barriers that existed between different companies.

The future of telecommunications is in integration. It is beginning to occur in many places. Long-distance companies are moving into the local telephone market. Local telephone companies are lining up to offer long distance. Cable television companies are joining with long-distance and competitive local telephone providers to

share facilities and offer packaged services. Technology is blurring the distinction between service offerings. Voice and data are transmitted interchangeably over common networks while entertainment services are becoming increasingly two-way.

GCI is the only company that has, in a single marketplace, combined all of the components necessary to offer a fully-integrated communication service. GCI has a profitable statewide long-distance business with a large market share, facilities-based local telephone services with direct access to 40 percent of the state's telephone lines, cable television services in 17 of the state's largest communities, and, a statewide wireless license in both narrowband and broadband spectrums.

Alaska is a unique market. It is remote and has an enormous land mass; yet it also has a small

Cable modems deliver up to 10 Mbits per second to home and businesses for hi-speed Internet access. GCI is the only company in Alaska providing the service.

GCI installed a 5-ESS digital switch for its local telephone service in Anchorage. The 5-ESS is the most advanced, integrated switch found in Alaska today.

population. The dispersion of population over a large land area makes telecommunications extremely important. The climate and geography of Alaska make the provision of telecommunications different and in many respects, more difficult. It is a market that places a high premium on Alaska expertise.

GCI is a company on the move. In the past three years, it has built 56 earth stations throughout rural Alaska, acquired a wired broadband network passing 74 percent of Alaska households, and con-

structed its own local telephone facilities using the industry's most advanced and reliable digital switching network.

In a global financing effort, GCI raised more than $550 million which it will use to construct additional facilities in Alaska over the next five years.

With these facilities, GCI will be able to link its network to a new generation of broadband capacity that it is introducing into both urban and rural areas of Alaska. This is being done with new satellite and fiber optic facilities.

GCI will secure state-of-the-art satellite coverage of the entire state when a replacement for Galaxy X is launched in 1999. This satellite should fulfill C-band and Ku-band capacity for the next 12 years and will use technology that doubles existing satellite efficiency.

Alaska United, the fiber-optic cable system, combines undersea and on-land fiber-optic systems to link Alaska's major urban centers to the lower 48 states. This will create a network of unprecedented reliability and capacity to meet current and future needs.

GCI pioneered demand assigned multiple access (DAMA) technology in its earth stations deployed throughout the state. DAMA brought digital, hi-speed communications to many remote locations for the first time.

Courtesy of GCI; Photo by Chris Arend

Courtesy of GCI; Photo by Greg Martin

The Global Sentinel *will be used to lay the Alaska United fiber optic cable system during the fall of 1998. Upon completion, the system will connect Anchorage, Fairbanks and Juneau with the Lower 48 states and is capable of carrying up to 129,000 simultaneous voice or data calls.*

ANCHORAGE INTERNATIONAL AIRPORT

Over 5 million passengers passed through the terminals last year. The visitor industry fueled an average 4 percent growth over the past five years.

The 4,800-acre Anchorage International Airport is modest in size when compared with its economic contribution to the local and state economy. The AIA complex, from its humble beginnings to its promise-filled future, is one of the economic engines of Alaska.

The future holds a $230 million expansion for the airport and another $120 million for related road access in a project called "Gateway Alaska." Major elements of the terminal redevelopment include four new jet aircraft gates, seven new regional aircraft parking positions, five new wide body aircraft remote parking positions, an expanded new ticket lobby, baggage claim area, and expanded curbside service and road improvements.

The changes will also provide for expanded retail space and replacement of the C Concourse, the airport's oldest section. The Alaska Railroad Corporation is considering an extension of its track to the terminal and the construction of a two-tiered train station. The sta-tion is planned to serve tour ships and other visitors, as well as commuters in the region.

While Gateway Alaska will remedy the needs of AIA's five million passengers per year, it is air cargo activity at Anchorage's airport that has grown most significantly in recent years. During fiscal year 1998, landings by cargo aircraft rose to an all-time high of 34,000.

That growth occurred in both international and domestic air cargo activity. However, it is the 22 international wide-body cargo carriers that fueled the largest gains — a 17 percent increase in landings, to over 450 per week. Private investments in improvements at the airport total more than $160 million from 1996 to 1998. AIA fuelers pump more jet fuel into cargo aircraft than fuelers in any other U.S. airport.

Opening the cargo door. Originating cargo such as seafood and cargo that is transferred "tail to tail" continues to transform the airport from a "technical stop" to a world class cargo hub. Logistics related business, currently in its infancy locally, promises to create cargo traffic.

Courtesy of Anchorage International Airport; Photo by Chris Arend

Overcrowded passenger facilities are driving "Gateway Alaska," a combined terminal and roads project totaling over $350 million to bring the airport into the next century.

Alaska's proximity to Europe, Asia, and the Americas continues to make Anchorage International Airport a convenient stopover on air-cargo routes. Cargo aircraft actually increase payload by making refueling stops at AIA. It makes Anchorage International the top-ranked air cargo airport in North America for "all-cargo aircraft landed weights."

Like much of Alaska's history, the development of Anchorage International Airport was closely tied to federal management of activity in territorial days. The Alaska Public Airport Act passed by the 80th Congress in May of 1948 authorized development of "international type" airports in Anchorage and Fairbanks by the Civil Aeronautics Administration, forerunner to the current Federal Aviation Administration.

In 1951, Anchorage International Airport opened with an 8,400-foot east/west runway and a north/south runway of 5,000 feet. The addition of a modest terminal in 1952 and a sewer and water system in 1959 were the only improvements made until the transfer of the facility to the new State of Alaska on May 1, 1960.

State ownership of the airport coincided with the dawning of the jet age in aviation. In 1960, seven international air carriers were using Anchorage as a regular stopover on routes between Europe and Japan and the U.S. East Coast and Japan. At the same time, Anchorage, the state population center, was emerging as the focal point for business and economic activity, including a growing interest in Alaska's oil, gas, and other resource-related potential. To keep pace with service demands, the state launched a series of improvements that lengthened the east/west runway to the west, bringing it to 10,600 feet.

The massive earthquake that struck Southcentral Alaska on March 27, 1964, increased the need for improvements at the airport. A development program over the next several years repaired the damage and began to address the long-term issues facing Anchorage International Airport.

In 1969, a new domestic and international concourse, ticket lobby, and baggage-claim area were constructed. This facility now serves as the domestic South Terminal. The following year, a new parallel 10,897-foot east/west runway was completed. A decade later, a 10,496-foot north/south runway was added to the complex and work began on an international facility, now known as the North Terminal, which was completed in time to handle the rapid growth of international passengers in the 1980s.

AIA is responsible for one of every ten jobs in Anchorage. With such a huge commercial influence, the airport will continue to be a driving force in both the city and the state economy. As the new millennium takes hold, Anchorage International Airport will be transformed and eager to meet its future.

Courtesy of Anchorage International Airport; Photo by Chris Arend

Enormous "lift." Over 34 air cargo carriers with over 450 all cargo flights per week land for fuel, maintenance. Diversity is a strength, as no single carrier accounts for more than 15 percent of aircraft revenue to the airport.

ALASKA AIRLINES

Alaska Airlines operates the youngest and quietest fleet of aircraft among the nation's major carriers. The centerpiece is the Boeing 737-400, which Alaska has equipped with highly advanced navigation technologies.

What makes a great—and lasting—team?

Complex strategic planning? Strong leadership? Plain old hard work and determination?

All that is part of the equation. But truly outstanding teams are a testament to the power of people working together in common cause for something bigger than the sum of the parts.

Business is the same way. Teamwork is key. To achieve it, though, you must have a unifying set of beliefs.

For nearly 70 years, Alaska Airlines and its people have been guided through thick and thin by a shared commitment to integrity, caring, resourcefulness, professionalism and spirit. Especially spirit—an *Alaskan spirit*, born in the land the airline is named after—a place where "can-do" and "neighbor-helping-neighbor" are facts of life.

The result? A long list of aviation milestones, as well as countless stories of people going out of their way to help others—both in the course of business and in the support of organizations that make our communities better places to live.

In the process, Alaska has grown from a small regional airline to one of the most respected in the nation. Carrying more than 12 million customers per year, Alaska's route system spans 46 cities and four countries. Its fleet of 80 Boeing jets is the youngest among all major airlines. And its reputation for outstanding service consistently earns best U.S. airline recognition from the likes of *Travel & Leisure* and *Condé Nast Traveler* magazines.

STORIED ROOTS

The foundation of this success was laid in 1932, when Mac McGee started flying his three-seat Stinson between Anchorage and Bristol Bay, Alaska. Finances were tight, but perseverance ruled the day; Mac and his team often worked round-the-clock, even though the next paycheck might be weeks away.

A merger with Star Air Service in 1934 created the largest airline in Alaska. After several more mergers, the name was changed a couple of times—until they found one that stuck: Alaska Airlines.

By the late 1940s, using surplus military aircraft, Alaska had branched into worldwide charter work, including the Berlin Airlift in 1948.

The Grumman Goose was a workhorse in Southeast Alaska from the 1950s into the '70s. This "Super Goose" was the first turbo-prop amphibian plane in the world. It became part of the Alaska Airlines fleet when the carrier merged in 1968 with legendary Alaska Coastal-Ellis Airlines.

Alaska Airlines used giant Lockheed Hercules aircraft to help kick-start North Slope oil development in the 1960s and Transalaska Pipeline construction in the 1970s.

Courtesy of Alaska Airlines; Ron Suttell Collection

In the late 1960s, Alaska strengthened its operating base by merging with Alaska Coastal-Ellis and Cordova airlines—legendary Southeast Alaska carriers owned by aviation pioneers Shell Simmons, Bob Ellis and Mudhole Smith. Alaska's world now stretched from Fairbanks south to Ketchikan and down to Seattle. And in some of the coldest days of the Cold War, Alaska made headlines with regular charters to the Soviet Union.

A New Era

When Fairbanks businessmen Ron Cosgrave and Bruce Kennedy came on board in 1972, the airline was in a financial fight for its life. They went to work setting goals and bringing people together. They won back the trust of creditors and improved on-time performance. One break that went their way was the construction of the Trans Alaska Pipeline; carrying supplies, equipment and workers gave Alaska a shot in the arm.

Bottom line, customer service became key in this new era. It put the airline on course for what would be a nearly unprecedented record in the industry: 19 straight years of profitability.

In 1979, the airline industry was deregulated. For many carriers, this was the end of the road. For Alaska, it was a new beginning. The airline expanded methodically throughout the West Coast and joined forces with two carriers similarly committed to outstanding customer service—Horizon Air and Jet America.

By the end of the 80s, Alaska had tripled in size. Its fleet had increased five-fold and the route map included scheduled service to Mexico and Russia.

Continuing The Legacy

Things haven't changed that much over the years. Alaska is still differentiating itself: offering more flights than any competitor in almost every market it serves; providing a superior level of customer service; and pioneering technologies that improve on-time performance and expand safety margins. And the awards just keep on coming.

Every time the history of commercial aviation is written, people ask how an obscure little airline in America's hinterland has continued to survive and thrive while once-proud giants have disappeared. Grit and determination will be part of the answer.

But more than that, it is the people. Their caring. Their resourcefulness. Their integrity. Their professionalism. And their spirit—the unique spirit of The Great Land where the airline was born.

Courtesy of Alaska Airlines; Ron Suttell Collection

In the 1940s, the Lockheed Lodestar was a familiar sight in The Great Land as Alaska Airlines flights between Anchorage and Juneau were operated with this 14-seat plane.

FAIRBANKS INTERNATIONAL AIRPORT

Fairbanks International Airport features a world class 11,800-foot (3,598-meter) air carrier runway.

Courtesy of Fairbanks International Airport

Some 50 years ago, a dirt airstrip known as Weeks Field served Fairbanks, the transportation and commercial hub of Interior Alaska. As the expanding community outgrew its modest airfield, the Civil Aeronautics Authority (CAA) — forerunner of the Federal Aviation Administration — began building a new airport eight miles south of town.

In 1951, Fairbanks International Airport opened with a paved, 6,000-foot runway as its centerpiece. By 1954, a new terminal building and modern control tower replaced temporary structures. Wien Air Alaska, the airport's primary tenant, constructed a large new hangar. In 1959, the CAA turned the title to Fairbanks International Airport over to the new State of Alaska.

In the ensuing years, Fairbanks International Airport grew to keep pace with a growing community and changing demands. The single largest improvement was lengthening of the runway to 10,300 feet in 1963 to accommodate a growing number of jet aircraft.

The construction of the Trans Alaska Pipeline System in the mid '70s brought unprecedented traffic to the Interior city's airport. In 1976, boarding passengers totaled 365,000, a record that stood for 19 years. Air freight peaked at more than 200,000 tons in 1974, a number unsurpassed to this day.

Fairbanks International Airport first experienced significant international air cargo traffic in 1978. A west coast jet fuel shortage prompted three Asian cargo carriers to move their freighter operations from Anchorage to Fairbanks. For Japan Air Lines, Korean Air, and China Air Lines, the move meant preserving their Anchorage ration of fuel for rapidly growing passenger services by taking advantage of

Passenger airlines, boarding over 400,000 travelers per year, link Fairbanks to Canada and the "Lower 48" U.S.

Courtesy of Fairbanks International Airport

an unlimited fuel supply from the newly opened North Pole Refinery near Fairbanks.

Air cargo operations peaked at over 80 flights per week and, with the passage of the fuel shortage, all three carriers reconsolidated their Alaskan operations in Anchorage. By the mid '80s, intercontinental cargo operations at Fairbanks had dwindled to occasional charters and weather diversions from Anchorage.

In 1986, a public/private partnership, working through the Fairbanks Industrial Development Corporation, undertook a market study for Fairbanks International Airport and the next year launched a marketing program on the airport's behalf. This effort, focused primarily on international cargo development, has moved the Fairbanks International Airport from an unranked position as recently as 1990 up to the United States' ninth-largest international airfreight gateway.

An extension of the runway to 11,800 feet, completed in 1997, allows wide-body cargo aircraft to take off year round with unrestricted payloads. Approximately 27 interconti-

nental cargo flights now pass through Fairbanks each week. The operators include Lufthansa Cargo, Air France, Cargolux, and Volga-Dnepr. Aircraft service, fueling, and crew changes occur during stopovers on routes between Asia and both Europe and North America.

Growth in domestic passenger service has kept pace with international operations. Now, more than 400,000 passengers annually board aircraft operated by Alaska Airlines, Delta Air Lines, and Northwest, as well as more than a half-dozen commuter airlines.

Today, passenger and cargo operations add up to impressive numbers for Fairbanks International Airport, a facility that provides vital transportation links, economic development, and jobs for the Interior Alaska community.

Intercontinental air cargo operations at Fairbanks International Airport.

Courtesy of Fairbanks International Airport

Courtesy of Fairbanks International Airport

Over 500 small aircraft — on wheels, floats, and skis — are based at Fairbanks International Airport.

NORTHWEST AIRLINES

Northwest Airlines has a fleet of 32 Boeing 747 aircraft. It is the primary aircraft used by Northwest to provide direct passenger service to Asia from nine U.S. cities.

Northwest Airlines has played a vital role in providing Alaska's transportation links to the world for more than five decades.

Minnesota-based Northwest envisioned a "Northwest Passage" to Asia in the early 1940s when it transported thousands of troops and military supplies to Alaska and the Aleutian Islands. Battling temperatures as low as 70 below zero, crews tackled the monstrous job of creating an "instant airline" to assist the nation's war effort.

Giant fuel tanks were cut apart, flown in, and welded back together; trucks and heavy equipment were sectioned and reassembled with a welder's torch; 25 buildings of varying sizes were erected; a network of

radio stations was created; and mountains of supplies were hauled in to all way stations. One newspaper wrote: "Winter problems were almost beyond belief. On occasion, the temperature went down to 70 below and ground crews working on

engines and parts could only put in a few minutes before they had to stop to warm themselves."

After the war, Northwest applied to begin the first regularly scheduled service from the United States to Asia via the "Great Circle" route across the top of the world. The route was inaugurated on July 15, 1947, with DC4 aircraft which covered more than 50 hours on the New York-Minneapolis-Edmonton-Anchorage-Shemya-Tokyo flight.

Northwest aircraft made trans-Pacific fuel stops at rocky, desolate Shemya, an island 1,461 miles down the Aleutian chain from Anchorage — an inhospitable, foggy little rock four miles long by two miles wide. On Shemya, Northwest remodeled abandoned Army Quonset huts into a staff house, crew quarters, commissary,

In 1947, Northwest Airlines inaugurated its historic flight from Anchorage to Tokyo. It was the first service of its kind from Alaska to Asia.

Alaska Governor Tony Knowles and First Lady Susan Knowles greet arriving passengers from Japan during inaugural fight ceremonies held in Anchorage on June 18, 1998.

laundry, mess hall, recreation lounge, maintenance shop, fuel depot and living quarters.

Nicknamed "Schmoo" by its inhabitants, Shemya housed 55 Northwest volunteers (one year per hitch) and even though a perennial pingpong tournament was one of the few local excitements, a number of employees ignored the rain, wind and fog to volunteer for three hitches in a row because "this is a great place to save money — there's no place to spend it."

Northwest's original service from Anchorage to Tokyo with 24-seat DC4 aircraft took 26 hours from departure to arrival. That compares to the seven hours and 30 minutes scheduled flight that Northwest reintroduced from Anchorage to Tokyo in June 1998 with wide-body jumbo jets. From Tokyo,

Northwest offers convenient connections to Northwest flights serving Beijing and Shanghai, China; Hong Kong; Singapore; Taipei, Taiwan; Bangkok, Thailand; Manila, Philippines; Seoul, Korea; Guam and Saipan. Northwest provides Alaska the most service of any carrier to Asia.

Through its alliance with KLM Royal Dutch Airlines, Northwest also links Alaska to the rest of the world. Northwest's convenient nonstop service from Anchorage to its hubs at Minneapolis and Detroit offers quick connections to its flights to more than 100 destinations in Europe, the Middle East, Africa and South Asia.

Northwest's commitment to Alaska does not end with passenger service. The airline

operates a major cargo hub at Anchorage International Airport with its fleet of eight all-cargo 747 freighters. Northwest's modern 50,000-square-foot warehouse allows five freighters to be loaded simultaneously. On average, Northwest handles more than 250 tons of cargo weekly at Anchorage International.

Northwest's year-around service to Anchorage is complemented by seasonal service from Fairbanks to Minneapolis and by its partnership with Alaska Airlines. Northwest is committed to remaining Alaska's transportation leader in the 21st century.

Anchorage International Airport plays an important role as the hub of Pacific cargo operations for Northwest Airlines. As many as 35 cargo flights per week are crossloaded in Anchorage.

CARLILE ENTERPRISES, INC.

Carlile Enterprises, Inc., together with K&W Transportation and Kuukpik Transportation, both subsidiaries of Carlile, is plugged into a national network that leads the way in exceeding the shipping industry's transportation standards. This network, along with a highly trained and experienced crew, is the reason Carlile can save businesses time and money by coordinating virtually every shipping need. Whether the shipment is hazardous waste, cold storage or a 180,000-pound piece of equipment, Carlile can ensure fast, affordable pick-up and delivery service anywhere between Alaska and the Lower 48 and beyond. And it's only a phone call away.

Carlile, an Alaskan-owned transportation company, offers cost-effective pricing options, on-site technical assistance and customized reports for all its customers. With an integrated multi-modal service, Carlile can expedite shipments — to the most remote site, or just down the street. A well trained team of logistics professionals has the expertise to provide their customers with the best possible service at the lowest possible price, whether its via barge, steamship, rail, air or the road system.

Carlile gives its customers options. With four weekly departures from Washington and Alaska, freight can be moved from most points within the Continental United States in less than a week. Carlile also offers daily service to Anchorage, Seward, Kenai, Homer and Fairbanks in Alaska, and to Seattle in Washington.

The Peregrine, with dimensions of 60 feet long by 24 feet wide by 16 feet tall, was transported from Anchorage to Prudhoe Bay by Carlile Enterprises. The boat is used for offshore oil exploration in the Beaufort Sea.

Courtesy of Carlile Enterprises; Photo by Frank Flavin

Courtesy of Carlile Enterprises

A few of Alaska's areas utilize ice roads to traverse rivers and normally soft ground. In some areas, these roads require little more than blading to keep snow clear and in other areas water is pumped and spread on the road to build up structural strength. In other applications, they are an acceptable alternative to the damage caused by permanent roads in sensitive landscapes.

Carlile has some of the best equipment available on the market today, including flatbeds, reefer vans and tankers. A new addition to the Carlile fleet is Cozad Lowboy, offering a capacity of 125 tons, more than double the capacity of previous lowboys.

Because its equipment is at the heart of Carlile's business, maintenance crews work to ensure everything is well taken care of by taking advantage of modern technological advances such as on board computers to improve safety as well as fuel and maintenance costs. Carlile also employs electronically-controlled engines in tractors making the trip from Fairbanks to Prudhoe Bay, saving 60 to 80 gallons of fuel each trip.

If the equipment is the heart of Carlile, the crew is its soul. Carlile's customer service philosophy is based on a desire to provide each customer with the best intrastate transportation service, whether it calls for meeting early delivery requirements, or designing special equipment to transport unique freight. It is this dedication to service that has allowed Carlile success and growth.

Carlile's drivers are among the best in the business. Each driver works to ensure that the customer's shipment reaches its destination safely and on time. After an initial employment screening, Carlile drivers are provided in-house training to properly handle different types of freight and are often rewarded with advancement opportunities in return for good safety records.

The company was founded in 1980 by Seward, Alaska residents John and Harry McDonald. John and Harry began their endeavor with two tractors, shipping timber, milk, bulk products and general freight. Nearly two decades later, Carlile has grown to include terminals in six locations with customers throughout Alaska and the Lower 48.

In early 1999, Carlile moved into a newly built terminal in Anchorage, consolidating the four buildings and small shop it had occupied. This growth is possible because of strong leadership, modern equipment and a commitment to the customer.

Carlile supports the community through the United Way, the Alaska Food Bank, the Alaska Trucking Association, and various youth activities and sports teams, among others.

Carlile moved into a new facility in early 1999.

Courtesy of Carlile Enterprises

Courtesy of Carlile Enterprises

Carlile partners with water carriers, air carriers and the Alaska Railroad to provide transportation service throughout Alaska.

Carlile's future is bright. With the addition of K&W Trucking and Alaska Native-run Kuukpik to the Carlile team; and with the company's commitment to fast, quality service at competitive prices; Carlile will to continue to serve not only Alaskans, but the rest of the country.

ASRC COMMUNICATIONS, LTD.

Specialists from ASRC Communications, Ltd. are designing the 2-way radio system for the new Alaska Native Medical Center in Anchorage.

ASRC Communications, Ltd. is an 8(a) certified Alaskan Inupiat Eskimo owned professional and technical services company with headquarters in Anchorage, Alaska and offices in Virginia, New Mexico, and Arizona. ASRCC's parent corporation is Arctic Slope Regional Corporation (ASRC), an Alaska Native Corporation (ANC). Glenn R. Edwards, President/CEO, has operated communications businesses within Alaska for over twenty years. Mr. Edwards' vision is to grow a high-technology business handling management, engineering, and services for government and commercial clients.

As an ANC, ASRCC is able to received sole-source contracts regardless of dollar amount.

ANCs are not subject to the $3 million limitation on sole-source contracts (the "competitive threshold") applicable to other 8(a) firms. ASRCC also qualifies under the DoD Indian Subcontracting Incentive Program, which allows prime contractors to receive a 5 percent bonus payment when they use Native subcontractors.

ASRCC was originally formed in 1978 to provide cable television services in Barrow as well as pipeline and oilfield services communication support. During the past year, ASRCC has seen important changes in structure and management. Along with the establishment of an 8(a) company, ASRCC acquired Correa Enterprises, Inc. (CEI), an information solutions company. A reorganization

of like business within ASRC resulted in the absorption of PMC Telecommunications (PMCT) into ASRCC.

With these recent acquisitions, ASRCC has the capability of offering its diverse client base a wide range of technical and professional services. ASRCC has a reputation for management integrity, technical competence, and customer responsiveness.

Correa Enterprises, Inc. (CEI) is a high-technology information solutions company. Based in Albuquerque, New Mexico, CEI began operations in 1980 servicing the federal sector. CEI offers Information Technology (IT) and Commercial-off-the-Shelf (COTS) hardware and software acquisition support.

ASRC Communications, Ltd. has completed numerous professional installations of critical 2-way mobile radios for public-safety communications as well as the private sector.

ASRC Communications, Ltd. provides remote-site satellite phone links to any location in the world.

Courtesy of ASRC Communications, Ltd.

ASRCC's 8(a) Company is based in Arlington, Virginia. Together with CEI, ASRCC's capabilities include but are not limited to the following areas:

TECHNICAL SERVICES

ASRC's highly trained staff provides a range of technical services to a diverse client base, the U.S. Air Force, U.S. Army, other DoD organizations, Bureau of Indian Affairs, General Services Administration and commercial firms.

COMPUTER AND NETWORK SERVICES

ASRCC has extensive experience providing quality computer and network services, which include requirements analysis, configuration management, hardware and software engineering and maintenance, training, and network installation and maintenance.

TECHNICAL CONFERENCE

ASRCC provides complete conference services. From site selection to document production, their Certified Meeting Planners (CMPs) will coordinate every aspect including program design, database management, reservations, travel arrangements, spouse programs, audiovisual support, documentation and security.

With offices in Anchorage, Fairbanks, and Wasilla, Alaska; PMC Telecommunications (PMCT) provides a customer base that stretches from Anchorage to Wasilla, and from Kotzebue to Barrow. PMCT provides nationwide engineering, installation, and maintenance of premier telephone, radio frequency and SMART cabling products. PMCT's staff is comprised of qualified technicians, engineers and managers, each with a proven track record for operating in harsh Alaska environments. Technicians at PMCT hold numerous industry certifications.

For both private and industrial applications, PMCT is expert at engineering, installing and maintaining sophisticated mobile and transportable radio systems. Product lines include microwave systems, community repeaters, short-range spread spectrum and radio systems. They also offer wireless modems for short-range and data telecommunications, mountaintop repeater-site construction and management, privacy analog radio and satellite communications networking.

PMCT also provides low-cost service in its modern repair facility. By utilizing factory-trained technicians, their long record of within-budget and on-schedule completion is a reflection of ASRCC's quality human resources.

ASRCC's broad range of services and products, extensive Alaska and remote experience, and dedication to quality service distinguish them from others in the industry. Their goal is to be a nationally recognized, full-service communications company, participating in partnerships and strategic alliances, the U.S. Small Business Administration's 8(a) program, and the Federal Buy Indian program. It is a vision of success derived from quality, employee stewardship, shareholder involvement, and customer participation. It is that participation in development, growth, and feedback that guides the direction of ASRC Communications' business.

Courtesy of ASRC Communications, Ltd.

Glenn R. Edwards is President and CEO of ASRC Communications, Ltd. He is shown here in front of a solar powered mountaintop radio repeater that was engineered and built by RF technical staff of PMCT.

EVERGREEN HELICOPTERS

Courtesy of Evergreen Helicopters and Wyndham Images

Evergreen provides a lifeline to small, isolated communities by delivering mail and food.

From delivering food and mail to residents on a remote island off the coast of Alaska to rescuing distressed mountain climbers off the top of North America's tallest peak, Evergreen Helicopters of Alaska has provided these services and more to residents of the nation's Last Frontier since 1963.

Alaska's harsh weather and unique geography can be very demanding. At times, people's lives literally hang in the balance, and every advantage is needed to tip the scales to a positive outcome. For this reason,

Gerard Rock, president of Evergreen, insists on the use of the latest, most innovative technology, and the best of pilots. For example, when a group of British mountain climbers recently ran into trouble high on the slopes of Mt. McKinley — a peak of more than 20,000 feet — one of Evergreen's award-winning pilots performed a heroic rescue in extreme conditions. With Evergreen's high-altitude helicopter, the pilot flew to 19,600 feet — the highest altitude ever accomplished at that time.

Evergreen was also there when Southcentral Alaskans were faced with losing their homes in the Miller's Reach forest fire. Evergreen's helicopters dropped fire retardant and water on the blaze, helping to control, and eventually extinguish, the flames.

Evergreen provides a different sort of lifeline to small communities like Little Diomede, a small village on an island in the freezing waters of the Bering Sea. Through Evergreen, the U.S. Postal Service delivers mail and food to these isolated residents.

Gerard Rock, President of Evergreen Helicopters.

Evergreen Helicopters of Alaska has four bases in the state: Anchorage, Nome, Deadhorse, and Cold Bay. The company also provides support services to Alaska's oil and construction companies, and will even give a lift to extreme skiers looking for an adventure in Valdez.

The company employs about 21 Alaskans and maintains seven aircraft during the winter months. During the busier summer season, Evergreen hires 40 additional mechanics and pilots for the 20 or more aircraft in order to provide residents with the services they need, when they need them.

Evergreen Helicopters of Alaska is a division of a world-wide endeavor, Evergreen International Aviation, which has corporate headquarters in McMinnville, Oregon. Founder and owner Delford Smith began the company back in 1960, and has shown the world that the helicopter can be both a work horse and an angel of mercy at the same time.

Today, Evergreen furnishes global aviation capabilities, from ground handling and flight operations to materiel and maintenance support, for more than 160 countries, while providing valuable jobs to more than 3,000 people. Through acquisition in 1975, Evergreen expanded its services to include heavy jet transport. As a result, the company has become the largest B747 cargo carrier in the world and the first U.S. B747 cargo carrier to fly directly to mainland China.

One of only three unlimited aircraft repair and maintenance stations in the nation, Evergreen Air Center in Marana, Arizona, has been a quality support depot for the world's fleets, including those of large financial institutions and government agencies.

The company does not limit its talents and expertise to the skies — they also look to the stars. By performing routine maintenance on the shuttle-carrier aircraft for NASA, Evergreen is an important part of the nation's space-flight program.

Evergreen also has agricultural and nursery divisions managed through the company's Agricultural Enterprises. These divisions have supplied international markets with select grains, seeds, and plants — even Christmas trees.

Humanitarian support and peace-keeping missions have occupied many of the company's helicopters. Evergreen pilots have dedicated many hours to working for the United Nations World Health Organization on the 20-year-long onchocerciasis program to eradicate the black fly, which is the cause of river blindness in parts of Africa.

Established on the principle that the customer is their reason for existing, Evergreen International has developed a wide scope of services to accommodate everyone, even those people who need out-of-the-ordinary assistance. Because of their philosophy, Evergreen Helicopters of Alaska provides its customers with both the usual and the unique services that their customers require.

By using the best pilots and the most innovative technology, Evergreen Helicopters has developed a reputation for getting the job done.

LYNDEN

Lynden Air Cargo and Lynden Air Freight increase Lynden's ability to move freight to, from and within Alaska.

In 1954, Lynden pioneered scheduled freight service to Alaska via the Alaska Highway. Today, the combined capabilities of the Lynden companies includes truckload and less-than-truckload highway connections, scheduled barges, intermodal bulk chemical hauls, scheduled and chartered air freighters, domestic and international air forwarding, international ocean forwarding, remote site construction, and multi-modal logistics.

Lynden's growth has paralleled Alaska's. In its early days, Lynden moved its first freight with one wagon and two horses based in Lynden, Washington. By 1921, its freight business

entered the motorized age with the purchase of a two-and-one-half ton Mack truck. As the company grew, regular runs to Seattle were added, more trucks purchased and new drivers hired. One of the new drivers hired in 1940 was Henry "Hank" Jansen. A few years later Jansen and his partner purchased the growing freight company which would later become

Lynden Transport. By 1949, the Alaska Highway opened new frontiers for a growing company ready to expand, and Lynden Transport began looking north toward the future.

Although Lynden has expanded and diversified over the years, its commitment to Alaska has remained a company touchstone. "We are, and always will be, primarily an Alaska company," says president Jim Jansen. Lynden Transport trucks still roll over the Alaska Highway, and, along with Canadian Lynden Transport, continue to serve the oil industry and other Alaska customers. Alaska Hovercraft delivers mail to remote villages over the tundra. Alaska West Express specializes in hauling bulk commodities, while Knik Construction builds roads and remote air strips in a state that boasts nearly as many pilots as drivers. This same Alaska commitment is shared by the

Alaska West Express, a subsidiary of Lynden, specializes in hauling bulk commodities.

people of Alaska Marine Lines, Lynden Air Cargo and Lynden Air Freight as they work to meet the needs of Alaska's citizens and businesses.

When the devastating Alaska earthquake hit in 1964, and later, when major flooding destroyed much of Fairbanks, Lynden responded by sending every available vehicle up the Alaska Highway with food, supplies and materials for rebuilding.

Beginning in 1972, construction on the 800-mile Alaska pipeline brought a new boom to the state's economy. Lynden Transport recorded its 10,000th trip north, as trucks rolled over the once-lonely Alaska Highway day and night, hauling supplies, equipment and building materials. Beginning in late summer of 1974, Lynden Transport began daily service between Valdez and Anchorage, Fairbanks, various construction camps and the Prudhoe Bay area hauling heavy oil-field equipment, pipeline materials, insulation, timbers for the base modular buildings, barrels of oil, parts, cats, cranes . . . and just about anything else one can imagine.

From the mid 1970s through the 1980s, the addition of new companies expanded the scope of the Lynden family. From delivering packages in Nome to providing service to isolated towns in Southeast Alaska to helping coordinate cleanup of the Valdez oil spill, Lynden companies have remained steadfast to their commitment to Alaska and its people.

Today, Lynden continues to serve the communities of Alaska in many ways. Every year, Lynden moves food around the state for community food banks by truck, barge and air. Lynden also trucks large blocks of ice cut from lakes in Fairbanks to Anchorage and other locations for various community ice carving events during the winter carnivals. Lynden is a major contributor to the arts, including helping arts groups to bring major events to Fairbanks, Kenai and Southeast Alaska by contributing its services for travel and shipping. Similarly, Lynden has supported various Iditarod dog sled racers for many years, providing transportation for dog food and other supplies, and returning the weary dog teams from Nome. Lynden continues to support the youth of Alaska with contributions to community and educational teams, scholarship programs, the United Way and Junior Achievement.

Lynden is proud to serve Alaska. At all levels Lynden's people work hard to maintain a small-company attitude with customers; but when it comes to accomplishing the job, they pull together to perform with big-company capabilities. Those capabilities are varied and complex, yet Lynden's corporate philosophy is simple and direct: work hard; deliver quality; be the best at what we do. The common goal of all Lynden companies is "to serve our customers well." Lynden looks forward to creating innovative new capabilities developed specifically to serve Alaska in the next century.

As a subsidiary of Lynden, Alaska Marine Lines provides an important barge-service link for Lynden Transport.

Lynden Transport expanded its service dramatically during the construction of the 800-mile Alaska pipeline and has since established itself as a valuable transport network that serves the oil industry and other Alaska customers.

CHUGACH ELECTRIC ASSOCIATION

Chugach has introduced a number of innovative services for customers in recent years.

Customer choice—it's the Chugach difference.

Chugach Electric Association is Alaska's largest electric utility. It is also an innovative provider of services to its customers.

For instance, customers can pick the day of the month they would like their bills to come due, under the flexible payment due date program. Construction performance guarantees assure customers that the utility will complete line extensions or service connections by an agreed-upon date, or begin paying them for the inconvenience—

General Manager Gene Bjornstad leads a team of 360 Chugach employees intent on providing the best electric service possible for customers of Alaska's largest electric utility.

assuming the delay is caused by something under Chugach's control. Chugach's "electric check" program lets customers tailor billing and payment options using a range of choices. And summary billing creates a single sheet bill that allows customers with multiple accounts to make comparisons and a single monthly payment—while still providing the individual account details on accompanying pages.

Programs like these and others have led to consistently high approval ratings for Chugach in customer surveys. The utility is also the leader in advocating for change in Alaska's electric utility industry.

Chugach has been virtually alone in saying that individual customers should have the right to choose the company that provides their electric service. The utility has championed customer choice before both the

Legislature and the Alaska Public Utilities Commission. That position is in line with repeated public opinion surveys that show that more than 90 percent of customers think they should have the right to choose their power provider.

Chugach serves a retail customer base of 55,000 members at 68,000 metered locations and provides power to about two-thirds of the homes and businesses in Anchorage. In addition, Chugach delivers power to Alaskans throughout the Railbelt region through wholesale and economy energy sales to other utilities from Homer to Fairbanks.

Chugach uses a mix of natural gas and hydroelectric resources to provide clean, reliable, affordable energy. Chugach owns and operates four power plants of its own—including Beluga, the largest power plant in the state. It is a co-owner of a hydroelectric project purchased from the federal government in

1997. Chugach also takes the largest single share of the State-owned Bradely Lake hydroelectric project, and dispatches a single-turbine plant owned by another utility. Chugach operates 1,973 miles of transmission and distribution line.

Most of Chugach's power comes from gas-fired turbine-generators. In 1997, 91 percent of the kilowatt-hours it sold were produced using natural gas as a base fuel for either single or combined-cycle combustion units. The other 9 percent come from hydro resources.

With most of its power coming from gas turbines, a steady supply of natural gas is crucial to Chugach. The utility has long-term contracts with multiple suppliers that will provide a stable, reliable, reasonably-priced supply of fuel until at least the year 2015.

In addition to its gas-fired and hydroelectric generation, Chugach is pursuing on-site fuel cell projects, and is investigating the practicality of wind-turbines to meet customer desires.

Despite the challenges of operating in Alaska, Chugach customers pay rates that are in line with the national average, and they enjoy very reliable service. In 1997, Chugach averaged only 1.24 outage hours per consumer—which translates to power being on 99.99 percent of the time.

With a combination of innovative customer services, excellent reliability and reasonable rates, Chugach plans to meet the needs of its customers today—and the demands of a competitive marketplace in the future, once customers in Alaska are free to choose their electric supplier.

Chugach's 115-kilovolt transmission line provides the only electrical link between Anchorage and the Kenai Peninsula.

Chugach's Beluga Power Plant is the largest generation facility in Alaska.

ALASKA FIBER STAR, LLC

An Alaska Fiber Star employee holding the fiber that transmits data by light.

Courtesy of Alaska Fiber Star

Alaska Fiber Star meet their commitment to the nation's largest state. Four hundred miles of fiber optic cable from Fairbanks to Anchorage has helped make accelerated high-speed data and voice transmission for businesses, education, and Alaskan residents possible. Better communications support improved medical care and educational opportunities, and offer a competitive edge for the state's businesses.

Alaska Fiber Star uses innovative technology that was virtually unheard of only a decade ago — technology offering a capacity and a clarity that is unmatched by satellite or other ground-based systems. One example is an all-digital Synchronous Optical Network, a base broadband medium capable of supporting the deployment of wideband and broadband digital services as

well as high-quality voice service. Because of this technology, a single-mode fiber optic cable network links Anchorage and Fairbanks for the first time ever.

Health care is a major concern for rural Alaskans, where many residents do not have direct access to experienced medical doctors. Technology provided by Alaska Fiber Star can close that gap. This new technology provides telemedicine for rural Alaskans. Transmissions such as medical x-rays or videoconference connections travel across the network in real time. A doctor in Fairbanks or Anchorage can look at an image, make a diagnosis, and relay treatment instructions to virtually any small village in the state. The cable can also link the super-computing center at the University of Alaska Fairbanks with users in Alaska and the

Alaska Fiber Star, LLC is linking Alaskans to the world. By using the most modern fiber optic technology, Alaska Fiber Star is providing limitless opportunities for all Alaskans through fiber optic extensions to Whittier and Valdez, and connections by submarine cable to Juneau, the Lower 48 and the world.

Their mission is simple: to provide new levels of capacity, quality and dependability to Alaska's telecommunications industry. The 49th state's newest pipeline will help employees at

Courtesy of Alaska Fiber Star; Photo by Chris Arend

Inside the operations center in Anchorage, employees provide quality-control monitoring, circuit provisioning and recovery operations 24 hours a day.

rest of the world, and can connect Alaskan's national defense networks to the Lower 48 in an instant.

The network and control center, based in Anchorage, is staffed 24 hours a day to provide quality-control monitoring, circuit provisioning and recovery operations. Alaska Fiber Star is a privately-owned Alaskan Liability Corporation, and is a subsidiary of World Net Communications, Inc. of Australia, which is developing

fiber optic cable systems throughout the United States. This partnerships provides the power to offer far-reaching services to Alaska's big industries. Alaska Fiber Star customers include a majority of the local telephone companies, the universities and the military.

Working in Alaska's unique territory and in temperatures that range from more than 80 degrees above to well below zero can be a formidable task, but the field staff at Alaska Fiber

Star can meet that challenge. Each of the men and women on Fiber Star's field staff is highly trained and specially equipped to work effectively in the state's harshest climates.

Alaska Fiber Star is the first company to install, connect and operate major fiber optic cable in Alaska, and the company will work to continue to promote this new network to stimulate growth in the Last Frontier. Alaska Fiber Star is lighting the way to a new technology.

A crew starts the installation of the fiber-optic cable from Anchorage to Valdez. The cable runs along the Alaska Railroad right of way to Whittier, where it connects to a 95-mile submarine cable link to Valdez.

CROWLEY MARINE SERVICES

One of Crowley's many Sea Lifts of module cargo to Prudhoe Bay.

CATCO's Rollagon balloon-tired vehicles transport an airplane over the frozen tundra of the North Slope.

Courtesy of Crowley Marine Services; Photo by Bill Kuper

For over 45 years, Crowley has been providing unique solutions for Alaska's logistics challenges. Beginning in the early 1950s, a Crowley company began operating railcar barge transportation to Southeast Alaska and, a few years later, began supplying the Distant Early Warning (DEW) sites for the U.S. Air Force. Since then, Crowley has provided solutions to the most complicated marine transportation problems.

In 1963, Crowley commenced regular rail-barge operations, known as the Alaska Hydro-Train, for the Alaska

A Crowley shallow draft barge delivers fuel in Western Alaska.

In 1968, Crowley began participating in sea lifts from the Lower 48 to Prudhoe Bay. Since the inception of the Trans-Alaska Pipeline in 1977, over 300 barges carrying in excess of 1.3 million tons of cargo have transported large modules and heavy cargo from the Lower 48 to Prudhoe Bay. Tugs and barges specifically designed and strengthened for module carriage and other cargoes have continued to support oilfield development on the North Slope and in the Beaufort Sea.

Crowley provides logistics support for oilfield development and heavy-lift overland transport on the North Slope using CATCO (Crowley All-Terrain Corporation) Rollagons — balloon-tired vehicles specifically designed for working on the tundra without damaging the delicate Arctic ecosystem.

Under contract to the Alyeska Pipeline Service Company since 1977, Crowley provides tanker escort and docking services in Valdez Harbor and Prince William Sound. Crowley's new 10,192-horsepower Prince William Sound Class enhanced tractor tugs, assigned to this service, are the most powerful tugs of their kind. These, and other Crowley vessels stationed in the area, provide a comprehensive marine service capability to Alyeska and its member companies.

Railroad, transporting rail cars by barge from the Lower 48 to the Alaska Railroad terminal in Whittier. For many years, Crowley barges have delivered containerized and general cargoes to ports throughout the state. Crowley continues to provide contract tug and barge services in support of infrastructure and resource development projects.

Crowley's state-of-the-art tug fleet escorts a tanker at Alyeska's Valdez terminal.

Unique expertise and equipment have propelled Crowley into its position as a leader providing quality, reliable services. Whether its over-the-tundra transportation, supplying subsistence fuel in remote areas, providing project cargo services, or state-of-the-art tug escort and response, Crowley creates solutions and develops the answers for Alaska's unique marine and logistics challenges.

Avis Rent A Car, Inc.

Customers can expect the "We Try Harder" service that makes AVIS second to none.

Courtesy of AVIS Rent a Car

Trying harder takes on a whole new dimension in Alaska, especially in vehicle renting. But that extra effort, for which Avis Rent a Car is so famous, has on many occasions made a big difference to customers residing in or visiting Alaska.

As the only statewide agency in Alaska, Avis is able to provide seamless integrated service across an area one-fifth the size of the contiguous United States. The exclusive "rent it here, leave it there" rentals available from Avis, allows customers to maximize their Alaskan adventure by incorporating nine different cities in which to leave their rental vehicles.

Avis serves an increasingly large number of tourists drawn to Alaska's vivid scenery and rich culture. These visitors are discovering there is a lot to see on the 14,000 miles of roads in Alaska, from the metropolitan feel of Anchorage to the rustic National Parks and sparkling rivers and lakes across the last frontier. From February's Fur Rendezvous in Anchorage, to the Summer Solstice celebrations in Fairbanks, Avis has been getting people where they are going in Alaska since 1955.

Regardless of their travel needs, customers have come to expect a high standard of performance from Avis. Service is delivered by a friendly, efficient, and well-trained staff from Fairbanks to Petersburg. Despite its large territory, the company prides itself on being able to immediately respond to customers in the event of mechanical problems. The statewide network of locations allows for prompt road service, to get the customer back on the road again.

The list of Avis amenities includes: the corporate rates that customers have come to expect from Avis agencies everywhere; a fleet of 1,400 vehicles including 4wds and 15-passenger vans; Alaska Airlines frequent-flyer miles with qualifying rentals; and a statewide network of locations in Anchorage, Fairbanks, Haines, Juneau, Kenai, Kodiak, Petersburg, Sitka, and Skagway.

AVIS features vehicles equipped to handle the many conditions one would find in Alaska.

Courtesy of AVIS Rent a Car

Courtesy of AVIS Rent a Car

Travelers with adventure on their minds discover that AVIS is ready to accommodate them with vehicles that can handle the elements.

GOLDEN VALLEY ELECTRIC ASSOCIATION

Courtesy of Golden Valley Electric

President and CEO Mike Kelly knows that computers can never replace the value of meeting customers face to face, but to meet customer expectations and the challenges of providing reliable electric service in Interior Alaska, GVEA's computerized dispatch command center is critical.

Golden Valley Electric Association, Interior Alaska's locally-owned rural electric cooperative, has a proud history of providing reliable electric service despite temperatures ranging from over 90 degrees to 50 degrees below zero. Yet Golden Valley Electric Association (GVEA) maintains an average service reliability of 99.9 percent. Their diverse power supply, with four fuel sources, is one reason why there has been no rate increase since 1982. GVEA has 224 megawatts of generation, over 200 employees and more than 2,300 miles of line throughout a 2,200 square mile service territory. Although the customer base is 85 percent residential, GVEA serves large commercial customers ranging from mining operations to oil refineries to retail shopping malls.

GVEA owns and operates a mine-mouth, coal-fired plant in Healy, Alaska and an oil-fired plant adjacent to a North Pole, Alaska, refinery. They also share in the output of a state-owned hydroelectric plant on the Kenai Peninsula. In addition, GVEA is the northern control for a 175-mile, 138-kV intertie connecting Alaska's two largest cities, Fairbanks and Anchorage. This intertie completes a Railbelt grid and enables the transfer of economy energy generated from natural gas in the Anchorage area.

GVEA plans to operate and purchase power generated by a state-of-the-art, coal-fired power plant at Healy by 2001. That plant is expected to provide 50 megawatts of competitively-priced electric power and demonstrate innovative clean coal-burning technologies. Combined with low-sulfur Alaska coal, these new technologies should result in one of the cleanest coal-burning plants in the world. The construction of

this 50 megawatt clean-coal plant is a joint venture between the U.S. Department of Energy (DOE) and the State of Alaska. The project received a $117 million grant from the DOE under their Clean Coal Technology Program. Once proven, this new technology can be used to retrofit existing coal-fired plants around the world.

Through the years, GVEA has met the challenges presented by increased military presence in the 1940s, statehood in the 1950s, the Good Friday earthquake and Fairbanks flood in the 1960s, the world oil crisis of the 1970s, the growth stimulated by the Trans Alaska Pipeline in the 1980s and the acquisition of the Fairbanks Municipal Utility System's 6,000 electric consumers in the 1990s. Today, GVEA is a progressive, stable utility planning for environmentally-sound expansion to meet Interior Alaska's energy needs well into the next century.

Courtesy of Golden Valley Electric

GVEA's commitment to provide low-cost, reliable power has remained the same for 50 years. To meet tomorrow's needs, the Healy Clean Coal Project is being constructed adjacent to GVEA's existing power plant.

BOWHEAD TRANSPORTATION COMPANY

Bowhead Transportation vessels lightering cargo across the very shallow Pt. Lay Lagoon.

Courtesy of Bowhead Transportation Company

Operating in the Arctic for more than a decade, with service recently expanded to include most Western Alaska ports, Bowhead Transportation Company (BTC) is a name that Alaska has learned to trust for fast and reliable marine transportation solutions. The company has shipped over 46,000 tons of materials to and from ports in Western Alaska and the North Slope, and the Lower 48.

"The people of Alaska depend on us to transport everything from groceries to modular housing, even to remote sites unnavigable by deeper draft boats and barges," says Robert Leonard, general manager at Bowhead. This need precipitated the design and construction of the *Sam Talaak*, the first of two 150' x 50' shallow draft landing crafts. Launched in 1998, the *Greta S. Akpik*, was the second vessel produced by Qayaq Marine, an LLC jointly owned by Bowhead and Seacoast Towing. These vessels have been very successful in providing cargo lighterage along the coastline and up the shallow rivers in Western Alaska.

BTC has a strong network of partnerships with a wide range of carriers in the Lower 48, which provides the company with the advantage of being able to quickly obtain the right vehicle for any job. The company has access to vessels up to 4000

HP and barges up to 330 feet. "Not only does this wide-reaching network of affiliates enable BTC to have flexible operations, but we can also offer customers a very competitive rate structure," says Leonard.

Bowhead Transportation Company is headquartered in Seattle, with an additional office in Anchorage. The company is wholly owned by Ukpeagvik Inupiat Corporation (UIC), the Native village corporation in Barrow. Named in 1995 as the tenth largest Alaska-owned corporation by Alaska Business Monthly, UIC and its family of companies provide a wide range of services in Alaska and the Lower 48, including transportation, construction, engineering and communications. Bowhead Transportation was recently certified under the Small Business Administration 8(a) program which allows certain priorities and advantages for Alaska Native Corporations in securing federal contracts. Under the 8(a) program, Bowhead's growth will extend from marine operations to government contracting.

Bowhead Transportation continues to grow and expand its services to keep pace with the unique needs of Alaskans and find solutions to their special transport requirements.

Courtesy of Bowhead Transportation Company

Cargo from Kaktovik and Prudhoe Bay is loaded on the Greta S. Akpik *and the barge* Qayaq 1, *headed for Pt. Lay.*

Sea-Land Domestic Shipping LLC

Anchorage is Sea-Land's largest Alaska port.

During the busiest fishing seasons, a Sea-Land Pacific Express Service vessel stops off in Dutch Harbor on the way to the Orient, takes on fresh frozen seafood, and speeds it on to waiting Asian markets.

In addition to ocean service, Sea-Land's linehaul truck service distributes freight arriving in Anchorage to final destinations throughout the railbelt and beyond. Special arrangements with connecting carriers allow cargo destined to villages without road access to be transferred quickly and to be dispatched to its final destination.

Sea-Land Domestic Shipping is proud to have served Alaskans for over 35 years. The company looks forward to serving the 49th state for many more, with a promise to continue developing new and innovative ways to meet the changing needs of the state and its people.

Just weeks after the 1964 Good Friday Earthquake in Alaska, Sea-Land Service began shuttling badly needed relief supplies between Seattle and the 49th state. That effort quickly expanded into the first regularly scheduled weekly maritime service between Seattle and Alaska's railbelt.

Today, thirty-five years later, Sea-Land has become Alaska's largest shipping company. Three specially constructed linehaul vessels ply the waters from Puget Sound to the Gulf of Alaska. The D-7 Class vessels, the *M/V's Sea-Land Anchorage, Kodiak and Tacoma,* link Alaska to mainland supply centers with two arrivals in Anchorage and Kodiak each week as well as one call a week to the busy fishing port of Dutch Harbor. Feeder service operates along the Alaska Peninsula, in Bristol Bay, and as far north as the Pribilof Islands.

Sea-Land links Dutch Harbor with mainland Alaska.

NORTHERN AIR CARGO

"Do what needs to be done to meet the customer's needs." For more than 40 years, this has been the philosophy of Northern Air Cargo. Beginning with founders Bobby Sholton and Maurie Carlson, employees at NAC have striven to meet any challenge presented to them by their fellow Alaskans.

Like other airlines, NAC began with a dream, a perceptive businessman and an astute aviator. But NAC, however, did things somewhat differently. Most rural Alaskan communities can only be reached by air. Seeing an opportunity, Bobby and Maurie set out to provide these residents with something they had never truly had before, and that was year round transportation and a connecting lifeline to the rest of the world. The two joined together to acquire a military surplus Fairchild C-82 "Flying Boxcar" cargo airplane. They founded Alaska's first and only all-cargo airline providing service from Barrow to Seattle and even beyond.

To continue meeting their customer's demands, Bobby and Maurie added DC-6 aircraft to the fleet mix. Eventually, the fleet of DC-6s became the largest operating in the world, at one time numbering as many 14 aircraft. The DC-6 has been particularly well suited to life in Alaska due to its large payload

and its ability to land at relatively short, unimproved runways. In addition, NAC has the only two "Swing Tail" DC-6s in the world. These planes allow for odd-sized cargo, including items up to 67 feet in length.

NAC supports more Alaskans with air freight than any other carrier, with scheduled or connecting service to well over 100 communities statewide. They fly more than 100 million pounds of cargo each year, including machinery, vehicles, fuel, fish, the U.S. mail, and anything else the residents of Alaska need.

NAC is a recognized expert in handling hazardous materials including explosives, flammables, corrosives and compressed gases.

In recent years, NAC has begun to expand its fleet by purchasing three Boeing 727-100 freighters. A new 36,000-square-foot facility at Anchorage International Airport, and the development of a new cargo tracking system, will also help NAC improve what is already a notable service to its customers.

As sponsors of the Iditarod Sled Dog Race, the Alaska Native Heritage Center, the Food Bank of Alaska and the "Flying Cans" program, NAC also works to support residents on a more personal level as well.

NAC has the only two "Swing Tail" DC-6s in the world.

It is this dedication to Alaskans that has made Northern Air Cargo the most sought-after air freight provider in the state. Its employees promise to do what it takes to continue this commitment to excellence and to live up to their slogan: "What you want, when and where you want it. No excuses!"

NAC's fleet of DC-6s.

FOSS MARITIME COMPANY

Early season lighterage operations at the Red Dog Mine.

Foss Maritime Company, an 110-year-old marine transportation services and support company, has a long history of regional and ocean transportation, harbor services, vessel repair, terminal operations, and shoreside marine support activities. The company serves every major port on the West Coast, and has ongoing operations from northern Alaska to southern Mexico, including the Columbia/Snake River System. Foss Subsidiary transportation companies also operate in Alaska, San Francisco, LA/LB harbors, the Gulf of Mexico, and the Caribbean Sea.

Foss Maritime Company provided the first tug and barge to Alaska in 1922, and since then has been providing services for remote construction projects, pioneering beach landings, and remote-site support throughout Alaska. Over the years, Foss has provided reliable tug and barge services for common-carrier operations to Southeast Alaska, Southcentral Alaska, and the Aleutian Islands year-round, as well as to Western Alaska in the summer months. The company has been in the petroleum transportation business in the 49th state for more than 75 years.

Foss is a recognized technology leader with 11 state-of-the-art tractor tugs, two specially-designed self-unloading offshore lighterage barges for the Red Dog Mine project, and the latest in support equipment.

Currently, the company is building a vessel for Boeing to transport rockets from Alabama to Cape Canaveral and Vandenburg Air Force base for launching commercial and Air Force satellites. Foss also has the capability to provide other specialized marine services, such as spill-response barges and camp barges.

Headquartered in Seattle, Washington, the company operates a total of 112 tugs and 99 barges. Foss Maritime Company prides itself on its versatility and capacity to supply customized equipment and expertise to fit the parameters of any job.

Three Foss tugs positioning a jack-up drilling rig in Kachemak Bay for loading on a submersible ship.

ALASKA MARINE HIGHWAY SYSTEM

Alaska Marine Highway's nine vessels sail around the clock, frequently passing each other as they deliver passengers and vehicles to their destinations.

A new road through southern Alaska was opened in July, 1998. Thousands of visitors, piloting everything from the largest RVs to multi-geared bicycles, rolled on to the new route in the Southeast Panhandle and rolled off in Valdez or Seward after a safe, comfortable trip. The "road" across the Gulf of Alaska was opened when the *Motor Vessel Kennicott* began her maiden voyage as the newest member of the Alaska Marine Highway System fleet.

It may seem like hyperbole to compare a single 382-foot-long ship to a road, but the ninth vessel in the Alaska state ferry fleet is serving a mission unlike that fulfilled by her sisters in their 35-year history. With monthly sailings from Juneau to Valdez and Seward during the summer months, the *Kennicott* has opened a travel express lane

for summer vacationers and commercial shippers to Alaska's urban centers and its primary road system.

The passage across the Gulf of Alaska is a notable travel adventure in itself. It offers motorists a leisurely alternative to the long-haul 1,500-mile Alaska Highway, or the popular ferry/drive route from Haines or Skagway to reach Alaska's Interior.

"A driver could travel from Bellingham (Washington) to Seward with little physical effort while enjoying a scenic, hassle-free experience," says Captain Robert J. Doll, the licensed merchant marine ship's master who manages the ferry system.

While slightly smaller than the 418-foot *M/V Columbia*, the *Kennicott's* maximum capacity is 748 passengers and up to 120 standard automobiles. "Anything that can make the 90 degree turn in the car-deck space, we can take aboard.

Fundamentally, that's almost anything that will go on a highway in terms of weight, width or length," Captain Doll explains. In the past, that "anything" has included herds of wild elk being transported to Southeast islands; whole circuses starting Alaska tours; the largest luxury motorhomes; cargo containers up to 48 feet; and — on very special occasions — Santa Claus. Even the jolly old elf sometimes needs a little extra help reaching remote island villages to bring holiday magic to Alaska's children.

While plying some of the world's most challenging waters, the Alaska Marine Highway System continues to maintain an outstanding record of safety. "The Alaskan public has come to take the safety and reliability of the marine highway for granted," Captain Doll notes. "Like a great cafe or the best mechanic, if the locals depend on something, you can too."

The M/V Kennicott set out on its sea trials in 1998.

TOTEM OCEAN TRAILER EXPRESS

TOTE terminal in the Port of Anchorage.

Totem Ocean Trailer Express Inc.(TOTE) has been providing cargo transportation between Alaska and the lower 48 states and Canada for more than two decades. Simplicity is the keynote of TOTE's fast and reliable roll-on/roll-off trailership system. Cargo of every type and dimension, even over-sized shipments, can be shipped easily and expediently. "We really pride ourselves on being versatile—if it has wheels, we can ship it," explains Jeff Keck, vice president of operations.

In addition to its three trailerships, TOTE has an extensive fleet of refrigerated and insulated trailers, dry vans, flatbeds, opentops and tankers available

to pick up and deliver cargo from anywhere in the Lower 48 and parts of Canada to Alaska. The lifeline of cargo transported by TOTE for Alaska's citizens includes groceries, construction materials, household goods, vehicles and other consumer products. TOTE also transports

military cargo and vehicles, as well as retail merchandise for stores serving Alaska, including Home Depot, Fred Meyer and Wal-Mart.

TOTE has earned a strong reputation as a solid member of the Alaska community as well as a first-rate business. "First and foremost, our goal is to serve the communities of Alaska that are our customers, business associates and neighbors," says Keck. "That means both community service and a strong commitment to our employees. There have been no layoffs in the company's history, which has created a strong and loyal workforce."

TOTE employees sit on both Anchorage and Fairbanks Community Advisory Boards, as well as contributing their time to a wide range of community services. One of many charity activities in which the company participates is transporting goods from the dock to the Food Bank of Alaska's facility at no cost.

Great Land *under power through Puget Sound.*

ALASKA PUBLIC RADIO NETWORK

Every weekday, 80,000 adult Alaskans rely on the local news provided by the Alaska Public Radio Network. It is in-depth news and information as only public radio broadcasting reports it . . . detailed, timely, informative and accurate. APRN is often the only immediate source of local and regional news and information, and is the only broadcast medium that reaches all of Alaska — the most culturally and geographically diverse state in the Union.

Simply stated, APRN is a producer of radio news and information programs. Though not a radio station, its organized network of 29 public broadcasting radio stations and their system of translators and repeaters provides broadcast coverage to all of Alaska, reaching into over 330 different communities.

APRN was created in 1978 to bring important news and information to isolated rural Alaskans. Beginning with fewer than a dozen public radio stations, and supporting only one news reporter in Alaska's state capitol of Juneau, APRN has grown to its current network of 29 member stations, with bureaus in Juneau, Anchorage, and Washington, D. C. Today, APRN remains committed to its initial mission — to work in cooperation with its member

Alaska Governor Tony Knowles talks with Alaska on APRN's popular LIVE program, Call-In With The Governor.

stations to provide Alaskan residents the most complete, timely and accessible source of Alaska news, current affairs and cultural information.

Each weekday, APRN collects news about Alaska from around the state and the nation, which is then reported via seven daily newscasts. APRN also produces a monthly call-in program with Alaska's governor, a weekly call-in program on key Alaskan issues, and other special event programs such as primary and general election coverage, legislative reports, Iditarod race updates, coverage of the Alaska Federation of Natives annual conference, and more.

The Alaska Public Radio Network *is* statewide Alaska radio news.

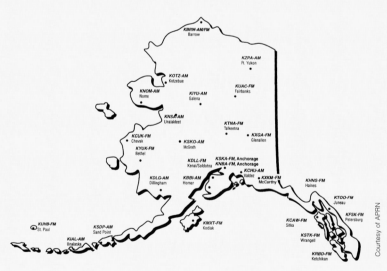

APRN Member Stations.

TESORO ALASKA

Courtesy of Tesoro Alaska. Photo by Ken Graham Photography

than 30 company-owned and -operated locations and the 160 independent dealers across Alaska and in Canada's Yukon Territory.

That strong dealer network got its start three decades ago when Tesoro began supplying the first made-in-Alaska gasoline. Over the years, Tesoro Alaska has become an integral part of the state's economy with customers ranging from individual automobile owners to large commercial enterprises, electric utilities, contractors, schools, governmental agencies, and military installations.

Founded in July 1969, the then Tesoro Alaska Petroleum Company was established to refine Alaskan crude oil and market finished products for use by Alaskans. Tesoro would open its new Kenai refinery several months later. The new facility came on-line with the capacity to process 17,500 barrels of Cook Inlet crude oil per day.

Tesoro's new image on display at the "Gateway" to Girdwood, Alaska.

As the dawn of a new century approaches, Tesoro Alaska Company looks to a bright future as it broadens its base in developing and marketing Alaska's resources. A 30-year partnership with the state of Alaska gives the company a sound foundation for expanding its leading role in oil refining and petroleum products distribution.

Building on the largest dealer network in the state, Tesoro's expansion plans call for the addition of seven new retail locations in 1999. The new locations are part of a long-term, $50 million marketing expansion program started in 1997 to construct new stations and remodel several existing sta-

tions. The program is focused on the Anchorage area, the state's largest motor-fuel market.

The company-owned locations will include Tesoro's new convenience store operation, "2Go," and will be graced by the new company logo. The new image will eventually cover more

Courtesy of Tesoro Alaska

Tesoro's Russian tanker Ingrim.

Tesoro's new image, shown here at a Tesoro location in Anchorage, will eventually cover more than 30 company-owned and -operated locations and the 160 independent dealers across Alaska and in Canada's Yukon Territory.

These relatively modest beginnings were the first steps toward correcting the irony that a state with abundant new oil reserves was importing almost all its refined products from refineries outside of Alaska.

Starting in 1973, Tesoro embarked on major upgrades and expansions at the refinery, investing hundreds of millions of dollars in the improvements.

Another expansion in 1975 provided the refinery with the ability to produce 252,000 gallons of gasoline per day. That same year, Tesoro completed construction of a 70-mile-long, 10-inch diameter pipeline from the Kenai refinery across the northern end of the Kenai Peninsula and under Cook Inlet to the Port of Anchorage. Tesoro's pipeline is designed to carry a variety of finished products including jet fuel, diesel, and gasoline to its tank farm and distribution center in Anchorage.

With the advent of world-class oil development on Alaska's North Slope, the state's economy began to grow dramatically. In concert with Alaska's growth during the 1980s, Tesoro Alaska substantially modified its plant

to accommodate this additional source of crude supply. In conjunction with this expansion, Tesoro processed the first cargo of Alaska North Slope crude loaded at the Port of Valdez into the very first gallon of gasoline manufactured from that source and sold in Alaska.

Modernization continued at the Kenai refinery with a near-capacity-doubling expansion of the gasoline-producing reformer, the construction of a new hydrocracker unit to produce more jet fuel and gasoline blendstocks, and an isomerization unit that increases the octane rating of gasoline components without using lead.

Due in large part to the dramatic increases in international air cargo traffic at Anchorage International Airport, Tesoro's

Tesoro's petroleum refinery on the scenic Kenai Peninsula is a major supplier of refined products.

Courtesy of Tesoro Alaska; Photo by Ken Graham Photography

Vaccum unit increases efficiency at Tesoro's refinery by reducing by half the amount of petroleum byproducts produced.

Moving into the next century, Tesoro Alaska's technology will continue to meet the demands of a changing market. A more recent addition to the Kenai operation was a state-of-the-art vacuum distillation unit. This $25 million investment has enabled the refinery to reduce the production and export of residual fuel oil and enhance its overall product mix.

The Kenai refinery also plays a role in trade with the Russian Far East. In July of 1996, the first load of Russian crude oil from Sakhalin Island was transported to the Kenai facility for processing. A Russian tanker under charter to Tesoro can transport a cargo of 13,000 tons of gasoline, jet fuel, and diesel to the Russian Far East. In 1997, nine round trips were made. Recently, Tesoro lent

marketing expertise to customers in Kamchatka, assisting in the development of two retail service stations; and the company anticipates expanding its presence in the region.

Closer to home, Tesoro has made inroads in the southeast Alaska market. In 1997, Tesoro purchased the Union 76 marketing interests in Alaska from Tosco Corporation. The purchase consisted of a 110,000-barrel capacity terminal in Ketchikan and three retail outlets, two in Juneau and one in Ketchikan.

An important aspect of Tesoro's continuing success is its commitment to environmental sensitivity. In the process of upgrading those service stations that sell refined products under the Tesoro brand, Tesoro strives to maintain strict compliance

jet fuel sales rose more than 10 percent in 1997 compared to the previous year. Anchorage has become one of the busiest air cargo ports in the world. More than 30 cargo firms use the airport in Anchorage as a refueling and trans-shipment point linking flights to Asia, Europe, and North America. Continuing traffic growth has created significant demand for jet fuel in a state that already relies heavily on aviation transportation.

Courtesy of Tesoro Alaska; Photo by Morton Beebe

Early Tesoro station at Kenai Lake.

Tanker taking on petroleum products at Tesoro's Terminal and Dock Facility in Nikiski, Alaska.

Courtesy of Tesoro Alaska; Photo by Ken Graham Photography

Alaska, who generate more than a $20 million payroll, to make a substantial contribution to the state's economy.

To ensure the company's future success, Tesoro's senior management is continuously improving its Alaskan refining and marketing processes. As part of that process, the company added asphalt production to its line in 1996.

With an eye towards maintaining its leadership in quality and customer service, Tesoro Alaska Company looks to the new century with optimism. Both on the home front and in the markets of the Pacific Rim, Tesoro sees opportunity that will both strengthen the company and provide benefits to the state of Alaska.

with laws regulating underground storage tanks and other industry-related concerns.

Tesoro also uses double-bottom tankers for transporting crude oil to its Kenai refinery. Tesoro believes that all such precautions are well worth the effort, and that the ultimate response to potential oil spills is to make every effort to ensure they do not happen in the first place.

Product quality is another area in which Tesoro Alaska can firmly stand behind its marketing claims. "Tesoro gasoline was tested by an independent, nationally recognized laboratory and determined to be the cleanest-burning gasoline produced in Alaska and one of the cleanest-burning fuels in the nation," stated Ronald E. Noel, Vice President and General Counsel. "Results like these are important

because Tesoro strives to be a good corporate citizen as well as a successful company," adds Noel.

Tesoro maintains a strong market share in Alaska despite the fact that it operates in an extremely competitive industry. The company's success enables its more than 550 employees in

Interior of Tesoro's new "2GO Mart" in Anchorage.

Courtesy of Tesoro Alaska; Photo by Ken Graham Photography

UDELHOVEN OILFIELD SYSTEM SERVICES, INC.

Established in 1970, UOSS has served the special needs of general contracting and oil production from Cook Inlet to Prudhoe Bay.

Over time, Udelhoven has expanded its services and become heavily involved in the construction industry.

Udelhoven Oilfield System Services, Inc. (UOSS), was established in Soldotna, Alaska by Jim Udelhoven in 1970. Originally from Wisconsin, Jim has called Alaska home for over 30 years. As company founder and CEO of UOSS, he has over 28 years experience as an entrepreneur, private businessman, oilfield service contractor and construction contractor. In addition to Udelhoven Oilfield System Services, Inc., he is also President and CEO of Harding Holding Inc.; Udelhoven General, Inc.; JU Construction, Inc.; and Udelhoven, Inc.

Jim currently is past president and director emeritus for The Alliance and serves on the Board of Directors for the Alaska State Chamber. He is also an active member of the Resource Development Council, Arctic Power, Commonwealth North, and the Kenai Peninsula Borough School District Vocational Advisory Committee.

UOSS specializes in mechanical and electrical inspection, instrumentation and controls, automation, functional checkout, commissioning and as-built programs in addition to electrical and mechanical construction, industrial and modular fabrication, plumbing, structural welding, and process piping.

UOSS capabilities include the design and installation of instrument network systems.

UOSS specializes in a wide spectrum of services including electrical and mechanical engineering, construction, maintenance and technical systems for oilfield structures.

Though a large portion of their business is from clients such as UNOCAL Corporation; Chevron USA Products Company; BP Exploration (Alaska), Inc.; and ARCO Alaska, Inc., they are also heavily involved in the construction industry. Some of these clients include Neeser Construction Company, Gaston & Associates, Inc., Watterson Construction Company and Cornerstone Construction. In the past two years, Udelhoven cites completion of mechanical work on the University of Alaska Anchorage's new dormitories, and the First National Bank of Anchorage new computer service center and executive offices. Three current projects are the electrical and mechanical contracts for the Alaska Native Heritage Park, the Joint Community Center and Commissary on Elmendorf AFB, and the Yukon Kuskokwim Health Center in Bethel.

A large portion of Udelhoven's business is from clients such as UNOCAL Corporation; Chevron USA Products Company; BP Exploration (Alaska), Inc.; and ARCO Alaska, Inc.

Image Copyright © 1999 PhotoDisc, Inc.

Courtesy of Udelhoven Oilfield System Services Inc.

UOSS monitored the construction and installation of this huge, multi-modal structure — a GHX-2 gas injection facility — and conducted its functional check out.

As the company grew, the corporate headquarters moved to Anchorage. They also have offices in Nikiski and Prudhoe Bay, Alaska; Bellingham, Washington; and Houston, Texas. In nearly 30 years of operation, UOSS has grown to employ almost 200 workers and up to 300 during the summer months. Safety has always been a major concern for the company. To help ensure the safety of workers and clients, UOSS became the first oilfield service company in the state of Alaska to require its employees to participate in pre-employment and random drug testing, before it was a federal requirement.

From the start, UOSS has operated with the mission of providing quality services by utilizing conscientious, professional employees. "Our employees are our biggest assets," Jim remarks. "At Udelhoven, the communication lines are open. We'll continue to work to make sure we keep our reputation for being fair." Jim's philosophy is that maintaining the company's reputation for fairness and honesty is up to the employees, so he makes sure they are treated with the same respect and dedication that they return to the company and its clients. Jim strives to provide his customers with the same commitment he gives his employees.

THE ALASKA FOREST ASSOCIATION

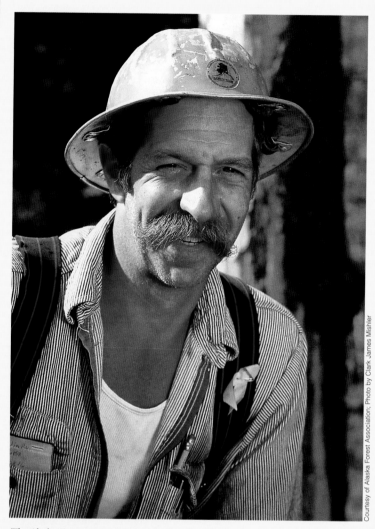

The Alaska Forest Association is a non-profit trade association that represents Alaska's forest-products industry.

Alaska's forest industry has spoken with a common voice since 1957, first as the Alaska Loggers Association, and now as the Alaska Forest Association. The Alaska Forest Association (AFA) is a non-profit trade association that represents the forest products industry in Alaska. Members of AFA include logging interests, cutting contractors, private land owners, saw mills, processors, consulting foresters, manufacturers and suppliers throughout the state.

Alaska Forest Association members produce the resources needed to manufacture thousands of wood-based products to meet growing global demand. As one of the only natural, renewable, biodegradable, and recyclable resource on Earth, wood serves many unique purposes. No other resource can replace wood in an environmentally sound or economically feasible way. That is why it is so important that AFA take an active role in maintaining healthy forests for today and tomorrow.

The Alaska Forest Association supports sound forest-management practices that protect fish habitat, water quality, and forest regeneration. We continue to fund scientific studies, ensuring that fish habitat and wildlife protections that are already in place are

effective. AFA cooperates with federal and state legislative and regulatory bodies to ensure a healthy, growing forest-based industry. AFA advocates a strong, sustainable forest-products industry based on the sound, scientific development of Alaska's timber resources.

Natural resource education is another area which AFA emphasizes and supports. AFA provides public information to schools, the public, the media, and its membership to increase awareness of forestry and forest-wide issues, and to accurately portray the facts about Alaska's forests.

Members of the Alaska Forest Association provide the raw materials for thousands of wood-based products.

ARCTIC SLOPE REGIONAL CORPORATION

Barrow in the winter.

At the top of the world lies a frozen land and its people, the Inupiat Eskimos. For thousands of years, the Inupiats have occupied this land, depending on the sea for their survival. However, during the last quarter century, the way of life for these ancient people has faced change, even extinction — a change from the traditional ways of survival and subsistence to a life of a cash-based economy. The Arctic Slope Regional Corporation was designed to help these people to help themselves in facing those challenges head on.

A negotiated settlement by the federal government in the early 1970s extinguished the aboriginal claim of the Native people to the lands of Alaska. The United States Congress passed the Alaska Native Claims Settlement Act, an act that allowed 12 regions in the state to select lands and to develop Native-run corporations to manage that land (an entity called the Thirteenth Corporation was also established to look after the interests of otherwise-qualifying shareholders living outside the state). Arctic Slope Regional Corporation was created for the Inupiat Eskimos of the North Slope region.

Today, ASRC is renowned as the most successful of those corporations, representing the business interests of nearly 8,000 Inupiat shareholders and the nearly five million acres of land chosen under the settlement act. To continue to be accessible to its shareholders, the corporation has kept its headquarters in Barrow, rather than relocating to a distant metropolitan area. It is this special attention to its shareholders — and to the land — that has made ASRC the state's largest Alaska-owned company, with nearly 5,000 employees and annual revenues reaching $500 million.

ASRC is a land owner, a resource developer, and a manager of a diversified portfolio of investments for its shareholders. As a careful manager and resource developer of some of the nation's most pristine property, ASRC is constantly pursuing a comprehensive

The Presbyterian church in Barrow celebrated its 100th anniversary in 1999.

A subsistence hunter cuts up a bowhead whale on the Barrow beach after a fall hunt.

exploration program for oil and gas, coal, gravel, and other hard-rock minerals.

ASRC's operating subsidiaries are involved in construction, oilfield services, engineering and architectural services, petroleum refining and fuel distribution, environmental services, government services and operations, tourism, and plastics manufacturing. While ASRC and its subsidiaries are determined to operate both efficiently and profitably by offering quality professional services, they are equally dedicated to doing so while maintaining and preserving the often delicate environment for the neighboring and migrating wildlife.

But this is only part of ASRC's mission. The Corporation is also committed to preserving the Inupiat culture and traditions. In a rare policy for large corporations in today's market, ASRC works to combine business with Native cultural missions. One of the favorite policies of ASRC employees is the provision of time off for whaling and other subsistence hunting and fishing.

ASRC also contributes to education on the Arctic Slope, encouraging today's Native youth to hang on to the traditions of their ancestors while understanding the ways of a modern, multi-cultural civilization. The Corporation supports Native dance groups and activities that preserve the tradition and culture of its people.

ASRC also funded a dormitory at the University of Alaska

Fairbanks. Here, students from rural areas can emotionally support each other in what can be a staggering transition from their homes to an urban environment, in their quest for a higher education.

Because the Inupiat people have such strong family ties, the shareholders of the corporation voted to allow its stock to be distributed to the children of the original shareholders. ASRC also takes extra strides to support Inupiat elders, giving longevity bonuses to those over 65.

The mission of Arctic Slope Regional Corporation is twofold. While the Corporation is certainly in the business of making money for the benefit of its shareholders, it is also in the business of preservation — preservation of the environment, and preservation of the traditions and culture of the Inupiat people. ASRC executives take into careful consideration how every business decision will affect every aspect of this unique mission. It is a job they do with pride.

Man and grandson look to the future on the frozen Arctic ocean ice off Barrow.

DOWLAND-BACH

During the early 1970s, the Alaska oil boom was in full swing. The oil was there, however, some of the necessary equipment to operate safely was not. Dowland-Bach was founded to meet that need.

The idea started with Ed Clinton, Lynn Johnson and Ron Tharp over Ed's kitchen table. These three men realized that conventional control systems often failed over time in places with extremely cold temperatures and severe winter conditions. Ed, Lynn and Ron felt they had the expertise to build a company to fill that need. They founded Dowland-Bach in 1975. During the last two decades, their vision has turned into one of the few Alaskan-owned and operated companies that specially build, install and maintain control systems for extreme environments.

Ed, Lynn and Ron hired the best technicians, engineers, and electricians. They were people with knowledge of local Alaskan environments. Together, the employees and the founders worked to form a company that can contribute innovative solutions to meet any oil company's needs. Thousands of Dowland-Bach's Wellhead Control Systems have been installed in oil fields — from the freezing icepacks of Prudhoe Bay on Alaska's North Slope, to the damp, humid jungles of South America.

Virtually every Wellhead Control System is specifically designed by Dowland-Bach

Sample of Dowland-Bach Corporation's stainless-steel inventory in the company's Anchorage facility.

engineers for each area. The systems use a combination of hydraulic and electrical power to monitor wellhead flow conditions and close the well in the event of an emergency or abnormal operating conditions.

Most of the equipment used for the system is contained in custom stainless-steel enclosures. A major part of the design philosophy is to provide easy maintenance accessibility within the smallest footprint possible. Another factor is proper selection of high-quality, vendor-neutral system components.

Their customers are some of the biggest in the industry, including British Petroleum, Arco and Alyeska Pipeline. Dowland-Bach also provides services for other industries,

Archie Poole of Dowland-Bach Corporation stands next to a custom-manufactured water-injection control panel being built for BP Exploration Colombia Phase II development.

such as telecommunications, aviation, construction and local government.

To help achieve the highest-quality service, Dowland-Bach houses one of the largest environmental test chambers in the state of Alaska. The sub-zero freezer is used to double-check manufacturers' specifications, and to collect performance data, before selecting system components. The test chamber can produce temperatures from 350 degrees Fahrenheit to minus 100 degrees Fahrenheit, with cycle times ranging from little more than an hour; or the temperatures can go from one extreme to the other.

"These control systems offer oil production companies an extra measure of protection," says Reed Christensen, Dowland-Bach's general manager. He adds that the Iraqis would not have been successful in setting dozens of oil wells on fire in Kuwait if those wells had been supplied with the company's control systems.

Since the company works almost exclusively with stainless steel, Dowland-Bach was able to expand its original vision to include the distribution of stainless pipe, fittings and metal goods — the same high-quality components and technology the company uses in its own

systems. Dowland-Bach is also a distributor of chemical and petroleum processing facility support equipment, and is an ETL and UL listed Original Equipment Manufacturer of industrial control panels, custom enclosures and mini-skids, for use in extreme environments.

Ed, Lynn and Ron struggled for years to build the American Dream. Sadly, too soon after the company had reached that goal, co-founder Ed Clinton passed away in 1997. He is sorely missed by those who knew him and all Dowland-Bach employees strive to make Ed proud of their continuing efforts.

According to Reed, their vision is clear, "We are a company of professional and technical personnel providing design, engineering and manufacturing services with an emphasis on long-term customer satisfaction. We supply and distribute equipment and solutions to a global market."

Those at Dowland-Bach will continue to expand and improve upon this vision in the years to come.

A 150-ton iron worker which is part of Dowland-Bach's Anchorage-based manufacturing facility.

NATCHIQ, INC.

Natchiq's Alaska Petroleum Contractors, Inc. (APC) offers expertise in all phases of construction, from fabrication through operation and maintenance.

The Natchiq family of companies delivers comprehensive oil field support throughout the world. From conceptual engineering to final design, project management, construction, and operations and maintenance, Natchiq delivers excellence in every aspect of oil field service and industrial systems development.

Natchiq, Inc. is a subsidiary of Arctic Slope Regional Corporation (ASRC), Alaska's largest regional Native corporation. ASRC is a private, for-profit corporation that manages the land and business interests of its more than 7,000 Inupiat Eskimo shareholders. The corporation is the largest Alaskan-owned and -operated company, and one of the largest minority-owned businesses in the United States. ASRC land holdings encompass five million acres across the North Slope, rich in mineral resources, including the Alpine oil field which is

currently under development. ASRC also has significant holdings in the Arctic National Wildlife Refuge, and its Western Arctic coal reserves constitute one of the world's largest deposits of low-sulfur coal.

Natchiq has developed one of the most technologically advanced fabrication facilities on the West Coast. Its Anchorage fabrication shop, combined with its deep-water sea-lift assembly site, facilitates construction and delivery of sophisticated production modules throughout the Western Hemisphere and Pacific Rim.

The Natchiq family consists of: Alaska Petroleum Contractors; Houston Contracting Company; ASRC Parsons Engineering, LLC; Omega Service Industries, Inc.; SPN de Venezuela C.A.; and Natchiq Sakhalin, Inc.

Alaska Petroleum Contractors, Inc. (APC) is one of the nation's largest merit shop oil

HCC, part of the Natchiq family, has built more miles of pipeline around the world than any other contractor in the Western Hemisphere.

field service contractors. Skilled APC craftsmen offer expertise in all phases of construction, from fabrication through operation and maintenance.

Houston Contracting Company (HCC) is one of the oldest union pipeline construction firms in the U.S. — a company renowned for its worldwide expertise in building pipelines, refineries, gathering centers and other industrial facilities, in some of the world's most challenging environments. HCC has built more miles of pipeline around the world than any other contractor in the Western Hemisphere.

Natchiq has formed an engineering procurement and construction management subsidiary, ASRC Parsons Engineering, LLC (APEL), with the ability to fully integrate oil and gas engineering services with existing facility and pipeline construction services.

Omega Service Industries, Inc. provides onshore and offshore construction and maintenance services for the complete life cycle of drilling projects. The company's two locations offer convenient waterway access for both the eastern and western regions of the Gulf of Mexico.

Natchiq Sakhalin, Inc. is the newest member of the Natchiq family and will specifically work to assist in the construction, development and operation of the emerging oil and gas industry in the Sakhalin Island region of Russia's Far East.

Finally, SPN de Venezuela C.A. is comprised of: SKW/Eskimos, a general construction company that built its reputation in Alaska; Petro Star, a fully integrated petroleum refining, distribution and marketing network; and Natchiq and its family of companies.

This is the Natchiq family of companies — home-grown in Alaska, and now serving the world.

ASRC Parsons Engineering, LLC (APEL), Natchiq's engineering procurement and construction management subsidiary, has the ability to fully integrate oil and gas engineering services with existing facility and pipeline construction services.

Courtesy of Natchiq, Inc.

Courtesy of Natchiq, Inc.

Natchiq's technologically advanced fabrication facility in Anchorage, combined with its deep-water sea-lift assembly site, facilitates construction and delivery of sophisticated production modules throughout the Western Hemisphere and Pacific Rim.

COMINCO ALASKA INCORPORATED

In the Northwest Arctic Borough, among Alaska's vast herds of migrating caribou and endless miles of tundra, lies Cominco Alaska's Red Dog Mine — the world's largest zinc and lead mine, containing 27 percent of all proven U.S. zinc reserves.

In the years before developing the Red Dog Mine, members of parent company Cominco, Ltd. worked with local Native Alaskans to reach an historic agreement. Not only does the mine share the land with the NANA (Northwest Alaska Native Association) people of the area; but it also shares its profits and its mission of maintaining the lands, the environment, and the commitment to train NANA shareholders in the business of mining.

NANA, a native corporation formed under the Alaska Native Claims Settlement Act of 1971, oversees the lands that lie north of the Arctic Circle and

Courtesy of Cominco Alaska: Photo by Chris Arend

The Red Dog Mine facility reflects in the nearby tailings pond.

the land which houses Red Dog. The NANA/Cominco Agreement gives Cominco the right to build and operate the mine, and to market zinc and lead concentrates. In return, NANA receives a royalty which converts to a percentage of the mine's profits, and will eventually hold a 50 percent share in the mineral profits.

Cominco Alaska's goal is to maximize the number of NANA shareholders who contribute to the success of the mine each year. Today, 55 percent of Red Dog employees are shareholders. Ultimately, the aim is to have 100 percent of its workforce filled with the Inupiat Eskimos who are the shareholders in the NANA Corporation. To aid this endeavor, Red Dog has developed education programs to encourage shareholders to earn degrees or learn skilled trades and to return to the mine to work. Offering scholarships and job-share programs; and the School-To-Work partnership with NANA, are a few of the ways Red Dog is working to meet its ultimate goal.

Courtesy of Cominco Alaska: Photo by Chris Arend

Summer students do archeological work near the Red Dog Mine.

Grizzly bears near the Red Dog Mine.

With the recent expansion of production, Red Dog is expected to process an estimated 3.2 million tons of ore each year. This is milled into 1.2 million short tons of lead and zinc concentrates which are transported year-round to a seaport 52 miles from the mine. Concentrate shipments to smelters occur during the 100 days of ice-free shipping season. The zinc and lead concentrates are shipped to Canada, Europe and Asia.

The road system was financed and constructed by the Alaska Industrial Development and Export Authority. The state's $160 million investment in the facility is being repaid with interest from Cominco's user and export fees over the life of the mine, estimated at more than 40 years.

Red Dog looks outside the mining industry and shows support for the local communities as well. Recognizing John Baker's dedication to children's education and his commitment to competing against insurmountable odds, Cominco Alaska decided to sponsor this NANA shareholder in his quest to win the 1,100-mile Iditarod Trail Sled Dog Race from Anchorage to Nome.

With its commitment to community, and a three-way partnership between state, local, and private sector groups, Red Dog has proven that such cooperation can be very profitable. Seeing this success, mining operations worldwide have striven to imitate Red Dog and its working relationship with NANA and the Native organizations of the Northwest Arctic Borough.

Cominco Alaska will continue to meet the engineering challenges of mining in an environmentally responsible manner, to develop the skills of NANA shareholders through education and training, and to support local interests while maintaining the traditions and culture of the region and its people.

Control room operators at the Red Dog Mine.

WGM

WGM exploration camp, Salmon Lake, Seward Peninsula.

Courtesy of WGM Inc.; Photo by Aimee Ruzicka

WGM office tent, Slate Creek exploration camp, Fortymile Mining District.

Courtesy of WGM Inc.; Photo by Bob Rogers

Alaska's mining saga includes tales of notorious Soapy Smith, legendary Chilkoot Pass, Iditarod Trail, and Nome's golden beaches. This saga continues with names like Red Dog, Green's Creek, Arctic and Pogo. What most of Alaska's major grass-roots discoveries share is Anchorage-based WGM Inc., with its nucleus of 12 permanent geologists. C. G. (Riz) Bigelow, a geologist with a 40-year Alaska track record, has been at the helm since WGM's 1972 founding.

WGM provides project management, technical consulting, acquisitions, permitting, and expediting services to its clients who include Native and mining corporations, joint ventures, property owners, and government agencies. WGM coordinated the first mineral exploration agreements between Alaska's Native corporations and mining companies, including the nation's largest private lands exploration project (13 million acres) on Doyon Ltd. land.

"The public record indicates WGM's Alaska discovery rate is second to none," says Bigelow, who set the stage for the emergence of WGM by discovery of the Ambler mineral district, including the high-grade Arctic deposit, for Kennecott in the 1960s.

WGM projects were responsible for the start-up of Alaska's four main modern-era mines, including discovery of the Red Dog ore body, currently being mined by Cominco and NANA; and Green's Creek, the nation's biggest silver producer (being mined by Rio Tinto's subsidiary, Kennecott). WGM's systematic delineation of ore bodies at Valdez Creek led to recovery of 700,000 ounces of gold by Cambior, and its drilling program resulted in definition of the Fort Knox ore body where Kinross is recovering 360,000 ounces of gold annually.

Among WGM discoveries is the widely acclaimed Pogo deposit. Public release of the tonnage and grade (10 million tons of 0.52 ounces per ton of gold) by Teck Corporation in 1998 triggered a major claims-staking rush. Discovered for Sumitomo Metal Mines in 1994, Pogo is approaching the development phase.

Bigelow envisions mining bringing families into the country to enjoy an Alaska experience too long restricted to a lucky few. He notes that, "Discoveries will be made in Alaska for as long as there is a geologist who knows that if it wasn't in the last basin, it must be in the next."

WGM geologist prospecting in the Wrangell Mountains of southcentral Alaska.

WGM exploration drill at Fort Knox, Monte Cristo Creek, Fairbanks Mining District.

AMERICAN SEAFOODS COMPANY

American Seafoods Company, one of Alaska's most progressive seafood harvesters and processors, attributes its success to having first-hand working knowledge of all aspects of the fishing industry. The company is known for its strong commitment to the environment, highly-motivated employees and sophisticated, state-of-the-art catcher-processors. The company produces 165 million pounds of finished seafood products annually, and generates revenues valued at nearly $200 million. American Seafoods' satellite office in Anchorage was established to facilitate recruiting in communities throughout Alaska. Offices are also located in Dutch Harbor, Dillingham, Naknek, and Seattle.

"Most of our management team started their careers at sea, working on boats and learning the business," says Michael J. Hyde, president and CEO of American Seafoods. "This hands-on experience has greatly contributed to our understanding of the processes involved with producing top-quality products," he adds.

Hyde knows commercial fishing from the deck up. In 1974, he started working as a deck hand on a commercial crab-fishing vessel in the Bering

Courtesy of American Seafoods Company; Photo by Natalie Fobes

The crew gears up for another trip.

Pollock fillet is being packed into a block on a catcher-processor vessel.

Sea. He ultimately worked aboard crabbers, seiners, gillnetters, and groundfish catcher-processors. He has been president and CEO of American Seafoods since 1998.

CONTRIBUTING TO OUR ALASKAN ECONOMY

American Seafoods is one of the seafood industry's largest employers of Alaska residents, providing hundreds of jobs each year and generating a steady stream of revenue within the state. In fact, more than half of all Alaskans working on at-sea processing vessels operating in the Bering Sea work at American Seafoods.

A key benefit of working at American Seafoods is the opportunity to grow professionally. The majority of promotions on its vessels come from within the company, allowing employees to establish careers in the industry that fit well with the rural Alaskan lifestyle. For example,

the pollock "A" fishing season takes place in the winter, allowing crew members to be home in time for hunting, fishing, and other seasonal activities during the summer. "A healthy fishery is crucial to all of us in Alaska who depend on it to sustain our livelihoods," says Tammy French, American Seafoods' vice president of human resources.

In addition to the jobs it provides, American Seafoods spends approximately $35 million annually with Alaska-based vendors to run its operations, from fuel on the dock in Dutch Harbor to vessel dry-dock repairs in Ketchikan.

GIVING BACK TO THE SEA AND THE COMMUNITY

The company actively participates in industry research projects such as designing nets to minimize the catch of undersized fish and testing measurement systems to improve the accuracy of total catch estimates.

"We depend on the sea for our livelihood, so of course responsible fisheries management is important to us," says Inge Andreassen, vice president of operations. "Our vessels are equipped with highly advanced, state-of-the-art equipment that

Crew members at the controls of a state-of-the-art catcher-processor.

The fishing vessel American Dynasty *heads out to sea.*

American Seafoods' highly-motivated employees have the opportunity to grow professionally, since a majority of the promotions come from within the company.

prevents waste and nearly eliminates bycatch. For example, our onboard fishmeal plants allow for 100 percent utilization of the fish."

American Seafoods donates $50,000 annually to help fund worthy programs and projects throughout Alaska. Its Community Advisory Board, made up of Alaskans from throughout the state, meets quarterly to review and vote on funding requests. A wide variety of non-profit organizations have received funds, including the Alaska Commercial Fishermen's Memorial in Juneau, Mothers Against Drunk Driving, Cordova District Fishermen's Union, the Kodiak Fishermen's Wives, the Pribilof Islands radio station, the Bristol Bay Native

Corporation, and Junior Achievement of Alaska. It is also contributing $600,000 over the next three years to the Alaska Sealife Center in Seward.

In addition, the company has been a partner with the St. Paul Island Community Development Quota (CDQ) program in Alaska since the program's inception in 1992. Another way that American Seafoods gives back to the community is by providing salmon to food banks to feed the needy, fish that are otherwise required to be returned to the sea, even if they are dead.

"Being a responsible corporate citizen goes hand-in-hand with doing business," says Hyde. "Giving back to the sea and the

community is a part of that and both are intrinsic to the philosophy of how we run our company. We are proud of the partnerships we've created in Alaska. We share Alaskan values of hard work, a diverse economy, and a healthy environment."

LOOKING AHEAD TO NEW MARKETS AND THE FUTURE

In an ongoing effort to expand its capabilities, American Seafoods continually looks for ways to better utilize its fleet of at-sea processors, and to create alternative markets for Alaskan fishermen. To meet the growing demand for seafood products, American Seafoods' sister company, Frionor USA, regularly develops new product lines,

Sorting fish on a factory trawler.

*American Seafoods is an active partici-
pant in industry research projects such as
designing nets to minimize the catch of
undersized fish and testing measurement
systems to improve the accuracy of total
catch estimates.*

which provides additional growth opportunities for the company and the Alaska seafood industry.

In recent years, the company has produced *teien*, an innovative salmon product for the Japanese market, on board two of its vessels operating as floating processors in Bristol Bay during the salmon season. According to Hugh Clark, manager of the company's Salmon Operations department, "*Teien* salmon is a high quality, value-added product. By processing at sea, we are able to produce it right in Bristol Bay. This creates additional employment for the people of Alaska. In contrast,

traditional methods add value to the product overseas. We are also experimenting with new machines that remove pinbones from wild salmon fillets."

Another exciting new opportunity emerged in the spring of 1998 for cod fishers in the Chignik area. The company stationed one of its at-sea processors in Chignik to process cod for local pot and jig fishermen. Because of operating efficiencies and the high-value product resulting from immediate processing, the company could pay the fishermen more than the going rate for cod.

American Seafoods is a premier example of the present and future of Alaska's seafood indus-

try. The company's goal to maximize the value of fishery resources and to keep as much of that value as possible in Alaska can only contribute to the quality of life for all Alaskans. Higher-valued resources mean increased tax revenues for the state, higher wages for crewmembers, higher fish prices to fishermen and the CDQ program, and a stable economy for the coastal communities dependent on our ocean resources. There are still many new opportunities in this industry and American Seafoods Company will be at the forefront, promoting Alaska's resources and contributing to a healthy economy.

*Processed fish is being offloaded at
Dutch Harbor.*

TRIDENT SEAFOODS

Located at the water's edge in Akutan Bay, the Safe Harbor Church and Community Center was completed in 1998. The new facility reflects Trident's ongoing commitment to its workforce and neighbors.

"It started with one boat," says Trident Seafoods' president Chuck Bundrant, glancing at the etching of the 135-foot *Billikin* that hangs above his desk. "We asked why we couldn't catch crab and process crab on the same vessel. They said it wasn't going to work."

That was in 1970. Chuck Bundrant was an Alaska king crab fisherman. So were Kaare Ness and Mike Jacobson, who would soon become his partners. Harvesting crab was profitable in the '70s. Nevertheless, the three fishermen understood that the key to their future lay beyond the docks where the boats simply unloaded the catch. Together they built the *Billikin*, adding crab cookers and freezing equipment necessary to process their own finished product. They embarked on a new course for themselves and ultimately the Alaska seafood industry — the fishermen were now in the seafood business.

Trident Seafoods was founded three years later, and the young corporation hooked its future to the bounty of Alaska's fishery resources and the demand for quality seafood that was building worldwide.

In 1984, the partners were joined by another successful forward-thinking fisherman, Bart Eaton, who stepped in to pioneer new fishing technologies and manage the company's rapidly expanding fleet of company-owned and independent catcher vessels. By that time, seafood buyers in Japan and Europe were regular customers, enjoying a full range of salmon, herring, shellfish and groundfish products caught by Trident fishermen and processed at Trident's Alaska facilities.

Over the years, the company had also joined forces with long-time Bellingham processor Edd Perry of San Juan Seafoods. By 1987, the two companies were fully merged, and Trident stepped up to the plate to meet the demands of America's domestic market and modern consumer tastes. Today, Trident's value-added processing facilities in Anacortes and Bellingham, Washington, turn out a wide selection of finished, ready-to-prepare seafood items for modern foodservice and retail distribution. From breaded whitefish fillets for popular fast-food outlets to herb-glazed salmon portions for family dining, to frozen halibut steaks and fancy king crab sections for

Trident's multi-species processing plant at Sand Point, Alaska, supports a large fleet of local vessels harvesting salmon, crab and groundfish from the abundant waters nearby.

Part of the surimi produced at this plant will be shipped to Trident's new analog plant in Fife, Washington which produces the premier brand of surimi seafood SEA LEGS®.

Executive chef Al Horcher creates a wide selection of new products at Trident's value-adding facility in Anacortes, Washington.

Courtesy of Trident Seafoods; Photo by Bart Eaton

white-tablecloth restaurants, Trident products reflect the company's diverse access to resources and its commitment to product quality and value.

It began with one boat. By 1998, Trident Seafoods was processing more than 480 million pounds of raw fish and shellfish annually. The company posted more than $360 million in sales, making it the largest, most successful seafood processor in Alaska and the Pacific Northwest.

Today Trident leads the Alaska industry in the production of crab, canned sockeye salmon and frozen Bristol Bay sockeye. Trident also ranks among the state's top five producers of pollock, cod, herring and canned pink salmon. But the company has not forgotten its roots.

"Make no mistake, our success begins with our fishermen," Bundrant says. Evidence of that partnership lines the walls and covers bulletin boards throughout the firm's Seattle headquarters. Scores of photographs pay tribute to the strength of the vessels and the determination of the fishermen who literally put their lives on the line to bring fresh product to the company's Alaska facilities. Trident operates six major primary processing plants, including a Southeast pink salmon cannery in Ketchikan; Bristol Bay sockeye salmon canning and freezing operations in North and South Naknek; and diversified processing plants handling Alaska pollock, Pacific cod, blackcod, halibut and crab in Akutan, Sand Point and St. Paul.

Trident's commitment to its harvesters is spelled out in a simple statement framed in Bundrant's office and displayed throughout Trident facilities from Seattle to Akutan. It reads in part: "Trident fishermen are not dependent on us, we are dependent on them. Trident fishermen are neither outsiders to our business nor an interruption to our work, they are an integral part and purpose of it.

Our growth and success is directly contingent upon a spirit of mutual respect, trust and the economic vitality of our fleets."

In 1998, Trident purchased $98 million worth of raw seafood products from Alaska fishermen. Its six shorebased facilities provided more than 2,000 jobs, delivering a total payroll in excess of $25 million into local economies.

Trident's partnership with its fishermen and processing crews extends to their families and Alaska communities as well. In 1998, the village of Akutan celebrated completion of the 14,000-square-foot Safe Harbor Church and Community Center, located at the water's

edge in Akutan Bay. The project was entirely funded by Trident employees and stockholders. The company continues to be a generous financial supporter of non-profit community services, fishing vessel safety training, school activities and scholarship programs for Alaskan communities, commercial fishermen and their families.

"Ultimately," Bundrant says, "the fruits of this partnership are shared by our seafood customers worldwide. We have a common goal: efficient production of high-quality fish and shellfish products — healthy seafood that our people and our customers are proud to put on the dinner table."

Courtesy of Trident Seafoods; Photo by Bart Eaton

Bering Sea king crabbers brave the elements aboard the F/V Amatuli.

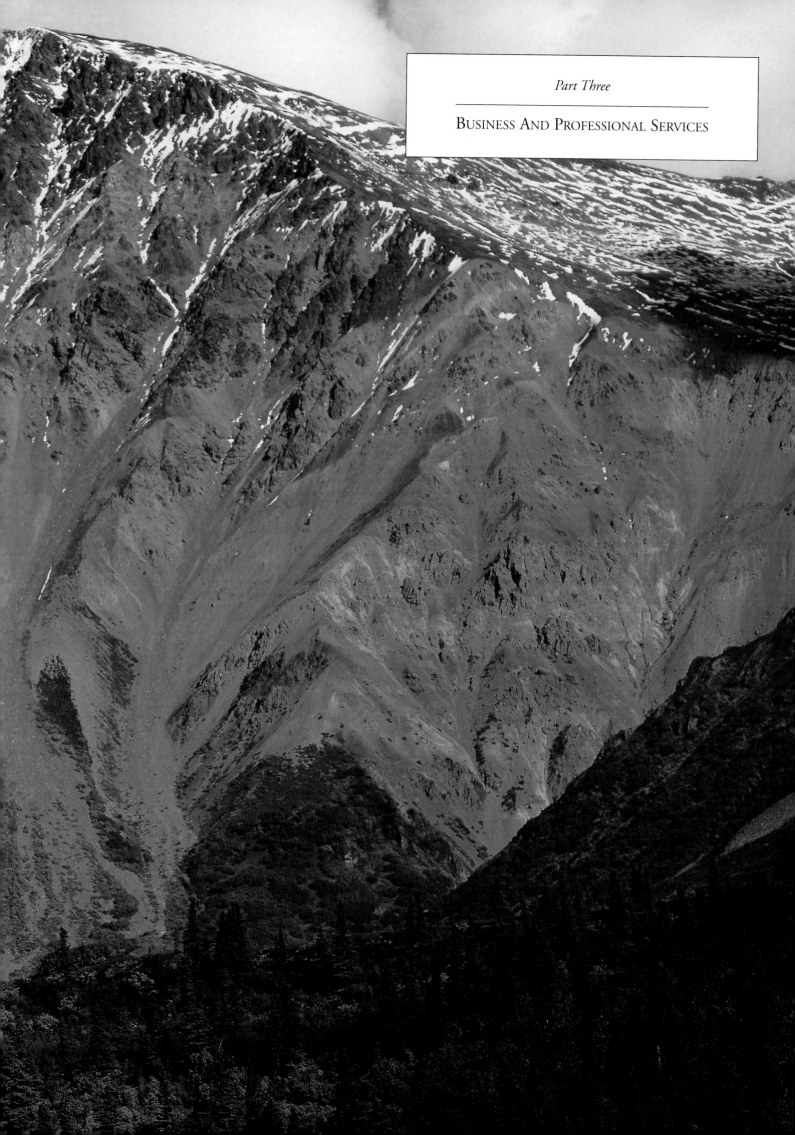

DELANEY, WILES, HAYES, GERETY, ELLIS & YOUNG, INC.

Alaska is a state whose growth and development are closely tied to the vast wealth and potential of its natural resources. The discovery of oil in the Cook Inlet region, and subsequent statehood in 1959, marked the beginning of Alaska's emergence as a participant in the global marketplace.

Alaska's growth and increasing sophistication also gave rise to a rapidly changing legal environment. During the past four decades, the law firm of Delaney, Wiles, Hayes, Gerety, Ellis & Young, Inc., has met the challenges of serving the legal needs of a growing state to emerge as one of the preeminent firms in Alaska.

As one of Alaska's oldest and most respected law firms, Delaney Wiles has grown and adapted to meet the rapidly

changing legal requirements of its clients. This growth and change has not altered the commitment made by the firm's founding partners to provide superior legal services in exchange for reasonable fees.

Today, the firm's 14 attorneys and team of paralegals maintain a practice that serves both the business community and government clients while also serving the vision of its founders. Along the way, former principals and associates of the firm have become judges at the state or federal levels. These include two Alaska Supreme Court justices, three Alaska Superior Court jurists, one Alaska District Court judge, and two who have served on the Federal District Court bench. Another former member of the firm served as Alaska Attorney General, the

A rare occasion when all firm attorneys gathered for a single photograph. Seated left to right are Andrew Guidi, Jeff Stark, Jim Friderici. Standing left to right are Bill Moseley, Don Thomas, Tim Lamb, Donna Meyers, Ed Sniffen, Cindy Ducey, Dan Gerety, Amy Headrick, Howard Lazar, Steve Ellis, Alex Young.

top law enforcement officer in the State, and other members of the firm served in the Department of Law, before joining the firm.

"We are extremely proud of our legacy of service to the legal profession," says Daniel A. Gerety, the firm's most senior member. "Among other things, we have seen more former attorneys of this firm placed as judges on the bench than any other firm in the state," he notes.

Joining Delaney Wiles in 1970, Gerety has seen the firm develop its practice in three areas. The firm's attorneys handle matters in all types of litigation, as well as transactions involving commercial and natural resources issues. While different members of the firm specialize in one of these areas of practice, there is collaboration

Bill Moseley and Steve Ellis discuss a commercial transaction.

among the lawyers in complex cases when it is advantageous to the client.

Delaney Wiles has developed a reputation for its ability to handle complex and difficult litigation. The firm has litigated cases involving product-liability questions, aviation issues, personal injury, professional malpractice, admiralty law, environmental incidents, and insurance coverage. The firm's lawyers have also litigated cases involving construction and operation of the TransAlaska Pipeline System, and other oil and gas issues. Delaney Wiles has participated, in one form or other, in a significant amount of major litigated conflicts in the state.

The firm has represented the State of Alaska in a variety of legal proceedings, including the defense of various state agencies in tort litigation, arguing the State's interest in major road right-of-way cases, and representation of state officials in civil rights matters. Many of the country's largest insurers, workers' compensation carriers, bonding companies and several Lloyds of London underwriting syndicates are clients of the firm.

The firm also has a commercial section through which services are provided for a diverse list of clients, ranging from sole proprietorships to international corporations. The State's largest ski resort, Alaska Native Corporations, an electric cooperative, construction and petroleum industry interests, major real estate owners and developers, hospitals, physicians and other professionals, as well as a variety of retail and service industry enterprises, are also among the firm's commercial clients. These varied clients are provided legal services from the acquisition and sale of existing businesses to the start-up of new business ventures. The firm also represents its commercial clients before various governmental agencies, boards, and legislative bodies at the state and local levels.

The natural resources section of Delaney Wiles serves major oil and gas and mining-industry

clients. The State's rich natural resource base offers both opportunity and complex legal issues to companies seeking to develop those resources. This section provides clients with legal guidance in major oil and gas exploration, leasing, development and marketing projects. Mining companies are also represented in the acquisition and development of properties throughout the state. Attorneys in this section offer clients an insightful understanding of the history and essence of Alaska's unique natural resource laws and their relationship to the environment. They also advise their clients on the latest developments in federal and state environmental laws.

Members of the firm successfully represented the cleaning and coating applicator in the litigation relating to the underground portion of the TransAlaska Pipeline System. The firm has represented entities in connection with projects in all parts of Alaska, from Ice Island in the Arctic Ocean to Amchitka on the Aleutian Chain, including Kodiak, Southeastern, Southcentral and Interior Alaska.

Firm president Dan Gerety oversees an office remodel project to bring the firm into the new millennium.

Andrew Guidi and Howard Lazar pose outside the new state court building in Anchorage, before entering to present arguments in a case.

Since 1989, Delaney Wiles has been the only Alaska member of the American Law Firm Association (ALFA), an international association of independent law firms. ALFA's basic objective, through its member firms, is to make available litigation, transactional, and other legal services for a reasonable and cost-effective price, through a network of select independent member firms committed to client service.

Membership in ALFA, also known as ALFA International, is based upon a peer evaluation of the candidate law firm and is extended to those firms having a broad spectrum of practice. Membership in the organization links Delaney Wiles with more than 100 member firms across

the United States and some two dozen international law firms in 17 foreign countries.

When a national or international legal effort is needed, ALFA firms coordinate their services for the benefit of the client. The firms represent many common clients with common problems.

Closer to home, Delaney Wiles attorneys provide pro bono work to the community through Alaska Legal Services and religious organizations. The firm's attorneys can be found in neighborhood recreation centers offering legal advice on such topics as wills and landlord/tenant issues. Members also serve on Alaska Bar Association committees and speak to professional associations and service clubs.

To support its staff in servicing clients, Delaney Wiles maintains an extensive in-house legal library and equally extensive local area network litigation support software including multiple databases, CD ROM based research materials, internet research access, Lexis and Westlaw computer research services, and company financial systems. The firm's lawyers are also individually accessible via e-mail on the internet.

Donna Meyers and Cindy Ducey discuss representation of an employer in an employment matter, in one of the offices overlooking Cook Inlet.

Members of the firm have enriched their experiences by involvement in the community through memberships on the Municipal Library Advisory Board, community councils, school curriculum committees, coaching youth ski racers and little league baseball teams, officiating at high school swim meets, serving on national swim committees, participating in local and national cross country and alpine ski events and bicycle races, and serving as officers and directors of the Alyeska Ski Club, the Alaska Ski Educational Foundation, Inc., the Aurora Swim Club, and the Arctic Bicycle Club. They have also been pleased to see their children achieve a number of noteworthy accomplishments, such as becoming valedictorian of a high school graduating class; achieving status as all-conference athletes; becoming a state wrestling champion, a U.S. Olympic skier, and members of high school championship football and swim teams; and being educated as lawyers, environmental designers, and environmental policy makers.

While the members work to attract top-quality lawyers and clients to the firm, there is no interest in growth for growth's sake. "We try to attract clients interested in furthering commerce and development in the State of Alaska," says Steve Ellis, the next senior member of the firm. In recruiting attorneys to the firm, he says, "We hire talent with the expectation they will be with us for years to come."

That approach has well worked for Delaney, Wiles, Hayes, Gerety, Ellis & Young, Inc. The Martindale-Hubbell Law Directory gives the firm its highest rating. Mindful of its founders' commitment to excellence and service, the members look to the new millennium with the confidence that comes with being one of the oldest and most well-established law firms in Alaska.

Don Thomas surprised at interruption in discussing a summary judgment matter with a client.

Courtesy of Delaney, Wiles, Hayes, Gerety, Ellis & Young, Inc.

Courtesy of Delaney, Wiles, Hayes, Gerety, Ellis & Young, Inc.

An electric cooperative, represented by the firm, brings power to approximately 35,000 customers.

ALASKA USA FEDERAL CREDIT UNION

Alaska USA is headquartered in Anchorage's midtown financial district.

Alaska USA Federal Credit Union is Alaska's largest consumer financial institution, the state's primary provider of consumer credit and a leader in developing electronic financial service options. The credit union is a not-for-profit cooperative, owned by over 210,000 members. In 1998, Alaska USA celebrated its 50th anniversary of providing members with affordable, quality financial services.

THE SELF-HELP PHILOSOPHY OF CREDIT UNIONS AT WORK IN ALASKA

Alaska USA was chartered in 1948 at Fort Richardson, Alaska. The 15 founding members of Alaska USA felt that local financial institutions were not adequately meeting the credit needs of the federal civil service personnel who had been recently transferred to Alaska. A credit union could satisfy those needs, as well as provide other financial benefits. Accordingly, the credit union was founded and members began pooling their savings and extending credit to one another, while volunteering their time to operate the credit union.

In 1953, after the separation of Elmendorf Air Force Base and Fort Richardson, the credit union expanded its field of membership to include military officers and enlisted personnel and, in 1959, the Board hired its first employee. During the next 10 years, membership was extended to personnel assigned to 24 remote Air Force stations in Alaska, as well as Naval Station Adak, located near the tip of the Aleutian Island chain.

THE MEMBER SERVICE CENTER IS CREATED

In order to effectively serve members who transferred out of Alaska, the Member Service Center was established in 1973. This was the first call center operation launched by an Alaska financial institution, and an innovation for credit unions nationwide. The center was originally located in Denver, Colorado, to compensate for Alaska's time-zone differences,

Since 1948, Alaska USA has provided financial services to military personnel and their families.

Self-Service Terminals provide members with quick, easy access to their accounts.

telecommunications limitations and postal delays. Today, the Member Service Center is located in Anchorage, and continues to provide members located around the world with toll-free telephone processing of their information, service and transaction requests.

THE MEMBERSHIP DIVERSIFIES

The credit union first expanded beyond its military roots in 1974, when it was authorized to serve the employees of companies building the trans-Alaska oil pipeline. In only four years, more than 20,000 pipeline technicians, welders, truck drivers and other personnel opened member accounts.

During this same period, the credit union's field of membership was expanded to include 10 of Alaska's Native regional corporations established under the 1971 Alaska Native Claims Settlement Act. The authority to serve the corporations' shareholders was to expire in 1978, but, after three extensions, Congress took action in 1981 to allow the credit union to continue serving Alaska Natives on a permanent basis. This is the first and only time the U.S. Congress has enacted legislation to authorize a credit union to serve a specific group of individuals.

ALASKA USA ATTRACTS
MEMBERSHIP

As Alaska USA expanded its services and branch network, it became an attractive merger partner for smaller credit unions. Between 1979 and 1996, Alaska USA became the credit union of choice for the members of six Alaska credit unions. Additionally, in 1981, Alaska USA was selected by the Department of Defense and the National Credit Union Administration (NCUA) as the credit union to serve U.S. military personnel at Clark Air Base in the Philippines. Service continued until the closure of Clark Air Base as a result of the eruption of Mount Pinatubo in 1991. Alaska USA also expanded into the Pacific Northwest in 1983 with the merger of a community-based credit union on Whidbey Island, Washington. This was followed by the merger of two Seattle-based credit unions, giving Alaska USA a strong presence in that area and enhancing geographic diversification of the credit union's membership.

Alaska USA is a pioneer in bringing electronic services to members.

Branches in retail locations around the state bring convenience to members.

Courtesy of Alaska USA Federal Credit Union; Photo by Ken Kolodge, Alaska Chromes, Inc.

CONGRESS REAFFIRMS PURPOSE

The 1980s brought credit union changes across America as the NCUA established a policy authorizing credit unions to serve occupational and associational groups that were without credit union service. As a result of this policy, over 4,000 employer and association groups requested and received NCUA approval to be included in Alaska USA's field of membership.

This NCUA policy was challenged in a lawsuit brought by the banking industry in 1990. After seven years of litigation, the lawsuit ended in a Supreme Court ruling which overturned NCUA's regulation permitting service to more than a single organization. In response to this decision, credit unions mobilized an overwhelming grassroots effort and petitioned Congress to ensure consumer access to credit union services.

In 1998, Congress passed the Credit Union Membership Access Act. This legislation enhanced consumer access to credit union membership and modernized the Federal Credit Union Act. It also reaffirmed Congress' commitment to a federal income tax exemption for credit unions, based on their social purpose of providing financial services to people of modest means, and doing so through a cooperative, not-for-profit structure.

SUBSIDIARIES SUPPORT SERVICE TO MEMBERS

Alaska USA has been responsible for introducing a number of innovations to the Alaska financial services market in order to improve and supplement its service to members. These efforts began in the 1980s with the formation of the Alaska Option Network. This organization was formed with other Alaska financial institutions to bring shared automated teller machine (ATM) and debit point-of-sale services to Alaska.

In later years, Alaska USA formed Alaska USA Insurance, Inc. and Alaska Home Mortgage, Inc. to provide additional product and service options to members. In 1997, Alaska USA established the Alaska USA Trust Company to provide investment custody and securities lending services to other credit unions and public units. The latest addition to Alaska USA's family of subsidiaries is EFT Alaska, Inc., which distributes and services proprietary ATMs to further expand consumers' financial choices and convenience.

MOVING INTO THE NEXT MILLENNIUM

The credit union's services and their delivery have evolved over the years in response to the membership's changing needs. However, since 1948, the credit union's commitment to its cooperative principles and the purposes for which it was chartered have remained constant. Alaska USA continues to strive to satisfy the financial needs of members from all walks of life and levels of income, providing them with the opportunity to be financially successful and to improve their standard of living.

Courtesy of Alaska USA Federal Credit Union; Photo by Chris Arend, AlaskaStock Images

Ten of Alaska's regional Native corporations are in the field of membership.

ALASKA USA TRUST COMPANY

Alaska USA Trust provides custody, securities lending, and related investment services.

Alaska USA Trust Company provides fiduciary and limited investment services to Alaska public units and to credit unions throughout the United States. Founded in 1997 as a subsidiary of Alaska USA Federal Credit Union, Alaska USA Trust is the only Alaska-based provider, and the only credit union-owned and -operated provider, of such services in the United States.

Alaska USA Trust specializes in investment custody and securities lending services. These programs help institutional investors protect and enhance their investment revenues. Alaska USA Trust offers Alaska public unit investors, such as those associated with state, municipal or regional governments, personal service through an experienced local agent familiar with the Alaska economic and political environment.

Alaska USA Trust also provides investment custody and securities lending services to credit unions throughout the country. Alaska USA is a respected name in the credit union community. Alaska USA Federal Credit Union's reputation for quality service, coupled with expertise in compliance with credit union regulatory requirements, has provided a solid foundation on which to build Alaska USA Trust. This credit union foundation has helped Alaska USA Trust customize services to this specific group of institutional investors.

Securities lending provides an opportunity for investors to leverage their current investment portfolios to achieve additional revenues. Alaska USA Trust, as agent, pairs security owners and borrowers to each party's mutual benefit. These opportunities are available as a result of the relationships developed by the company's experienced staff with some of the world's finest investment firms. These Wall Street connections make available a wide array of securities lending options. Additionally, Alaska USA Trust provides the necessary custodial and other fiduciary services to complete the transactions on a full-service, cost-effective basis.

State-of-the-art systems and "real-time" transaction-processing capabilities support Alaska USA Trust's ability to perform for their clients. Professional expertise in both public unit and credit union markets, together with long-term relationships and a proven track record, make Alaska USA Trust an important addition to Alaska's financial marketplace.

Alaska USA Trust is a subsidiary of Alaska USA Federal Credit Union, one of America's largest federal credit unions, with over $1.8 billion in assets, and it is located in Anchorage's midtown financial district.

Alaska USA Trust can provide securities lending services to credit unions with smaller portfolios.

NORTHERN TESTING LABORATORIES, INC.

Sunset at midnight over a lake on the Summer Solstice. Northern Testing Laboratories' motto is "Alaska's Water Quality Professionals since 1980."

The Prudhoe Bay lab performs rapid environmental analysis to 365 days per year.

The state of Alaska has more than 3 million lakes and 3,000 rivers flowing across its pristine lands — more than any other state in the nation. Abundant wildlife splash through many of these waters, looking for food and sustenance, while often leaving behind bacteria and other contaminants that can cause health problems to humans who also rely on this valuable resource. Northern Testing Laboratories, Inc. is working for Alaskans to make their drinking water safe for consumption.

An Alaskan-owned corporation founded in Fairbanks in 1980, NTL operates analytical laboratories in Fairbanks, Anchorage, and Prudhoe Bay. NTL provides state-of-the-art environmental testing services for Alaska's business, industry, government and military endeavors.

NTL has recently moved to an international market by opening an affiliated lab in Buenos Aires, Argentina. This lab is designed to provide certified potable water and environmental testing in a country with limited testing resources.

NTL Fairbanks Trace Metals Lab provides low detection limit analysis for potable water and environmental studies.

NTL employees carry a full listing of certifications for testing of microbiology, inorganic and organic chemical contaminants. These valuable employees have developed extensive service capabilities in the areas of water and wastewater systems, asbestos and materials testing, and environmental chemistry testing.

As Alaska's largest provider of professional potable water testing services, NTL operates labs holding the widest scope of Alaska Department of Environmental Conservation and Environmental Protection Agency certifications of any firm in the state. NTL currently monitors more than 500 public water systems statewide, and provides process control and discharge permit monitoring for more than 50 wastewater treatment facilities from the North Slope to the Aleutians Islands.

Water contaminated with Cryptosporidium and Giardia can be harmful to humans. NTL has the expertise to assess groundwater that is influenced by surface water, to help ensure its safety for utility customers.

NTL Anchorage Organics Lab performs volatile and semivolatile chemical analysis.

In addition to its testing services, NTL provides a variety of professional operations support services for water and wastewater utilities, performing both in-house and remote-site pilot and bench-scale testing of water and wastewater treatment processes. NTL is also the state's largest provider of ADEC certified operator training services, and provides independent third-party monitoring of industrial pretreatment and domestic wastewater systems.

The Fairbanks lab is National Voluntary Laboratory Accreditation Program (NVLAP) accredited for bulk asbestos analysis, and participates in the American Industrial Hygiene Association's Proficiency Analytical Testing program for air particle counting. NTL is one of the largest providers of independent testing of air and bulk asbestos samples for government agencies in Alaska.

NTL maintains a high standard of quality control in its analytical services. The lab's analyses are performed using procedures approved by federal, state, and professional associations. NTL's biologists, chemists, and environmental

scientists have both university training and many years of experience providing professional services in Alaska. High-quality, professional jobs for more than 25 Alaskans are provided by NTL. During the busier summer months, NTL hires additional staff, generally high school and college students, to provide education and training support to the next generation of Alaska job-seekers.

Employees at NTL are encouraged to participate in a variety of community programs. NTL directly invests in youth sports and a host of environmental-awareness and public-service activities. NTL also directly sponsors several valuable organizations such as the Anchorage and Fairbanks Chambers of Commerce, the Alaska Water Wastewater Management Association, Water Environment Federation (WEF), American Water Works Association (AWWA), the World Trade Center, and Rotary International.

NTL's reputation includes cutting-edge environmental testing technology and advanced scientific procedures and research; but at the core, Northern Testing Laboratories is a home-grown business that is dedicated to ensuring a clean water environment for its fellow Alaskans.

NTL's Fairbanks lab is NVLAP approved for asbestos analysis.

NTL president Mike Pollen prepares a report on the Prudhoe Bay lab computer system.

NTL's Prudhoe Bay lab operates year round in the severe arctic climate to support the operation of America's largest oilfield.

Space Mark, Inc.

Operations and maintenance services which Space Mark provides to the U.S. Coast Guard Base at Kodiak include maintenance of buildings, roads, and grounds; wastewater treatment plant maintenance; environmental protection and hazardous materials services; and supply and warehousing support.

HERITAGE

Space Mark, Inc. provides seamless support to government and commercial operations around the world. Founded in 1986 as a professional consulting firm, Space Mark restructured its business base to become a leader in providing a wide array of support services to government and commercial clients.

Space Mark takes pride in its unique ownership as a wholly owned subsidiary of The Aleut Corporation of Anchorage, Alaska. The Aleut Corporation (an Alaska Native Corporation) acquired the assets of Space Mark in late 1991, allowing Space Mark to be eligible for the U.S. Small Business Administration's 8(a) program. Such status has made it possible for Space Mark to serve a variety of

customers who have been enriched by their association with a minority-owned business. Forty-five percent of Space Mark's FY98 revenues of $67 million was generated in the state of Alaska.

In addition to its corporate headquarters in Colorado Springs, Colorado, Space Mark has regional offices in Anchorage; Lompoc, California; and Christchurch, New Zealand. Space Mark's projects encompass contracts with Federal Government agencies and commercial clients at locations from California to Florida, and from Alaska to Antarctica.

With a customer-focused approach, extensive resources, and a highly skilled staff, Space Mark has consistently achieved high levels of repeat business and recognition for outstanding performance in its core areas of specialization:

- Operations and Maintenance keeping a wide array of operations running smoothly with comprehensive support services. Through close communication between its highly skilled staff and project management teams, Space Mark ensures responsive and proactive customer support.
- Supply and Services supporting a broad range of essential, day-to-day activities, from supply warehousing to record-keeping, janitorial service, and multimedia production.
- Telecommunications providing project engineering, planning, system design, installation, testing, finished product documentation, onsite and offsite support, emergency troubleshooting, and maintenance for a variety of voice and data communication in both commercial and industrial environments.

Space Mark maintains vital communications systems for space launches at NASA's Kennedy Space Center.

The 8(a) program has contributed greatly to Space Mark's explosive growth. Since 1991, the company has experienced an 85% annual growth rate, expanding from a handful of employees to more than 900 dedicated workers. Space Mark is ranked (in revenues) the number two, and number 52 overall, minority-owned contractor in the state of Colorado [Colorado Business Journal]. In September 1998, Space Mark was ranked 5th in *Washington Technology* magazine's list of top 25 8(a) information technology companies (based on revenues) for 1997.

FUTURE GROWTH

Since 1991, nearly 90 percent of Space Mark's business has come from the Federal Government. As Space Mark comes to the end of its 8(a) status, CEO Robert Bills is mapping new strategies for continued growth into the next century. Over the next five years, Space Mark plans to grow its commercial business from the current 10 percent to 30 percent, partly fueled by expansion of its telecommunications work. Space Mark is also establishing more partnerships with larger companies to provide access and experience on larger projects.

Finally, the company plans to expand into international markets. With the recent establishment of Space Mark, New Zealand Pty Ltd., Space Mark is now turning its focus to potential opportunities in Australia.

COMMITMENT TO COMMUNITY

As a 100 percent Native-Alaskan-owned company, Space Mark is committed to improving business conditions for the Native American Indian community through an Aleut scholarship program and is a member and strong supporter of the Colorado Indian Chamber of Commerce. The company also provides preferential employment opportunities for the Aleut people. In addition, Space Mark:

- Contributes to the Alaska Native Justice Center and Alaska Native Heritage Center in Anchorage;
- Supports the Native Youth Olympics in Kodiak, Alaska;
- Participates in the Jesse L. Carr Golf Tournament that supports various charities in the Anchorage area;
- Is a major participant and contributor to the annual Muscular Dystrophy Telethon in Anchorage and Colorado Springs;
- Supports projects and activities at various communities in the Aleutian region;

- Is a member of the Chamber of Commerce in Anchorage, as well as in Colorado Springs and Pueblo, Colorado;
- Is an active member of the Association of the US Army;
- Contributes to various Colorado Springs organizations (Boy Scouts, Junior Achievement);
- Is a member of the Falcon Business Partners at the Air Force Academy;
- Is a major supporter and contributor to the Colorado Springs Independence Center for the Rehabilitation of the Severely Disabled.

Space Mark assists in unloading supplies at McMurdo Station in the Antarctic.

ALASKA USA INSURANCE, INC.

Members can select a plan to suit their needs, with information from insurance professionals.

Alaska USA Insurance, Inc. was founded in 1986 as a wholly owned subsidiary of Alaska USA Federal Credit Union. For decades, the credit union offered loan and life savings insurance products to members. As the number of credit and deposit products available from the credit union grew, so too did the demand for a wider variety of insurance products. The credit union responded by creating Alaska USA Insurance, Inc. This independent insurance agency allows the credit union to offer a much broader array of insurance products and services to members, on a competitive and affordable basis.

The credit union's goal in operating Alaska USA Insurance is to deliver insurance with the same high level of service, value and convenience that Alaska USA members have grown to expect from the credit union. Since its inception, the company's product line has expanded to include a wide range of programs tailored to the Alaska lifestyle. Popular programs include a variety of life and health plans, as well as unique coverages, such as life and disability insurance for pilots. Most programs are available with the advantages of group rates. While programs have been expanded to meet a growing range of individual insurance needs, this expansion has occurred only through careful product screening and with a commitment to quality and affordability.

Alaska USA Insurance has used these same standards to help small- and medium-size employers and associations secure affordable and meaningful employee and member benefits. Long needed in the Alaska marketplace, the company offers a full range of employee benefit products, including life, health, long- and short-term disability, dental, vision, retirement and Section 125 Cafeteria plans.

Alaska USA Insurance is committed to helping consumers and businesses meet their personal and employee insurance needs, and is continually exploring ways to add value to its portfolio of available programs.

Alaska USA Insurance, Inc. helps employers with employee insurance benefits programs.

ALASKA OPTION SERVICES CORPORATION

Point-Of-Sale is expanding as a popular payment system, thanks to Alaska Option.

Alaska Option Services Corporation introduced shared automated teller machine (ATM) service to Alaska. In 1983, eight credit unions and two banks formed the Alaska Option Services Corporation to provide electronic switching and settlement of ATM financial transactions among its member financial institutions. Initially, 10 institutions offered service through 21 ATMs in Alaska. Within a few short years, all of Alaska's major financial institutions had joined the founders in providing shared ATM service to Alaskans throughout the state.

Today, there are over 300 Alaska Option ATMs in the state, and, with the help of the Alaska Option Network, Alaskans are linked to the world through a variety of regional, national and international networks. In 1997, Alaska Option was ranked the 36th largest regional network in the U.S., processing over 13 million transactions that year.

ATMs are only part of the Alaska Option story. Together with Alaska's dominant grocery retailer, Alaska Option developed the state's first debit point-of-sale program, thus allowing cardholders to pay for purchases with their ATM debit cards. Response to this convenience has been overwhelming. The result is that more and more merchants and customers are benefiting from the security, convenience and cost savings associated with electronic financial transactions. Alaska Option cards are now accepted at over 750 retail merchant locations statewide.

In 1997, in response to a 1996 Congressional mandate, the State of Alaska and Alaska Option partnered a pilot program to distribute government benefit payments to individuals electronically. As a result of this program, Alaskans can now receive many state and federal benefit payments through the convenience of electronic benefits transfer (EBT). Through Alaska Option and its member institutions, the majority of ATMs and most major retail locations accept state-issued EBT cards for electronic access to government cash benefits.

Alaska Option Services Corporation is operated under management contract by its majority shareholder, Alaska USA Federal Credit Union. Its administrative offices are located in Anchorage's midtown financial district. Twenty-two financial institutions participate in the network, representing over 97 percent of the debit cards issued in Alaska.

Alaska Option drives financial-institution ATMs throughout Alaska.

ALASKA HOME MORTGAGE, INC.

From recreational property to dream homes, Alaska Home Mortgage finds Alaskans the right financing.

Alaska families need quality, affordable housing, and Alaska Home Mortgage, Inc. assists them in finding the right financing to put home ownership within reach. Alaska Home Mortgage provides comprehensive, cost-effective and professional mortgage services for the purchase or refinance of one- to-four-family residential properties.

Alaska Home Mortgage works closely with Alaska's real estate professionals to ensure high-quality, convenient and responsive mortgage lending services to their clients. Obtaining a mortgage can be one of life's stressful events, but mortgage financing through Alaska Home Mortgage is quick and convenient. Alaska Home Mortgage's highly experienced mortgage originators guide Alaskans through the entire process, working hard to identify the best program to meet each applicant's individual needs. Their commitment to quality is an important attribute to Alaska Home Mortgage's borrowers, real estate professionals and secondary-market investors.

Alaska Home Mortgage is committed to local servicing of its mortgages. This is an important feature, since most borrowers prefer to have their

Alaska Home Mortgage's First-Time Homebuyer programs are turning more families into homeowners.

loans serviced locally. Alaska Home Mortgage was also one of the first mortgage lenders in the state to provide 30-minute mortgage loan approval through FANNIE MAE's Desktop Underwriter program. This approach has revolutionized the mortgage lending process and is one example of how Alaska Home Mortgage utilizes the latest innovations to better serve its clients.

Because of its commitment to service, Alaska Home Mortgage is one of the fastest growing mortgage lenders in Alaska. Alaska Home Mortgage makes available a full line of mortgage loan products to meet the diversified and unique needs of the Alaska market. Conventional, FHA, VA, Alaska Housing Finance and Jumbo loans are available, with a wide range of additional options for first-time homebuyers and borrowers with special needs.

Alaska Home Mortgage is a wholly-owned subsidiary of Alaska USA Federal Credit Union and is located in the heart of Anchorage's midtown financial district, with a branch office on the Kenai Peninsula. Although a separate corporate entity from the credit union, the two share a commitment to quality service, professionalism, affordability and convenience.

E & S DIVERSIFIED SERVICES

Hard work and perseverance, blended with support from family members and experience gained over 26 years of military service, are the building blocks that support the success of E & S Diversified Services. Those elements have served President and CEO Mayfield Evans well. As a result, this leading Anchorage-based company has consistently provided quality janitorial, carpet-cleaning, warehousing, laundry, dry-cleaning, local moving, and food services over the past 20 years.

The company was founded in 1978 with partner Willie O. Sims while both were stationed at Elmendorf Air Force Base in Anchorage, Alaska. Their first janitorial contract was for the Alaska State Troopers headquarters building in Anchorage. Evans remembers well the challenges he and Sims, along with their teenage sons, faced that first night on the job. "The building was new to us, and we didn't finish until seven in the morning — just in time to go to work on base!"

The business grew over the years as the company added other janitorial contracts to their client list and offered new services to their customers.

In 1983, Evans retired from the Air Force after 26 years of commissary/warehouse service and base support experience at several different duty stations.

Twice during his military tenure, Evans was honored with Services Superintendent of the Year awards. In 1985, Evans bought out Sims' interest in the venture, and the business would then become more of a family operation.

The family connection remains an important part of the business to this day. Evans' son, Barry, serves as the company's Operations Manager. Daughter Jacqué is the Finance and Administrative Manager and Secretary-Treasurer for the business that services contracts in several Alaska communities and at military bases in four other states. Growth has increased the E & S Diversified Services payroll to more than 200 employees, placing the company in the ranks of the top 100 employers in the state.

While building his business, Evans has not forgotten the importance of serving his community. He sits on the United Way Board of Directors; chairs the Mountain View Task Force (a neighborhood organization working to improve conditions in the low income community); is Vice President of Gateway Rotary; acts as advisory commissioner for the Anchorage Police Department; and works with the NAACP to assist children in learning computer skills.

Evans rejects the idea of a second retirement, anticipating instead the possibility of putting in fewer hours as he helps his family with a successful and growing business.

Courtesy of E & S Diversified Services

Mayfield Evans has been a resident of the state of Alaska since 1976. He has been married to Willie Mae Evans for 41 years and they have three children, Melphine, Jacqueline and Barry, and also two grandchildren, Jamila and Jelani.

Courtesy of E & S Diversified Services

Mayfield Evans (right) stands with his wife, Willie Mae, and his son, Barry.

ALASKA INSTRUMENT COMPANY

President Daniel Conrad and Chief Financial Officer Sherrie Bancroft purchased Alaska Instrument Company in 1997.

Courtesy of Alaska Instrument Company

The founder of Alaska Instrument Company, J. Gary Anderson, traveled north from Pennsylvania in 1967 with a briefcase and a dream. That dream turned into the largest manufacturers' representative company in the state of Alaska. AIC, which was purchased by Daniel Conrad and Sherrie Bancroft in 1997, holds sales accounts with the biggest oil, gas and mining companies operating on The Last Frontier.

For 30 years, the Alaska-owned and -operated company has provided this quality process control instrumentation to the state's largest companies, including BP Exploration (Alaska), Arco Alaska, Alyeska Pipeline Service Company, Tesoro, and Mapco Refineries. Other AIC accounts include the City of Anchorage, the State of Alaska,

and several utility companies and military bases. Additionally, AIC supports Alaska's environmental concerns with continuous emission monitoring and remediation equipment.

AIC has historically introduced new, state-of-the-art technology to the state's industries, including the latest innovative technology—the Multi-Phase Flow Meter, designed to measure the ratios of water, oil and gas. Daniel Conrad has the flow meter fabricated locally as a way to provide jobs in the local community. "It is going to be integral to oil companies throughout the state," Conrad says.

The future looks strong for the Anchorage-based company. Potential sales in the Russian Far East may prove productive as the oil industry investigates those largely untouched lands.

Conrad also sees future development occurring on the North Slope as an open door to expanding services provided by his company. "Prospective development in the North Slope will offer a stable, positive environment for our future, especially with our current relationship with oil companies," he says.

Conrad, in addition to running the company, has recently completed a term as a member of the Health Curriculum Committee for the Anchorage School District, assembled to develop, improve, and modernize children's education in health

studies. He has also served on the board of directors for the Crisis Pregnancy Center and traveled on a three-week mission to Albania with a local church. AIC employees, too, work to better their communities through charitable work, such as coaching young adults and children at the local Boys and Girls Club and the YMCA. The company itself is an annual supporter of the United Way and other local charities.

The close-knit group of individuals at AIC has worked to improve their surroundings both within the community and throughout the state. It is this dedication and reliability that makes AIC the largest and best company of its kind.

Courtesy of Alaska Instrument Company

AIC owners Daniel Conrad and Sherrie Bancroft are at the helm of the largest manufacturers' representative company in the state of Alaska.

ALASKA INDUSTRIAL DEVELOPMENT AND EXPORT AUTHORITY

Some years ago, the management team at the Alaska Industrial Development and Export Authority (AIDEA) wanted to define, in very simple terms, what the agency with the tongue-twisting name does. It was not direct lending. It was not financing "pie in the sky" projects. Then it came to them. "What we're really about is financing Alaska's future."

The tagline stuck because that is exactly what AIDEA was set up to do when it was established by the Alaska Legislature

in 1967. For all the changes in Alaska and AIDEA since then, financing Alaska's future is still what AIDEA is all about.

AIDEA provides capital to finance economic growth all over Alaska, creating and retaining jobs for Alaskans—from multi-million-dollar mining projects to small family-owned businesses; from urban centers to small towns and rural villages.

Regardless of project size or location, all AIDEA-financed projects must enhance the state's economy and provide or main-

The Red Dog Mine, in the DeLong Mountains of Northwest Alaska, is the world's largest producer of lead and zinc. AIDEA financed the original road and port that made the mine commercially viable. AIDEA continues to provide financing, allowing the mine to stay competitive and profitable.

Courtesy of Alaska Industrial Development and Export Authority; Photo by Chris Arend

Courtesy of Alaska Industrial Development and Export Authority; Photo by Mark Kelley

Spruce Mill Mall in Ketchikan is prime retail space in a charming location. A recent addition to the mall was financed in part by AIDEA.

tain jobs for Alaskans. The projects also must clearly show the ability to repay their debts.

AIDEA's highest-profile projects are those it develops, owns and operates. These projects—which must be financially feasible and bring economic benefits to the people of Alaska—typically provide infrastructure support to private sector projects. Examples include the DeLong Mountain Transportation

System (road and port that supports the Red Dog Mine, the world's largest zinc mine) and the Federal Express Aircraft maintenance facility.

AIDEA also participates in bank loans providing long-term financing for business projects, provides loan guarantees for Alaskan business and export transactions, and issues tax-exempt revenue bonds for eligible projects. Focusing on economic diversification and jobs for Alaskans, AIDEA is helping finance Alaska's future.

Part Three

QUALITY OF LIFE

UNIVERSITY OF ALASKA ANCHORAGE

Quiet areas for study are found across the UAA campus.

The University of Alaska Anchorage (UAA) enters the 21st century as an innovative and dynamic metropolitan university. Accredited by the Commission on Colleges of the Northwest Association of Schools and Colleges, many of UAA's professional and technical programs — such as business, nursing, and civil engineering — are accredited by their respective associations. Based in

the state's population and service center, UAA is the center of professional and technical higher education, serving over 15,000 traditional and non-traditional students at its four college campuses and extension sites located in the major cities of south-central Alaska and on various military sites.

Through teaching and learning, inquiry and discovery, and service to others, UAA strives to make profound, significant differences in the lives of its students, in the affairs of the communities in which its faculty, staff, and students live and serve, and in the professions and vocations taught. UAA offers academic programs in the liberal arts and sciences as well as in a host of professional and technical fields. Academic specialties include health and biomedical sciences, business and international trade, public policy and administration, and special education. New programs, such as logistics management, are added to the curriculum in response to community needs and opportunities. As an open-enrollment university UAA is committed to helping all students succeed with their educational goals while retaining high academic standards.

UAA's main campus is located in Anchorage with extension sites at Eagle River, Fort Richardson, and Elmendorf Air Force Base. For students residing in the Palmer-Wasilla region, Matanuska-Susitna College offers two-year degrees and certificates as well as access to baccalaureate and some advanced degrees. Students from Kodiak Island and the Kenai Peninsula are similarly served by Kodiak College, Kenai Peninsula College (KPC) and KPC's Kachemak Bay Branch in Homer. Administratively attached to UAA, Prince William Sound Community College (PWSCC) serves students in Valdez, Cordova and Copper Center. The university also serves students across Alaska via various media through the Center for Distributed Learning.

Seawolf Jim Hajdukovich scores in the Carrs Great Alaska Shootout.

Within minutes of the UAA campus, the Chugach Mountains provide year-round outdoor activities.

TEACHING

In today's world, higher education equates to lifelong learning. UAA takes its motto "We Learn for Life" seriously. Whether recently graduated from high school, making a career change, or learning for self-enrichment, UAA students have the opportunity to pursue exciting and challenging opportunities for academic excellence, vocational-technical mastery, or personal fulfillment. In all instances, students have extraordinary opportunities to learn in small classes taught by dedicated faculty. The University of Alaska Anchorage offers certificate, associate, baccalaureate, and master's degree programs and instruction in 115 major study areas. Students have access to scores of tailored short courses,

workshops, and seminars throughout the year with special summer study and conference programs offering students and faculty from around the world the opportunity to study and experience the natural grandeur of Alaska.

UAA's University Honors Program challenges academically advanced and gifted students to expand their intellect in both depth and breadth. Students desiring an international educational experience have a rich diversity of study-abroad opportunities from which to choose. UAA also offers a host of study opportunities at other universities, including, for example, a special agreement with the University of Washington School of Medicine that allows Alaskans to pursue their first year of medical training in Anchorage and their family-practice residency in cities throughout Alaska.

Three academic schools and four colleges form the base of the university's academic mission. The College of Arts and Sciences hosts over 22 academic disciplines in the natural and social sciences, the humanities, and the fine and performing arts. The Community and Technical College houses a full suite of technical, vocational and allied health programs as well as the university's Adult Learning Center which offers adult basic

education programs and the G.E.D. The College of Health, Education and Social Welfare encompasses the School of Education and the School of Nursing, as well as the departments of social work, human services, and justice. The College of Business and Public Policy offers studies in accounting, management, economics and computer information systems. The School of Engineering offers programs in geomatics, civil engineering, environmental quality and engineering management.

RESEARCH

Faculty and student research, scholarship, and creative activity are fostered across the curriculum and throughout the university. An annual Student Showcase emulates professional meetings wherein student

research and creative expressions are reviewed by faculty and culminate in a university publication. Faculty routinely win accolades for their creative works in music, theatre, and creative writing, including *The Alaska Quarterly Review*, cited by Washington Post Book World as one of the nation's top literary magazines. Scores of faculty advance the frontiers of science through their research activities sponsored by the National Institutes of Health and the National Science Foundation.

UAA capitalizes on the unique scientific and cultural opportunities and needs of Alaska through its various centers and institutes. The Environment and Natural Resources Institute; the Center for Alcohol and Addiction Studies; the Center for

The UAA campus comes alive with flowers in the summer.

A state-of-the-art radar control room simulator provides the latest in instruction for aviation students.

UAA has a beautiful new residence hall which was recently constructed to meet the growing demand for on-campus housing.

Economic Education; the Institute for Circumpolar Health Studies; the American Russian Center; the Center for Human Development: University Affiliated Program; the Justice Center; the Institute of Social and Economic Research; and the Center for Economic Development all make significant and sustained contributions to the advancement of their respective disciplines of study and to the welfare of Alaska.

Working with Providence Health System in Alaska, the university operates the Alaska Telemedicine Project that coordinates a consortium of health care providers, telecommunications carriers, and the State of Alaska, all of which are committed to enhancing the delivery of health care and medicine within the state. The School of Engineering works with compa-

nies such as Alyeska Pipeline Service Company to address arctic construction and environmental aspects of development, while UAA's state-of-the-art Aviation Technology Center works with the FAA to improve air transportation safety in Alaska. All advance UAA's mission to be of help to society by applying research knowledge and skills.

SERVICE

Providing service to the communities in which we live and work is an integral part of UAA's mission. More than 400 faculty and staff regularly lend their experience, as a public service, to various public and private groups and organizations. Students also participate in a range of internships and service-learning settings as part of their professional or technical education and training. A number of UAA centers organize formal programs of service. For example, the Small Business Development Center (SBDC) helps budding entrepreneurs create new jobs and garner millions of dollars in loans for their businesses. The BUY ALASKA program, administered by SBDC, provides sourcing services for hundreds of buying needs identified by Alaskan

businesses. The American Russian Center has over a decade of success in operating four business centers in major cities and regions of the Russian Far East, and has trained over 8,000 Russians in the theory and practice of small business enterprise.

STUDENT SERVICES

Helping students achieve their academic goals is the mission of UAA's support service. University students are supported by centers that focus on academic excellence, student health, learning resources, advising and counseling, career development, educational

Surveying students check out the lay of the land on campus.

Mainstage Theatre students prepare for a production.

opportunity, and study abroad. Other services assist students with financial aid, or special needs or interests. The African-American, Hispanic, Asian, International and Native America (AHAINA) office and Native Student Services (NSS) foster an appreciation for cultural diversity and support students of color or diverse ethnic ties. The Union of Students governs vital aspects of student life and fosters student leadership as does Club Council, which represents over 67 student interest clubs. The student-run radio station (KRUA) and newspaper, *The Northern Light*, have both won national and state awards, as has the UAA Speech and Debate team.

The new, $33 million Student Housing project, which opened in 1998, added three state-of-the-art residence halls and a Commons to the existing cluster of condo- and apartment-style student housing facilities. Student housing serves as a hub for student activities and has enhanced a rich and diverse campus life.

Adding excitement to UAA's campus life are its intercollegiate sports programs. Nicknamed the Seawolves, University of Alaska Anchorage's athletic teams compete as members of the NCAA Division II in basketball, volleyball, gymnastics, and skiing for women, and basketball, swimming, skiing, and cross-country running for men. UAA competes in Division I ice hockey (WCHA). Seawolf teams regularly rank among the nation's best and have produced many All-American and Academic All-American performers.

A Community Resource

The University of Alaska Anchorage is a major cultural and social resource for Alaska, hosting activities as diverse as Engineering, Canada, Japan, and Jazz weeks, the PWSCC Edward Albee Theatre Festival, and the nationally renowned Carrs' Great Alaska Shootout basketball tournament. In return, major state corporations such as Key Bank; Holland American Lines, Westours; ARCO; BP Exploration; the Anchorage Daily News; and others help to fund university programs and scholarships.

Nationally celebrated speakers regularly visit UAA campuses, and have included historian James McPherson; authors Jane Smiley, Michael Ondaatje, Richard Ford, and Tobias Wolff; linguist Noam Chomsky; psychologist Dr. Ruth Westheimer; comedian Paula Poundstone; and historian Pierre Berton. Recent performers have included Jewel, The Reduced Shakespeare Company, and Rockapella.

Trails winding through the wooded Anchorage campus beckon summer bikers and winter cross-country skiers. With skating rinks, swimming pools, gyms and other athletic facilities around Anchorage, UAA is a rewarding place to both study and experience the Last Frontier year-round. The academic excellence and lifelong learning opportunities it offers students are as great as the state of Alaska.

UAA Chancellor Edward Lee Gorsuch, center, meets with students during the annual fall convocation.

PROVIDENCE HEALTH SYSTEM

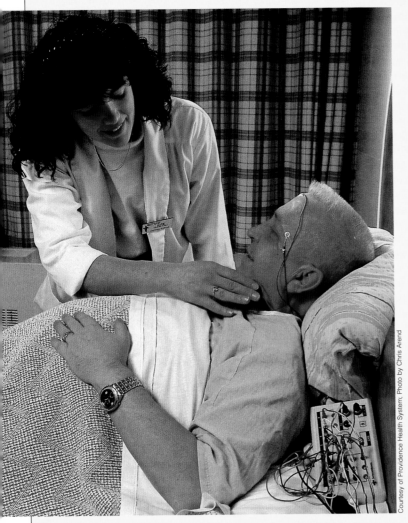

Providence Health System offers a wide range of rehabilitative services for Alaskans, including an accredited sleep disorders center.

the same: to offer the healing ministry of Jesus with a special concern for those with little or no ability to pay.

Providence Health System is a unique network of experienced health care providers and health care facilities in Anchorage, Seward, and Kodiak. Providence Alaska Medical Center is located in Anchorage, the state's largest and most populous city. This 341-bed acute-care general hospital is the primary referral center for the state of Alaska.

Specialty care services include the state's most comprehensive Heart, Cancer, Surgery, Maternity, Rehabilitation, and Behavioral Medicine (mental health) Centers, plus the Children's Hospital at Providence, a "hospital within a hospital" concept specifically designed, clinically and architecturally, for children.

The Emergency Services Department at Providence Alaska Medical Center responds to any minor or major crisis 24 hours a day, with approximately 50,000 visits per year. For critical-care emergencies that occur in remote areas of the state, LifeGuard Alaska provides fixed-wing and helicopter flight service.

For the elderly, Providence's Senior Services provide a range of services, including long term care, home health care, and assisted living housing.

Providence Health System in Alaska also offers a variety of preferred provider contracting arrangements to the state for both medical and behavioral medicine services.

To care for health needs in the community of Seward, Providence Health System operates the Providence Seward

When Mother Emilie Gamelin began the Sisters of Providence Religious Community in Montreal, Canada, in 1843, she wanted to develop a loving ministry for people in need. The start of the Providence ministry in Alaska began when these pioneering Sisters arrived in the gold rush town of Nome in 1902. Here, they built the foundation for modern health care in the state of Alaska.

Since then, new hospitals have been constructed and services have been expanded, but the mission has remained

Providence Alaska Medical Center, part of the Providence Health System, is the state's largest hospital, providing a comprehensive range of services for Alaskans statewide.

Medical Center. Family care clinic services, in-patient care, rehab therapy, diagnostics, home health care services and 24-hour emergency room care are all available in the new medical building.

On Kodiak Island, the Borough-owned Providence Kodiak Island Medical Center is managed and operated by Providence Health System. With a new building, 25 hospital beds and 19 extended-care beds, it includes a significant range of inpatient and outpatient care services including emergency department, surgery, maternity, general medicine, rehab therapy, specialty clinics, diagnostics, and home health care. Providence is also responsible for Kodiak's community mental health services.

Thirty-six miles south of Anchorage, Providence Girdwood Medical Clinic serves the community of Girdwood, home to Alyeska Ski Resort. Specializing in family medicine, the Clinic also serves as an urgent care clinic, with treatment provided by a full-time nurse practitioner.

Providence Health System also has a special collaborative relationship with Valley Hospital Association in Palmer. Sharing a very similar mission philosophy with Providence, Valley Hospital is a fully accredited not-for-profit, community-based health care organization providing care to residents of Matanuska-Susitna Valley. It has 36 beds and offers both inpatient and outpatient services with surgery, maternity, general medicine, diagnostics, emergency care, rehab therapy, home health care and hospice. It has an outpatient campus in Wasilla. The Providence-Valley relationship allows for shared resources, educational opportunities and value-added contracting opportunities.

Children's Hospital at Providence is a unique facility creatively designed especially for the care of children.

Courtesy of Providence Health System; Photo by Chris Arend

Courtesy of Providence Health System; Photo by Chris Arend

Providence LifeGuard air ambulance service provides rapid air transport and in-flight medical attention throughout Alaska and the North Pacific.

KETCHIKAN GENERAL HOSPITAL

For 75 years, PeaceHealth, through Ketchikan General Hospital, has provided quality health care to the residents of one of Alaska's most populous islands. Arriving by steamship in 1923, two Catholic Sisters began a tradition of compassionate, dedicated health care services to all in Southern Southeast Alaska — a legacy which continues to grow and flourish today.

As the world has changed and evolved, so has the health care ministry of the Sisters of St. Joseph of Peace. Establishing a health care corporation in 1974, known today as PeaceHealth, the Sisters had the foresight to bring Catholic health care into the realm of modern business. PeaceHealth is a non-profit corporation with health care systems in Oregon, Washington,

and Alaska. Each system works individually to meet the needs of its community, but also shares resources to provide a computerized patient medical record system which spans three States and will take PeaceHealth to the cutting edge of health care in the next century.

Ketchikan General Hospital is a unique combination of private enterprise and public support. The City of Ketchikan owns the building and leases it to PeaceHealth to operate the hospital debt-free. PeaceHealth, in turn, provides up-to-date equipment, technology, and medical care as well as charity care for all those in need.

The voters of Ketchikan agreed to fund a $10.7 million hospital expansion project in 1996. By the end of 1999, Ketchikan General Hospital will

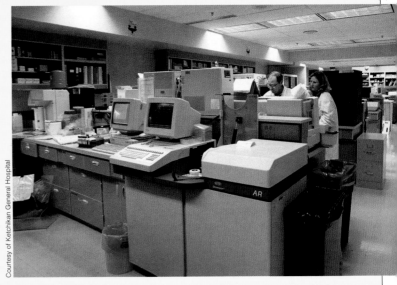

The KGH lab boasts state-of-the-art facilities.

realize the results of this public support with the addition of a new Patient Care Wing, new Radiology department, and an entirely new infrastructure.

With over 350 employees including 12 physicians and five medical clinics, Ketchikan General Hospital is the largest private employer in Ketchikan. Patients travel from outlying communities, including Prince of Wales, Petersburg and Wrangell, for doctor appointments and outpatient surgery.

As the community has supported PeaceHealth through building expansion, PeaceHealth has expanded services to include non-traditional hospital services. Over the last eight years, Ketchikan General Hospital has added home health care services, recovery services for alcohol and drug addiction, psychiatry and psychology services, cardiac rehab services, and outpatient rehabilitation therapy services.

KGH offers compassionate long-term care.

KGH's new addition is adjacent to the hospital's main entrance.

Technology has allowed Ketchikan General Hospital the ability to diagnose illnesses with a new Computerized Axial Tomography (CT) Scanner, new Nuclear Medicine Camera and new Bone Mineral Densitometer.

Because Ketchikan General Hospital is a part of PeaceHealth, a truly unique program for treating and caring for cancer patients has developed. Using video teleconferencing, Ketchikan General Hospital works directly with St. John Medical Center, a PeaceHealth Medical Center in Longview, Washington. The Affiliate Cancer Program allows Ketchikan physicians face-to-face meetings, via video conferencing, with cancer specialists in Longview in real time. The physicians in Alaska and Washington view the same X-rays and pathological slides and come to agreement on the best treatment methods for the cancer patient. The Affiliate Cancer Program is only the second of its kind in the nation accredited by the American College of Surgeons, Commission on Cancer. The program allows cancer patients in Southeast to stay close to home while undergoing cancer treatment.

Ketchikan General Hospital is looking to the future as well. By forming a partnership with Alaskans for Drug Free Youth, two full-time drug prevention educators work throughout the Ketchikan School District to inform children from kindergarten through 12th grade about the damaging effects of drug use.

Ketchikan General Hospital also supports the PATCHWorks Community Initiative which is working to create a community that values its youth. Through the use of Search Institute's Developmental Asset model, Ketchikan hopes to define itself as one of the healthiest places for youth and families to live.

PeaceHealth remains committed to the mission in Southern Southeast Alaska which the Sisters began 75 years ago. Providing quality health care with the newest technology, the latest medical care and the spiritual dedication of the Catholic health care legacy is what sets Ketchikan General Hospital apart from most other rural health care systems.

These Sisters continued the tradition of compassionate, dedicated health-care service in Ketchikan during the difficult decade of the 1930s.

BLUE CROSS BLUE SHIELD OF ALASKA

Leonhard Seppala, key figure in the Nenana to Nome Diphtheria Serum Run and the most renowned musher of all times, symbolizes the courage and strength of Alaskans helping Alaskans.

In January 1925, the 2,000 citizens of Nome were in the middle of a cold winter and a deadly outbreak of diphtheria. Chances for getting the serum they so desperately needed were as dark as the winter days, since the railroad ended at Nenana almost 700 miles away. But Alaskans, then as now, were not going to let their neighbors suffer.

Braving temperatures that dropped to 70 below zero, 20 teams of dogs and mushers covered 674 miles in seven days — a trip that usually took four weeks — to deliver the serum and save lives. This first serum run is a prime example of how Alaskans, throughout the history of the state, have gone the extra mile for each other.

The memory of the heroic deeds of these mushers and their dogs lives on in the Iditarod. The teams are faster and the equipment better, but the can-do spirit, courage, and strength of the mushers remain crucial. Now supported by skilled volunteers who offer the needed logistics, food, supplies, shelter and rest, these modern teams make the run solo from Anchorage to Nome in times that surpass the speed of that original run. Then as now, the Iditarod symbolizes the Alaska spirit, which brings the people of Alaska close together over vast distances.

Blue Cross Blue Shield of Alaska also has a proud history of service and support in Alaska, working to go the extra mile so Alaskans can get the high-quality, affordable health care they need. Our work in Alaska spans more than 40 years, beginning before statehood. Blue Cross Blue Shield of Alaska provides health insurance to almost

Like the mushers of the serum run, the Blue Cross Blue Shield of Alaska staff is dedicated to removing barriers for Alaskans to high quality affordable health care.

Staff in the Anchorage office work as an integral part of the community to meet the needs of fellow Alaskans, both on and off the job.

Courtesy of Blue Cross Blue Shield of Alaska

90,000 Alaskans, and to provide greater strength, we draw on the resources of the Premera family of Health plans, which serves more than a million people in Alaska, Washington, and Oregon.

The practice of medicine also has changed. Now, along with their healing touch, Alaska physicians and other providers have access to powerful technologies, surgical advances and effective pharmaceuticals that enhance health and well-being. However, advances in medicine also have brought challenges, including keeping access to services affordable. This has required Blue Cross Blue Shield of Alaska to work diligently with providers, business, and government to develop solutions that work in the unique Alaska environment.

Many challenges remain, but the purpose is still the same. Like the Iditarod volunteers, Blue Cross Blue Shield of Alaska works behind the scenes, removing barriers to high-quality, affordable health care for Alaskans, whether they are here at home, or traveling outside the state. Further, recognizing that there is no single right answer in this increasingly complex world, Blue Cross Blue Shield of Alaska offers a wide range of choices

for both individual and groups ranging from traditional indemnity plans to the Alaska Prudent Buyer option.

To meet the ever-increasing challenge, Blue Cross Blue Shield of Alaska renewed its commitment to Alaska and changed its name to reflect that commitment. The company has added new technologies to provide better service to customers. But more importantly, the Alaska based staff has been more than doubled. Because in the end, it is people, going the extra mile, that will enable Blue Cross Blue Shield of Alaska to help Alaskans access affordable, high-quality health care services for at least another 40 years.

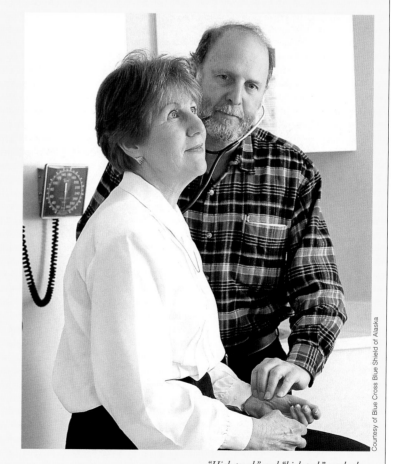

Courtesy of Blue Cross Blue Shield of Alaska

"High touch" and "high tech" are both vital ingredients in the practice of Anchorage Cardiologist, Dr. William Mayer.

Bartlett Regional Hospital

Bartlett Regional Hospital in Juneau, Alaska.

In Alaska's isolated state capital, Juneau's Bartlett Regional Hospital combines state-of-the-art technology with old-fashioned patient care.

Surrounded by the waters of Gastineau Channel and the Tongass National Forest, Juneau's 30,000 residents live nestled between snow-capped peaks and glacial ice fields. The city's pristine beauty draws more than 500,000 annual visitors. Juneau is the world's fifth most popular port-of-call.

"I think we've got the best of both worlds here," says Bartlett Administrator Robert F. Valliant. "We have a small-town hospital atmosphere, but we've got big-city technology. We can provide services equivalent to medical facilities in much larger towns."

During his tenure, Valliant has attracted a broad range of medical specialists not previously available to the region's residents. The physician-recruiting program he developed added more than 15 new doctors, including several general practitioners, and specialists in OB/GYN, urology, ear/nose/throat, psychiatry, physical rehabilitative medicine, neurology, and orthopedic and plastic surgery.

Bartlett Regional Hospital has also added state-of-the-art technology ranging from Southeast's first Magnetic Resonance Imaging scanner, to a tele-medicine project linking Bartlett physicians with doctors at Seattle's Virginia Mason. Fully licensed by the State of Alaska as an acute-care general hospital, Bartlett Regional now offers numerous ancillary services ranging from radiology and nuclear medicine to labor and delivery. The hospital even has a hyperbaric chamber which is used in treating both diving-accident victims and other medical problems. This year the hospital installed a computer system that will enable health professionals throughout the region to access integrated patient records.

"We're finding more and more people stay in Juneau for their health care," Valliant said. "And we are able to help people throughout Southeast access needed services closer to home and more economically."

About the only services Bartlett Regional Hospital does not offer are neurosurgery, open-heart surgery and head-injury procedures. In those cases, a Lear Jet equipped as an intensive-care unit medivacs patients to Seattle trauma centers.

Bartlett is operated by a nine-member board appointed by the Juneau Assembly and is managed by hospital management corporation Quorum Health Resources Inc. It is certified by the Medicare/Medicaid program, is a participating provider with Blue Cross, and is accredited by the Joint Commission on Accreditation of Healthcare Organizations and the College of American Pathologists.

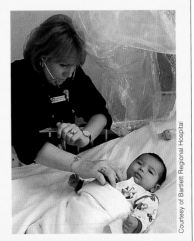

Bartlett combines modern technology with old-fashioned patient care.

ALASKA REGIONAL HOSPITAL

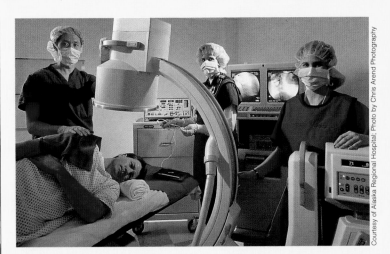

The Pain Management Center at Alaska Regional Hospital provides patients suffering from chronic pain an in-state option for care.

For more than a generation, Alaska Regional Hospital has fulfilled the medical needs of Alaskans, continually seeking ways to improve the scope of services, skills and technology available in the state. The Pain Management Center at Alaska Regional is a good example, providing Alaskans who suffer from chronic pain a program tailored to individual needs utilizing current pain management modalities, under the medical direction of a physician specifically trained in alleviating chronic pain.

In addition to inpatient and outpatient health care, Alaska Regional Hospital's specialized medical services include: cardiovascular services including surgery and cardiac rehabilitation; critical care units; diabetes and health management services; cancer treatment and care; pulmonary rehabilitation; acute rehabilitation unit; neurological services; wound program; and women's and children's services.

Located in Anchorage, Alaska Regional has services adapted specifically to Alaska's unique

climate and geography. The hospital's "LifeFlight" critical care air-ambulance program gives rural residents everywhere in Alaska access to the hospital's trauma facility the only hospital in the state where fixed-wing aircraft can taxi to the door.

With more than 700 employees and over 400 independent physicians, the hospital is dedicated to meeting the total health-care needs of Alaska. At Alaska Regional Hospital, the mission is to be Alaskans' partner in life.

Alaska Regional Hospital is a sponsor of the Alaska Nordic Skiing Center's Gold 2002 training program. Alaska Regional provides sports medicine and testing for the Alaska-based athletes training for the 2002 Olympics cross-country competitions. Alaska Regional's support of Gold 2002 is another example of the hospital's commitment to being Alaskans' partner in life.

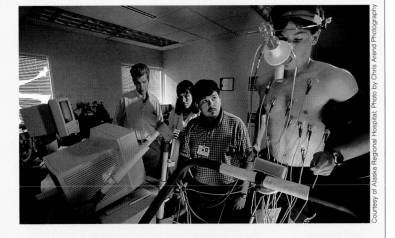

Alaska Regional Hospital is committed to meeting the health needs of Alaskans from throughout the state.

Part Three

BUILDING ALASKA

ALEUT CORPORATION

The Aleut Plaza in Anchorage.

Alaska's Aleut people occupy some of the most rugged and isolated regions of the state, stretching the length of the Aleutian Chain and including the Pribilof Islands in the Bering Sea. It is from this limited land base that the Aleut Corporation, one of the 13 regional corporations established in 1972 under the terms of the Alaska Native Claims Settlement Act (ANCSA), looks to the future for its shareholders as it recognizes the history of its people.

That history reaches back some 8,000 years on the Aleutian Islands and at least 200 years in the Pribilofs. The pre-Russian population was thought to have numbered 12,000 to 15,000 people whose lives were sustained by the sea.

The early Russian period some 250 years ago brought profound change to the Aleut

people. Russian fur traders enslaved entire villages — their inhabitants pressed into service hunting sea mammals for fur and were relocated to serve the Russian's colonization goals. Many species of sea mammals were nearly wiped out and the Aleuts who survived numbered fewer than 2,000. The Aleut culture suffered to the point of being nearly non-existent in some villages.

With the purchase of Alaska by the United States in 1867, the Russian dominance ended, but the Russian influence on Aleut culture remains to this day. The Russian Orthodox faith continues to be a strong element of Aleut cultural heritage.

Today, that enduring heritage is blended with 20th-century business endeavors by the Aleut Corporation. Launched with an ANCSA settlement of $19.5

million, 66,000 acres of surface land and 1.5 million acres of subsurface estate, the corporation issued stock to 3,249 shareholders.

The corporation's early economic activities centered on the commercial fishing industry. Investments in fishing and processing vessels and marine transportation operations came naturally to a people whose heritage was so closely tied to the sea.

Investment in real estate, primarily in Southcentral Alaska, along with rock and gravel extraction from corporate land, marked other early activities. Unlike some of the other regional corporations created under ANCSA, the Aleut Corporation does not have a

Aleut dancer, Mary Swetzof.

rich natural-resource base on which to build its business enterprises. There were no commercially viable deposits of gold, zinc, silver or other minerals found elsewhere in Alaska. The oil, gas, or timber resources that fueled the development plans of other Native groups were not available to the Aleuts.

The Aleut Corporation changed its investment policy to move from the fishing industry to real estate. Real estate holdings, including several commercial properties in Anchorage, were added to the corporation's investment portfolio. In 1984, construction was begun on the Aleut Plaza in midtown Anchorage. The three-story class-A office building houses corporate headquarters in 4,500 square feet of the 30,000 square foot building. The balance of the space is leased to other commercial tenants.

In 1991, the corporation made a major business move with the acquisition of Space Mark, Inc. (SMI), an enterprise that concentrates on federal government operations and maintenance contracts. By 1997, SMI, a wholly owned subsidiary of the Aleut Corporation, had 15 federal contracts in seven states, including Alaska, and Antarctica.

SMI, which is based in Colorado Springs, Colorado, is certified in the Small Business Administration's (SBA) 8 (a) program. The certification provides competitive advantages to minority-owned companies that pursue federal contracts. In 1993, SMI was named "Prime Contractor of the Year" by the SBA and later received that agency's "Administrators Award for Excellence." The Aleut Corporation has invested in other 8(a) subsidiaries, TAC Services Inc. and Akima Corporation, to promote Alaska's interests in governmental contracts.

The Aleut Corporation also established a permanent fund for the benefit of its shareholders. The purpose of the fund is to accumulate investments in marketable securities that will provide for future dividends to be paid to shareholders. Earnings of the fund will be reinvested until its assets reach $10 million. After that, 50 percent of the earnings will be reinvested in the fund and 50 percent will be distributed to shareholders.

The greatest opportunities and challenges for the corporation are yet to come, according to President & CEO Elary Gromoff, Jr. With military downsizing, the Adak Island Naval Air Facility was selected for closure. A virtual city that once housed up to 6,000

military and civilian support personnel, the facility includes a deep-water port, two 7,800-foot paved runways and bulk fuel storage facilities that can hold more than 20 million gallons of fuel. It is a future city, burgeoning with potential, ready to become Alaska's "Gateway to Far East Russia."

Through land swaps with the federal government and with political support at both the state and federal levels, the Aleut interests are poised to take title to the land and most of the facilities at Adak. As the transfer process moves forward, the Aleut Corporation is developing an economic feasibility study and looking to the future development of an economically viable community at Adak which will benefit its shareholders and all Alaskans.

The board of directors reaffirmed the corporation's long-term goals to increase profitability, further diversify its investment portfolio, increase shareholder benefits, and to improve Aleut relationships within the region. It is with this determination, and with a strong sense of cultural identity that the Aleut Corporation faces the next century.

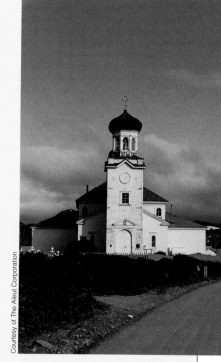

The Russian Church at Unalaska.

N.C. MACHINERY COMPANY

Front-end loaders are used in construction and mining projects throughout Alaska.

N.C. Machinery Company, the Pacific Northwest's oldest Caterpillar dealer, has been a vital part of Alaska's growth since the early 1800s, including having provided machinery and other goods needed for the Gold Rush. A steadfast commitment to providing customers with world class equipment, parts, technical support and service has resulted in N.C. Machinery becoming one of the leading Caterpillar dealerships in the world. The Seattle-based Tractor and Equipment Company serves Washington; Alaska; Magadan, Russia; and parts of Montana, North Dakota, and Wyoming.

The Northern Commercial (N.C.) Company was started in 1776 by two Russian fur

traders, who organized the first company to do business in Alaska on a continuing basis — a fur-trading post on Kodiak Island. The company moved into transportation and mercantile in the early 1800s, and was named Caterpillar dealer for Alaska and Yukon territory in 1926. The company's heavy equipment immediately went to work building the new frontier's basic infrastructure, as well as exploring and developing Alaska's vast resources.

Today, N.C. Machinery Company operates under third-generation, family-owned Tractor & Equipment Company (T&E), which took the reins in 1994. Formerly based in Billings, Montana, T&E shared N.C.'s history of over 65 years of service as a Caterpillar dealer. "The joining of two long-lasting industry leaders in the heavy equipment, power generation, and engine business made sense for both companies, as well as our customers," says John Harnish, President and CEO of T&E.

N.C. MACHINERY SHARES RICH HISTORY WITH ALASKA

N.C.'s rich history in Alaska exemplifies the company's focus on mutual success with its customers. Caterpillar equipment was instrumental in finding the

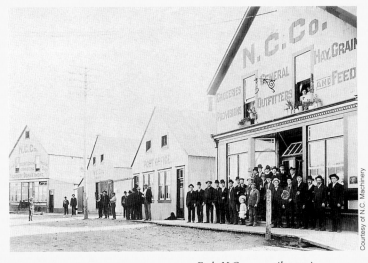

Early N.C. mercantile store in Fairbanks.

N.C. Machinery Company is one of Caterpillar's older dealers.

Courtesy of N.C. Machinery

N.C. Machinery Company will deliver and assemble machines in remote locations not accessible by road, like this isolated spot outside Juneau.

Courtesy of N.C. Machinery

first arctic petroleum reserves, as well as building the 800-mile transAlaska Pipeline. Today, N.C. supports all the primary industries in Alaska, Washington, and Montana with 35 branches, more than 1,000 employees, and modern systems that solve support problems overnight.

"During the past century, N.C. Machinery has expanded its services and geographical reach to support growth in Alaska's developing territories," says Harnish. "Caterpillar equipment has played a major role in supplying villages with electrical power, enabling petroleum engineers to discover oil, supporting miners looking for gold and other natural resources . . . the list goes on and on."

The opening of N.C. Machinery's Caterpillar dealership in Magadan now allows the company to sell and service the same Caterpillar equipment on both sides of the Bering Sea. Economies of scale have always provided the company's Alaska customers world-class service and parts-inventory support, and this expansion makes N.C. even stronger.

The Siberian dealership brings the company full circle, back to its roots in the Russian-American Company formed by two enterprising Siberian fur traders more than two centuries ago.

ARCTIC FOUNDATIONS, INC.

HAARP Antenna in Gakona, Alaska.

A sound foundation is the key to building a successful business. For Arctic Foundations, Inc., making sure that structural underpinnings are sound in the permafrost conditions that underlie much of Alaska has made for business success.

Permafrost is a condition of permanently frozen ground. Climatic changes and surface damage due to development have caused thawing and degradation of permafrost. A cycle of ground thawing and freezing causes movement that can destroy foundations in just a few seasons.

Arctic Foundations' business is based on a thermo or heat-transfer process developed by President and CEO Erwin Long in the late 1950s. He worked for the U.S. Army Corps of Engineers at the time. The Corps used the process Long patented to maintain permafrost stability at two communications sites built in 1960. The commercial product — Thermo Pile — used in the construction of towers at the Aurora and Glennallen sites remains functional to this day.

Over the years Long refined his ideas and in 1972 Arctic Foundations, Inc. was launched with headquarters in Anchorage. Initially, he hired a geo-technical engineer to run the company, but soon realized that the new enterprise would require his undivided attention. Long retired from the Corps of Engineers a short time later and has not looked back since.

Today, Arctic Foundations provides the technology and product line that makes the company a worldwide leader in innovative solutions to the challenges of foundation construction in the arctic. This technology gives planners, architects and engineers the ability to design stable foundations in permafrost conditions.

In Alaska, that means being able to build on land that was once inhospitable to development. It means being able to build roads, drill pads, airfields, communications sites, and whole cities with housing, stores and schools.

School in Galena, Alaska.

*Communications Tower in
Glennallen, Alaska.*

Arctic Foundations produces four products and can develop hybrid solutions to meet special arctic construction needs. Helixpiles are structural, non-refrigerated pilings. They permit the transfer of stress and prevent the premature failure of the upper bearing surfaces. Thermo Piles are structural, passively-refrigerated pilings for reducing the soil temperature to increase safety or allowable bearing when permafrost must be created or upgraded, or when frost heaving

must be prevented. Thermo Probes are non-structural, passively-refrigerated units for subgrade refrigeration. Hybrids are combination units incorporating both passive and active refrigeration. Arctic Foundations builds these systems specifically for each job and its individual requirements.

The largest single project utilizing Arctic Foundations technology and products was the Maniilaq Health Center (Hospital) in Kotzebue, built by the U.S. Public Health Service. The 80,000-square-foot facility was constructed on a pad of beach gravel using Thermo-helixpiles and Thermo Probes to stabilize the permafrost that was located at a depth of five feet during the summer.

While the largest, the Kotzebue project is only one among the many different challenges that Arctic Foundations meets in providing products and services to clients across Alaska. The list includes projects large and small for government, industry and private citizens. Since 1978, Arctic Foundations has fabricated its products at the Anchorage facility. This results in a high-quality product that can be delivered to customers quickly.

In 1983, the company took the next logical step in expansion when it established Arctic Foundations of Canada in Winnipeg, Manitoba. The subsidiary is licensed to design and manufacture products for projects located in Canada. More recently, the Canadian division has completed passive frozen-core dams in the Russian Far East and at diamond mines of the North West Territories.

Long has also taken his company in another direction, this one far from the permafrost conditions of the Arctic. In a demonstration project for the U.S. Department of Energy at Oak Ridge, Tennessee, Arctic Foundations technology is being used to contain high-level radioactive contaminates.

The company's Thermo Probes are being used to create a subsurface frozen-soil barrier that surrounds and contains the contaminants. The frozen barrier forms a 75- foot square around the site and prevents the migration of pollutants through the groundwater.

Long's innovative thinking has been recognized by his peers. In 1978, he received the Alaska Engineer of the Year award, and in 1991 he was cited with an American Society of Civil Engineers award for Cold Regions Engineering.

It is because of innovative engineering solutions and products that Arctic Foundations, Inc., a small Alaskan company, has become a world leader in frozen-ground technology.

*Cryogenic Barrier Demonstration
Project in Oak Ridge, Tennessee.*

KIEWIT CONSTRUCTION GROUP, INC.

Alyeska Prince Hotel in Girdwood.

From small, everyday jobs to multi-million dollar projects, Kiewit Construction Company and Kiewit Pacific Company — both part of Kiewit Construction Group, Inc. — provide Alaskans with the construction work they need.

As the contracting arms of Peter Kiewit Son's, Inc., a national conglomerate based in Omaha, Nebraska, KCC and KPC have the power and the backing to complete any construction job. Through KCC, which erects buildings, and KPC, which constructs roads, Kiewit builds anything from elegant hotels and theaters in the heart of the city, to highways and bridges through areas populated only by a few bears.

They will even work under mountains. The train to Whittier, Alaska, has historically been a favorite for residents and tourists alike. After the work of Kiewit is completed, private automobiles will be able to safely pass through miles of tunnels and experience the glories of Whittier and Prince William Sound.

Kiewit can do all this on schedule and within budget because the local offices are supported by Peter Kiewit Son's. Kiewit owns more large equipment than nearly any other construction company in the world — holding equipment with a replacement value of more than $555 million, so there is no excuse for not getting the job done right.

Kiewit maintains a decentralized network of district and area offices located across the United States and in Canada. If the local office does not have something it needs, then other offices lend resources and additional support for the project, regardless of size.

Safety is a big issue with Kiewit. Accident prevention is a line responsibility, beginning with the president and regional managers of the operation to the district managers, job superintendents and individual supervisors. If an accident happens, in even the most remote site, the company's Board of Directors knows about it within the week — and the company never fails to investigate.

The 4,600 cubic yard foundation for the Marriott Hotel in Anchorage.

Military Family Housing, Eielson AFB.

Courtesy of Kiewit Construction Company

Kiewit employees know that accidents can adversely affect productivity, costs and employee relations — something that can directly affect them financially. At Kiewit, nearly one-half of the employees own stock in the company. As shareholders, they have a direct stake in the success of the work they do.

"Employee ownership is what sets this company apart from the rest," said David Zemek, KCC's Alaska area manager. "And as far as safety, we want to make the workplace safe and send a worker home in the same shape as when he came to work."

"It's this dedication from the company that makes Kiewit employees want to stay with the company," adds Shawn Lannen, KPC's area manager. "Management tenure at Kiewit averages 24 years for executives and 14 years for superintendents."

A company founded in 1884, Peter Kiewit Son's, Inc. has survived wars and depression as well as economic booms. Over the years, the company has branched out into mining, telecommunications, and energy and infrastructure privatization.

Few other companies can match that experience.

The managers at KPC and KCC are not passive contractors. The same local people organize, plan and build the work, lending continuity and organization to each project. This hands-on contracting strategy allows for tighter control over the production and performance of the job.

While the Alaska Kiewit offices are supported by the parent company in Nebraska, Zemek stresses that these are local companies. The local KCC office has been in business since before Alaska was a state, more than 50 years ago.

Decisions about the job lie in the hands of the people closest to the work, people who live in Alaska. These are people who have extensive knowledge about the local labor force, material suppliers and subcontractors. Both KCC and KPC hire locally when they can, and they purchase supplies from businesses in the state, supporting the local economy — and their neighbors.

No job is too big or too small for Kiewit. From construction of the foundation for Anchorage's courthouse to building the renowned Alyeska Prince Hotel, Kiewit works hard to make Alaska a better place.

Courtesy of Kiewit Construction Company

Bird Point Pedestrian Bridge.

ALASKA INTERSTATE CONSTRUCTION, LLC

Alaska Interstate Construction's specially designed all-terrain "snowbirds" making an ice road on the Arctic Ocean.

Completing projects ranging from roads and pads to islands and bridges, on time and on budget is an Alaska Interstate Construction, LLC (AIC) hallmark. The company is known for its ability to work in some of the harshest conditions on earth while providing its clients with cost-saving alternatives. AIC is the preeminent support contractor in Alaska for resource development.

AIC specializes in developing a project by fulfilling all necessary heavy civil construction requirements, including access and haul roads; containment ponds; earth dams and channel systems; drilling and blasting; excavating and hauling waste materials; building tank farms; installing containment systems; and providing camp and facility maintenance. These services allow AIC's clients to do what they do best—extract and refine resources.

New technology in oil recovery has made Alaska's North Slope alive with activity. More drilling rigs than ever before are reaching record depths, searching for and finding new oil fields. Smaller footprints in today's resource development means a significant challenge in project planning and execution. By participating in the design phase, AIC can offer ideas which result in substantial cost savings to their clients. A recent example is the new Badami oil field where development costs

were reduced by more than half of the original estimate. Another advantage to early project involvement is keeping in mind the overall goal which includes minimizing impact on the environment.

AIC's North Slope base of operations at Deadhorse is home to a 30,000-square-foot maintenance shop, block fabrication plant for the manufacturing of slope protection, and Thermal Remediation Unit—the only permanent thermal remediation unit based in Prudhoe Bay. AIC has completed several major environmental clean-up projects, restoring hundreds of acres of contaminated sites to their natural conditions. The company has also excavated and remediated thousands of cubic yards of contaminated soil.

An AIC crew driving pile at the Northstar Dock project in Anchorage.

AIC is committed to hiring Alaska Natives.

AIC pioneered many of the construction techniques used in the arctic today and is the leading expert in offshore gravel island and causeway construction. These islands are built during the harsh, cold winters off Alaska's northernmost coast, on the Arctic Ocean. Frozen sea-ice is not thick enough for use in transporting the equipment and materials required to construct gravel islands. Unique, specially-designed all-terrain vehicles called "Snowbirds," built specifically for AIC, are used for building and maintaining on- and offshore ice roads. The recently completed Badami project utilized ice roads constructed by AIC to haul all the gravel necessary to build the remote 16-acre pad and three miles of road that comprise the foundation of the development.

The sheer size of AIC's heavy civil fleet, the largest in Alaska, offers a glimpse into the vast number of completed contracts since the company was started. AIC supports both mineral and hydrocarbon extraction including ongoing work at the Red Dog Mine in northwestern Alaska, the world's largest lead and zinc mine, and mine development projects at the Fort Knox gold mine near Fairbanks, Alaska's biggest gold producer. Most recently, all roads, pads and bridges were constructed on schedule and on budget for ARCO Alaska's Tarn oilfield, and BP Exploration's Badami project was brought on line with significant participation from AIC.

The Kubaka Gold Mine in Russia is a notable example of AIC's ability to bring new resource development on line. Located over 500 air miles from Magadan, AIC overcame numerous challenges presented by political uncertainties, severe weather and the remote roadless location to bring the new, modern gold mine into production.

AIC is continually striving for improvements in every facet of the company. It has become a leader in the construction industry by constantly seeking new and innovative techniques. The company's employees live and work in Alaska and are actively involved in their communities.

In looking toward the future with projects such as BP's Liberty and Northstar islands, ARCO's new developments, and with other areas in Alaska being opened up for exploration in both mining and petroleum industries, Alaska Interstate Construction is ready with ideas, equipment and experience to make it happen.

Aerial view of the Badami development. Alaska Interstate Construction built the dock, road and pad for the new field.

WILDER CONSTRUCTION COMPANY

This barge unloading shows the special handling equipment designed by Wilder Construction and fabricated specifically for the Unalaska Airport Dolos project.

At the top of the world along the northern regions of the ring of fire, the people at Wilder Construction Company cover Alaska like no other civil construction company can. Through the numbing temperatures in Deadhorse and the strong winds and rain that blow over the Aleutian Chain, the employees at Wilder know that every job they do in the state will bring new challenges. Wilder's experienced personnel welcome the challenges and look forward to facing them head-on as they have for the past 22 years.

Alaska is a huge tourist destination and reconstructing a major runway at the Anchorage International Airport during the tourist season is a significant challenge; however, it is one of the easier jobs for Wilder's employees in recent years. To rebuild and rearmor the runway at the Unalaska Airport in Dutch harbor, Wilder's crew took on a more difficult situation. The runway is a mere 20 feet above sea level and subject to heavy, pounding surf that builds up from deep in the expansive Pacific Ocean. Wilder's crews placed 1,450 eight-ton concrete dolos to protect the runway structure and safely complete the project.

Another extraordinary effort by Wilder's crews occurred near Illiamna, a remote area of the Alaska Peninsula. Wilder's crews constructed the Tazimina Hydroelectric Project adjacent to the falls on the Tazimina River. The new structure receives water above the falls and through a shaft drilled in the rock delivers the water to generators in a cavern carved out of the rock at the base of the falls. The drilled shaft is approximately 30 feet in diameter and drops eighty feet. The remote project required crews to construct 6.5 miles of road just to reach the site.

Wilder crews returned to Illiamna the following year to construct a runway. Equipment for both the projects was barged across Cook Inlet, and transported by mountain road over the pass to Illiamna Lake, where it was barged to the work location. Access is restricted to summer months, since the pass is closed by snow and the lake is thick with ice in the winter.

While nearly half of the work performed by Wilder in 1997 consisted of airport construction around the state, the company has the exceptional versatility for a wide range of civil construc-

In the initial stages of the Tazimina Hydroelectric Project, the excavation and construction of the intake structure above the falls of the Tazimina River begins.

tion work. Highways, dams, bridges, docks, and environmental remediation work are all typical of Wilder's extensive experience.

Wilder showcased its versatility during the Standard Steel Metals and Salvage Yard Superfund Cleanup Project. Wilder's broad range of experience was perfect for the excavation, chemical treatment, soil stabilization, sheetpile, erosion control structure, dewatering and water-treatment activities required to complete the highly technical cleanup project. Add the discovery of unexploded ordinances to the project and you have a very volatile challenge. The owner was left with a useful piece of property and the threat from contamination was eliminated.

Wilder's crews have built roadways and bridges all across Alaska. One of the more notable projects was the construction of the Seward Highway from Bird Flats to Milepost 111. Contracted in 1982, the Bird Flats project was then the largest highway project ever commissioned by the Alaska Department of Transportation. The Work consisted of 12 miles of extensive drill and shoot for rock excavation, grading, drainage, and paving. Through innovative approaches and cooperative efforts between Wilder and the State of Alaska, the job

was completed ahead of schedule and within budget, saving the state millions of dollars.

Supporting Wilder's construction capabilities are the resources of Wilder's subsidiary, Central Paving Products (CPP). CPP owns numerous gravel resources in Alaska and produces aggregate products with their plants for screening, crushing, washing and asphalt production. Coordination with the Alaska Railroad allows for unique customer service and efficient supply of products to Wilder and the rest of the construction industry.

Remote locations, changing weather, inhospitable seasons, and unique arctic conditions are obstacles that have been overcome by Wilder's crews since the beginning. Founded in the Pacific Northwest in 1911, Wilder Construction Company started as a small operation in a big territory. The company has since expanded its operations and now annually performs upwards of $160 million of work volume. Wilder's work is done predominantly in Washington, Alaska, Oregon and Idaho.

With offices in six cities in three states, Wilder Construction services a large area and a wide range of businesses. Wilder also believes in giving back to the communities it serves, and provides support for numerous

organizations helping others, especially children, who face challenges of their own. Wilder sponsors youth sports, the Make-A-Wish Foundation, Junior Achievement, United Way and several local charities. Wilder's engineers also participate in judging for Block Kid's programs that help introduce young children to the rewards of working in the construction industry.

The commitment that Wilder Construction maintains to its customers and community is what makes Wilder stand above the rest. Wilder maintains a high work ethic for its employees and strives to provide the highest quality to their customers and community.

This is the finished Unalaska Airport Dolos project. The dolos dissipate the wave energy.

Recognizing the importance of positive role models, Wilder Construction sponsors weekly youth baseball clinics held by the Anchorage Bucs, a local summer collegiate baseball team.

Part Three

MARKETPLACE, ACCOMMODATIONS,
TOURS AND JOURNEYS

HILTON ANCHORAGE HOTEL

Situated in the heart of Downtown Anchorage, the Hilton Anchorage is just a few short steps from business, shopping, tour companies, Egan Convention Center, performing arts, and entertainment.

Lying in the heart of downtown Anchorage, within walking distance of shopping and local attractions, is the Hilton Anchorage Hotel. The Hilton Anchorage operates under a policy of providing first-class service and accommodations not only to traveling businessmen and vacationers, but to the local community, as well.

During local celebrations, such as the Mayor's Annual Ball, Fur Rendezvous, and the start of the 1,100-mile Iditarod Trail Sled Dog Race from Anchorage to Nome, the Hilton Anchorage focuses on serving Alaskans, as well as guests visiting the state. The Hilton Anchorage and its employees are especially proud of the work they do in support of local and statewide community efforts. The hotel has donated furniture to the Salvation Army and has given

toiletries and blankets to local charitable organizations. The Hilton also donated furniture to the local university to offer a more comfortable atmosphere for students. Many local students work at the hotel in a work-study program to gain practical experience while furthering their education.

Hilton employees have participated in promoting the United Way, the March of Dimes, and several Alaska Native organizations—and Hilton General Manager, Robert Southall, is a participant in the notorious Polar Bear Plunge, where participants take a dip in freezing water to raise money for the fight against cancer.

The Hilton Anchorage strives to provide equal access to the disabled by embracing the requirements of the Americans with Disabilities Act. This commitment to all its guests has allowed the Hilton Anchorage the opportunity to host the athletes participating in the Special Olympics, coming to Alaska in the year 2000, and to host the People First Convention in the past.

The Great Alaska Shootout is a huge event in the state, and the Hilton is proud to have hosted from two to four teams during the widely-publicized basketball games aired world-wide during the Thanksgiving holiday weekend.

The Hilton Anchorage provides a level of service unsurpassed in Alaska. The hotel's professionals go the extra mile to create the perfect atmosphere for guests while they enjoy the finest amenities during their visit.

The business traveler can rely on the Hilton Anchorage to meet their business needs. "Smart Rooms" are specially equipped with two phone lines, voice mail, data ports, and a working desk designed just for the business traveler.

Courtesy of Hilton Anchorage

Part of the Hilton mission is to provide quality, first-class service to everyone involved in the day-to-day process of keeping the hotel running. All employees work hard to ensure that all customers have memorable experiences during their stay in Alaska's heartland. These dedicated people work equally as hard to ensure that their vendors also are treated with due respect.

Hilton guests in Anchorage enjoy the same luxury found in its other hotels throughout the world. However, in Alaska, Mother Nature provides an added bonus. Look out of virtu-ally any of the 591 guest rooms and you can see the pristine beauty that can be found only in Alaska. The hotel houses 23 suites and three Executive floors with a bird's-eye view of this spectacular scenery. Gourmet dining, elegant shops, indoor swimming, and an exercise room are just a few of the luxurious accommodations located in the hotel.

Within walking distance are opportunities to see a play, visit a museum, go shopping, experience a controlled earthquake, or even catch a 50-pound Alaska King Salmon. For a relaxing evening, one can watch a glorious midnight sunset while strolling along part of Anchorage's 70-mile-long Coastal Trail.

Near the Hilton are local touring companies offering visitors a host of opportunities to see Alaska's most popular destinations, including

Courtesy of Hilton Anchorage

The Hilton Anchorage Business Center allows guests to keep the office at home. Services include: faxing capabilities, computer rentals, pagers, cell phones, photocopier, and package handling — everything needed to address business needs.

For excitement or just a relaxing drink, the Sports Edition Bar offers around-the-world sports via satellite available on 20 screens situated throughout the bar.

and the Chart Room, which has a nearly 360-degree view of the surrounding mountains, city-life and the waters of Cook Inlet.

Full catering services are available for conventions or business meetings. Hilton's catering professionals vow to go the extra mile to create the perfect atmosphere and to prepare a customized menu for any event—from a quiet breakfast on the top of a glacier, to a luncheon theme with the feel of the old Gold Rush town of Skagway, to an elegant dinner with quiet background music.

Businesses have grown to rely more on technology and the Hilton Anchorage has already begun to keep up with the pace

by creating "Smart Rooms." Within a year, every room is expected to be specially equipped to allow easy access to computer hookups on top of a desktop; or business representatives can visit the hotel's Business Center, where they can have access to virtually everything needed to run a successful company, including fax lines, photocopiers, secretarial services, pagers, cell phones, computer rentals, and package handling.

These are just a few of the amenities available at the Hilton Anchorage, where all the luxury and comfort are available for a quick business trip, an extended vacation, or just a weekend getaway.

Mt. McKinley, the Seward SeaLife Center, or any of several glacier tours. By developing a partnership with Holland America and Princess Tours, the Hilton Anchorage can also provide visitors with the opportunity to see many of Alaska's remote touring sites, making the state one of the top five cruising destinations in the world.

The Hilton Anchorage contains 16,000 square feet of premier banquet and meeting facilities, including two ballrooms, an executive boardroom,

The dining experience at the Top of the World Restaurant, located on the 15th floor, offers both visual wonder and exquisite gourmet cuisine served with Anchorage's best view of the Cook Inlet and Mt. McKinley.

ALASKA'S FISHING UNLIMITED LODGE

Since 1976, Alaska's Fishing Unlimited Lodge, a family owned and operated facility, has been providing a premier Alaskan fly-out fishing experience. Owner and operator Lorane Owsichek has created a little piece of paradise amongst Alaska's wilderness and rugged beauty, nestled on the shores of Hardenburg Bay on Lake Clark.

Clients from the United States as well as abroad fly out daily to fish areas surrounded by some of the most breathtaking vistas and wilderness imaginable. Packages available consists of a three-, three-and-one-half-, or seven-day stays. While at the lodge, anglers enjoy the luxury of nine private cabins set amid the trees near the shoreline, as well as two fully-stocked lodges, two wood-fired wet saunas and hot tubs and fabulous cuisine. Daily fly-out's in one of the Lodge's two Cessna 206 or two DeHavilland Beaver floatplanes allow exploration of some of the most productive fishing waters and wilderness in the Bristol Bay Drainage. The pilots/guides stay with the anglers the entire day, giving clients maximum freedom and flexibility to fish various locations and species. Guests have the opportunity to catch the five (5) species of Pacific Salmon (King, Red, Silver, Pink and Chum), Rainbow Trout, Arctic Char,

Arctic Grayling, Lake Trout and Northern Pike. Not only does Alaska's Fishing Unlimited Lodge endeavor to provide a premier fishing experience but also an all-encompassing Alaskan adventure.

As with many other Alaskan businesses, the Lodge is continuously striving to grow and improve its level of service to both its clients and community. The Lodge's business growth has expanded to include adventure packages featuring such activities as hiking, clam digging, sightseeing excursions, scenic float trips, and more. The hope is that guests will experience a broader range of activities in addition to, or instead of, just fishing. The facility also has the capability to provide corporate clientele with a complete conference/meeting environment in which to conduct a combination of business activities and personal relaxation.

Community enrichment, both locally and nationwide, is an important part of the company's overall philosophy. Every year trips, time, and money are donated to organizations locally and throughout the U.S. Some of these recipients include Wish-Upon-A-Star Foundation, Girl

Some of the most beautiful and productive fishing waters for both fly and spin fishermen are located in the Bristol Bay region.

Scout Council, Anchorage Museum Association, National Multiple Sclerosis Society and several other preservation and conservation organizations.

Alaska's Fishing Unlimited Lodge welcomes those from all over the world to experience Alaska and its unlimited country, unlimited fishing adventure, and unlimited memories!

Early morning fog rising over Alaska's Fishing Unlimited Lodge.

ANCHORAGE CHRYSLER DODGE

The automobile dealership that was the forerunner to the current Anchorage Chrysler Dodge Center had barely opened its doors when the roof fell in. Back in April of 1963, then 5th Avenue Chrysler was chartered as a new dealership and conducted business out of a trailer on Anchorage's east 5th Avenue. Less than a year later, a new building constructed to house the fledging operation was struck by the March 27th Good Friday earthquake of 1964, bringing the roof down.

No serious injuries resulted from the devastating quake as employees took cover under desks and tables. The task for founders and owners of the company, Kenneth B. Davis and Glen Phillips, was the same one that faced the entire community, rebuilding.

The 1996 Iditarod Champion Jeff King (left) accepts a Dodge Ram pickup truck from Rod Udd at the end of the race in Nome.

That challenge was met as a new building was constructed on the same site. It served as the principal structure for the business until 1972 when a second showroom and service facility was built nearby. The original structure become the Dodge Building and the new facility housed the Chrysler/Plymouth operations and became known as the Chrysler Building.

The ensuing years saw the dealership grow and change hands as first Davis acquired full ownership of the business, and

then sold it to another team of owners in 1979. Along the way, the combined dealership became a stellar performer, outselling all other dealers in the Chrysler Corporation's Northwest Zone.

By 1990, new leadership emerged as Anchorage Chrysler Dodge Center was acquired by Rod Udd, the current president, who started at the dealership several years earlier as a member of the sales staff. Udd credits the success of the business to several factors.

"The K-car helped revive Chrysler," said Udd, making reference to the front-wheel-drive model that closely followed Lee Iacocca's emergence as

Rod Udd, President, Anchorage Chrysler Dodge.

Anchorage Chrysler Dodge is an official sponsor of the Iditarod Sled Dog Race.

Courtesy of Anchorage Chrysler Dodge

Chrysler Corporation president. Iacocca took the reins of the company in 1981, a harrowing time for America's third-largest automaker.

The K-car platform and, in 1984, the introduction of the minivan, turned Chrysler's fortunes around and set a pattern of growth for the company that persists to this day. That good fortune is shared at the local level. "Chrysler has developed some extremely good products," adds Udd.

Another factor in the success of the dealership can be found in the approximately 140 employees that staff the sprawling complex at the eastern edge of downtown Anchorage. "We have some excellent long-term employees," says Udd.

The combination of a successful product backed by a dedicated staff accounts for the dealership's continued leadership in sales among Chrysler dealers. "We are expanding market share and have been doing so for years," Udd notes.

The success of the business translates to a broad range of support for community events and charitable causes. The most notable event is the dealership's annual sponsorship of the Iditarod Trail Sled Dog Race through its Dodge Truck division. The 1,110-mile Anchorage

Courtesy of Anchorage Chrysler Dodge

Rod Udd, President of Anchorage Chrysler Dodge, has the pleasure of turning over the keys of a brand-new Dodge Ram pickup to Three-Time Iditarod Champion Jeff King and his lead dog Jenna.

to Nome event, run each March, draws dog teams and mushers from across Alaska and the U.S., as well as international competitors.

Other beneficiaries of Anchorage Chrysler Dodge Center support range from the Big Brothers/Big Sisters and the Boys & Girls Club programs to sponsorship of the Lions Club District Convention. When Intervention Helpline, a local drug and alcohol counseling program, lost its refurbished 1984 van to theft and vandalism, Anchorage Chrysler Dodge Center came to the rescue.

"Rod's generosity put our program back on the road," says Bob Young, Intervention Helpline's Executive Director. The dealership lent the program

a minivan for use until they were able to take delivery of a new, full size Dodge van that was then donated to the program.

"Over the years, some of our employees have had alcohol or drug problems. I know how devastating that can be for a family," says Udd. "I appreciate what a program like Intervention Helpline does for people with those problems," he adds.

Optimistic about the future for Anchorage Chrysler Dodge Center, Udd recently acquired nearby property to allow for expansion. For a company with a well-established presence and enjoying record sales, that move seems like a safe bet.

CLARION SUITES

Anchorage's newest downtown hotel.

Since its grand opening in the spring of 1998, Clarion Suites has offered Anchorage visitors a unique opportunity for comfort, while still meeting the needs of business travelers. Located in the heart of downtown Anchorage, Clarion Suites is within walking distance of not only the city's shopping district, but the Federal Building, Arco Alaska, and the Bank of America buildings.

The hotel's 111 suites have something for everyone, from the vacationing family to the weary business traveler. Each suite has two separate rooms — a bedroom and a living room. Suites are complete with two televisions, two phones, microwave, refrigerator, coffee-maker, sofa sleeper and data ports. The hotel also features a nine-restaurant food court, swimming pool, whirlpool, exercise room and a business center.

The Anchorage Clarion Suites was founded by Steel Group, comprised of owners John Blomfield and George Swift. John, a third generation Alaskan, was born and raised in Anchorage and has been active in developing the city for many years. He designed and built the Federal Bureau of Investigations building on 7th Avenue, and owns several other buildings in Anchorage, including Ashley Home Stores, Boniface Plaza and an export company.

Currently residing in Seattle, Washington, George was part of the Anchorage construction boom of the 1980s. He is the president and owner of Western Steel, Inc., the hotel planning and development company that constructed the Clarion Suites in Anchorage.

In order to become increasingly involved with the community that supports the hotel, each member of the management team of Clarion will become partners with a non-profit organization. Clarion Suites has already become involved with the Food Bank of Alaska and the March of Dimes.

In the future, Clarion Suites plans to stay competitive in the marketplace by continually visiting target markets and cities to establish and maintain close sales relationships. Clarion employees will strive to maintain excellent service to its guests, going beyond what it takes to make each guest feel as if he or she is the most important person in the hotel.

Courtesy of Clarion Suites

Courtesy of Clarion Suites

Luxury and comfort await.

KEY PLAYERS

ALASKA AIRLINES
P.O. Box 68900
Seattle, Washington 98168
Telephone: (206) 433-3200
Facsimile: (206) 433-3379
Web Site: www.alaskaair.com/
Page 216

ALASKA DEPARTMENT OF
COMMUNITY AND ECONOMIC
DEVELOPMENT
P.O. Box 110804
Juneau, Alaska 99811-0804
Telephone: (907) 465-3961
Facsimile: (907) 465-3767
Web Site:
www.commerce.state.ak.us/trade
Page 202

ALASKA FIBER STAR, LLC
1029 West Third Avenue, Suite 150
Anchorage, Alaska 99501
Telephone: (907) 365-7250
Facsimile: (907) 272-0081
Web Site: www.akfiberstar.com
Page 232

ALASKA FILM OFFICE
DEPARTMENT OF COMMUNITY AND
ECONOMIC DEVELOPMENT
550 West Seventh Avenue,
Suite 1770
Anchorage, Alaksa 99501
Telephone: (907) 269-8137
Facsimile: (907) 269-8136
Web Site: www.alaskafilmoffice.com
Page 204

ALASKA FOREST ASSOCIATION
111 Stedman, Suite 200
Ketchikan, Alaska 99901
Telephone: (907) 225-6114
Facsimile: (907) 225-5920
Web Site: www.akforest.org
Page 255

ALASKA HOME MORTGAGE
P.O. Box 196850
Anchorage, Alaska 99519-6850
Telephone: (907) 563-3033
Facsimile: (907) 261-6401
Web Site:
www.alaskahomemortgage.com
Page 290

ALASKA INDUSTRIAL DEVELOPMENT
AND EXPORT AUTHORITY
480 West Tudor Road
Anchorage, Alaska 99503
Telephone: (907) 269-3000
Facsimile: (907) 269-3044
Web Site: www.aidea.org
Page 293

ALASKA INSTRUMENT CO., INC.
P.O. Box 230087
Anchorage, Alaska 99523-0087
Telephone: (907) 561-7511
Facsimile: (907) 561-0762
Web Site: akinstr@alaska.net
Page 292

ALASKA INTERSTATE
CONSTRUCTION, LLC
P.O. Box 233769
Anchorage, Alaska 99523
Telephone: (907) 562-2792
Facsimile: (907) 562-4179
Web Site:
http://www.aicconst@alaska.net
Page 318

ALASKA MARINE HIGHWAY SYSTEM
1591 Glacier Avenue
Juneau, Alaska 99801-1427
Telephone: (800) 642-0066 —
Reservations
Facsimile: (907) 465-2476
Web Site: www.dot.state.ak.us/
amhshome.html
Page 243

ALASKA NATIONAL GUARD
P.O. Box 5800, Camp Denali
Fort Richardson,
Alaska 99505-5800
Telephone: (907) 428-6031
Facsimile: (907)428-6035
Web Site: www.ngchak.org/dmva
Page 196

ALASKA OPTION SERVICES
CORPORATION
P.O. Box 196233
Anchorage, Alaska 99519-6233
Telephone: (907) 563-0078
Facsimile: (907) 563-7668
Page 289

ALASKA PUBLIC RADIO NETWORK
(APRN)
810 East 9th Avenue
Anchorage, Alaska 99501
Telephone: (907) 277-2776
Facsimile: (907) 263-7450
Web Site: www.aprn.org
Page 245

ALASKA RAILROAD CORPORATION
P.O. Box 107500
Anchorage, Alaska 99510-7500
Telephone: (907) 265-2300
Facsimile: (907) 265-2312
Web Site: www.akrr.com
Page 208

ALASKA REGIONAL HOSPITAL
2801 DeBarr Road
P.O. Box 143889
Anchorage, Alaska 99514-3889
Telephone: (907) 276-1131
Facsimile: (907) 264-1143
Web Site: www.alaskaregional.com
Page 307

ALASKA'S FISHING UNLIMITED
P.O. Box 190301
Anchorage, Alaska 99519
Telephone: (907) 243-5899
Facsimile: (907) 243-2473
Web Site: www.alaskalodge.com
Page 327

ALASKA STATE CHAMBER OF
COMMERCE
217 Second Street, Suite 201
Juneau, Alaska 99801
Telephone: (907) 586-2323
Facsimile: (907) 463-5515
Web Site: www.alaskachamber.com
Page 205

ALASKA STATE LEGISLATURE
SPEAKER OF THE HOUSE,
STATE CAPITAL
Juneau, Alaska 99801
Telephone: (907) 465-4930
Facsimile: (907) 465-3834
Web Site:
www.akrepublicans.org
www.akdemocrats.org
Page 198

ALASKA STATE LEGISLATURE
JOINT HOUSE/SENATE OFFICE OF
INTERNATIONAL TRADE POLICY
216 West 4th Avenue, Suite 630
Anchorage, Alaska 99501
Telephone: (907) 269-0160
Facsimile: (907) 269-0161
Web Site:
ronda-thompson@ legis.state.ak.us
Page 199

ALASKA USA FEDERAL
CREDIT UNION
P.O. Box 196613
Anchorage, Alaska 99519-6613
Telephone: (907) 277-5577
Facsimile: (907) 561-4857
Web Site: www.alaskausa.org
Page 280

ALASKA USA INSURANCE, INC.
P.O. Box 196100
Anchorage, Alaska 99519-6100
Telephone: (907) 272-6611
Facsimile: (907) 786-2085
Web Site:
www.alaskausainsurance.com
Page 288

ALASKA USA TRUST COMPANY
P.O. Box 196757
Anchorage, Alaska 99519-6757
Telephone: (907) 562-6544
Facsimile: (907) 561-8404
Page 283

THE ALEUT CORPORATION
4000 Old Seward Highway,
Suite 300
Anchorage, Alaska 99503
Telephone: (907) 561-4300
Facsimile: (907) 563-4328
Web Site: www.aleutcorp.com
Page 310

AMERICAN SEAFOODS COMPANY
Market Place Tower
2025 First Avenue, Suite 900
Seattle, Washington 98121
Telephone: (206) 448-0300
Facsimile: (206) 448-0505
Web Site: http://www.amsea.com
Page 268

ANCHORAGE CHRYSLER
CENTER, INC.
2601 East 5th Avenue
Anchorage, Alaska 99501
Telephone: (907) 276-1331
Facsimile: (907) 264-2202
Web Site: dodge@alaska.net
Page 328

ANCHORAGE INTERNATIONAL
AIRPORT
P.O. Box 196960
Anchorage, Alaska 99519
Telephone: (907) 266-2525
Facsimile: (907) 243-0663
Page 214

ARCTIC FOUNDATIONS
5621 Arctic Blvd.
Anchorage, Alaska 99518-1667
Telephone: (907) 562-2741
Facsimile: (907) 562-0153
Web Site:
www.arcticfoundations.com
Page 314

ARCTIC SLOPE REGIONAL
CORPORATION
301 Arctic Slope Avenue,
Suite 300
Anchorage, Alaska 99518
Telephone: (907)349-2369
Facsimile: (907) 349-5476
Page 256

ASRC COMMUNICATIONS LTD
201 East 56th Avenue,
Suite 210
Anchorage, Alaska 99518
Telephone: (907) 563-1176
Facsimile: (907) 261-2663
Web Site: asrcc.com
Page 224

AVIS RENT A CAR
P.O. Box 190028
Anchorage, Alaska 99519
Telephone: (907) 243-4300
Facsimile: (907) 249-8247
Web Site: avis.com
Page 236

BARTLETT REGIONAL HOSPITAL
3260 Hospital Drive
Juneau, Alaska 99801
Telephone: (907) 586-2611
Facsimile: (907) 463-4919
Web Site: www.bartletthospital.org
Page 306

BLUE CROSS BLUE SHIELD
OF ALASKA
2550 Denali Street, Suite 600
Anchorage, Alaska 99503
Telephone: (907) 258-5065
Facsimile: (907) 258-1619
Web Site: www.premera.com
Page 304

BOWHEAD TRANSPORTATION
P.O. Box 84982
Seattle, Washington 98124
Telephone: (206) 623-6036
Facsimile: (206) 623-6371
Web Site: bowhead.com
Page 239

CARLILE ENTERPRISES, INC.
1800 East 1st Avenue
Anchorage, Alaska 99501
Telephone: (907) 276-7797
Facsimile: (907) 278-7301
Web Site: www.carlilekw.com
Page 222

CHUGACH ELECTRIC ASSOCIATION
P.O. Box 196300
Anchorage, Alaska 99519-6300
Telephone: (907) 563-7494
Facsimile: (907) 562-0027
Web Site: www.chugachelectric.com
Page 230

CITY OF VALDEZ
P.O. Box 307
Valdez, Alaska 99686
Telephone: (907) 835-4313
Facsimile: (907) 835-2992
Web Site: vdzacm@alaska.net
Page 178

CITY OF WHITTIER
P.O. Box 608
Whittier, Alaska 99693
Telephone: (907) 472-2327
Facsimile: (907) 472-2404
Web Site Address:
JQFV74A@prodigy.com
Page 190

CITY OF WRANGELL
P.O. Box 531
Wrangell, Alaska 99929
Telephone: (907) 874-2381
Facsimile: (907) 874-3952
Web Site: www.wrangell.com
Page 186

CLARION SUITES
325 West 8th Avenue
Anchorage, Alaska 99501
Telephone: (907) 274-1000
Facsimile: (907) 274-3016
Web Site:
http://www.clarioninn.com/
hotel/AK017
Page 330

COMINCO ALASKA INCORPORATED
P.O. Box 1230
Kotzebue, Alaska 99752
Telephone: (907) 426-2170
Facsimile: (907) 426-2177
Web Site: www.cominco.com
Page 262

CROWLEY MARINE
SERVICES, INC.
2525 C Street, Suite 303
Anchorage, Alaska 99503-2639
Telephone: (800) 248-8632
Facsimile: (907) 257-2828
Web Site: www.crowley.com
Page 234

DELANEY, WILES, HAYES, GERETY,
ELLIS & YOUNG, INC.
1007 West Third Avenue,
Suite 400
Anchorage, Alaska 99501
Telephone: (907) 279-3581
Facsimile: (907) 277-1331
Web Site: dwhge@alaska.net
Page 276

DOWLAND BACH CORP.
P.O. Box 230126
Anchorage, Alaska 99523-0126
Telephone: (907) 562-5818
Facsimile: (907) 563-4721
Web Site: www.dowlandback.com
Page 258

E & S DIVERSIFIED
SERVICES, INC.
P.O. Box 140905
Anchorage, Alaska 99514-0905
Telephone: (907) 276-2018
Facsimile: (907) 276-6587
Web Site:
ESDMQC@worldnet.att.net
Page 291

EVERGREEN HELICOPTERS OF
ALASKA, INC.
1935 Merril Field Drive
Anchorage, Alaska 99501
Telephone: (907) 276-2454
Facsimile: (907) 279-6816
Web Site: Jerry@EvergreenAk.com
Page 226

FAIRBANKS INTERNATIONAL AIRPORT
6450 Airport Way, Suite 1
Fairbanks, Alaska 99709
Telephone: (907) 474-2500
Facsimile: (907) 474-2513
Web Site:
www.dot.state.ak.us/external/
aias/aias_fairbanks.html
Page 218

FOSS MARITIME COMPANY
660 West Ewing Street
Seattle, Washington 98119
Telephone: (206) 281-3800
Facsimile: (206) 281-4702
Page 242

GCI
2550 Denali Street, Suite 1000
Anchorage, Alaska 99503
Telephone: (907) 265-5600
Facsimile: (907) 265-5676
Web Site: www.gci.com
Page 212

GOLDEN VALLEY ELECTRIC
ASSOCIATION, INC.
P.O. Box 71249
Fairbanks, Alaska 99707-1249
Telephone: (907) 452-1151
Facsimile: (907) 451-5633
Web Site: www.gvea.com
Page 238

HILTON ANCHORAGE
500 W. Third Avenue
Anchorage, Alaska 99501
Telephone: (907) 272-7411
Facsimile: (907) 265-7140
Web Site: www.hilton.com
Page 324

KETCHIKAN GATEWAY BOROUGH
344 Front Street
Ketchikan, Alaska 99901
Telephone: (907) 228-6625
Facsimile: (907) 247-6628
Web Site: www.ktnboro.com
Page 182

KETCHIKAN GENERAL HOSPITAL
3100 Tongass Avenue
Ketchikan, Alaska 99901
Telephone: (907) 225-5171
Facsimile: (907) 228-8322
Web Site: http://www.ktn.net/kgh
Page 302

KIEWIT CONSTRUCTION COMPANY
1577 C Street, Suite 101
Anchorage, Alaska 99501
Telephone: (907) 222-9350
Facsimile: (907) 222-9380
Web Site:
http://anch.Kiewit-pbd.com
Page 316

LABORERS INTERNATIONAL UNION
OF NORTH AMERICA LOCAL 341
2501 Commercial Drive
Anchorage, Alaska 99501
Telephone: (907) 272-4571
Facsimile: (907) 274-0570
Web Site: laborers@alaska.net
Page 201

LYNDEN INCORPORATED
6441 South Airpark Place
Anchorage, Alaska 99502-1809
Telephone: (907) 245-1544
Facsimile: (907) 245-1744
Web Site: www.lynden.com
Page 228

MUNICIPALITY OF ANCHORAGE
632 West 6th Avenue, Suite 840
Anchorage, Alaska 99519-6650
Telephone: (907) 343-4431
Facsimile: (907) 343-4499
Web Site:
http://www.ci.anchorage.ak.us
Page 175

NATCHIQ, INC.
6700 Arctic Spur Road
Anchorage, Alaska 99518-1550
Telephone: (907) 344-5757
Facsimile: (907) 267-3166
Web Site: www.natchiq.com
Page 260

NC MACHINERY CO.
6450 Arctic Blvd.
Anchorage, Alaska 99518
Telephone: (907) 561-1766
Facsimile: (907) 786-7580
Web Site: www.ncmachinery.com
Page 312

NORTHERN AIR CARGO
3900 W. International
Airport Road
Anchorage, Alaska 99502
Telephone: (907) 243-3331
Facsimile: (907) 249-5190
Web Site:
www.northernaircargo.com
Page 241

NORTHERN TESTING
LABORATORIES, INC.
3330 Industrial Avenue
Fairbanks, Alaska 99701
Telephone: (907) 456-3116
Facsimile: (907) 456-3125
Web Site:
mrpntl@eagle.ptialaska.net
Page 284

NORTHWEST AIRLINES
5101 Northwest Drive
St. Paul, Minnesota 55111
Telephone: (800) 225-2525
Web Site: www.nwa.com
Page 220

PROVIDENCE HEALTH SYSTEM
P.O. Box 196609
Anchorage, Alaska 99519
Telephone: (907) 261-3145
Facsimile: (907) 261-3048
Web Site:
www.providence.org/alaska
Page 300

SEA-LAND DOMESTIC SHIPPING
COMPANY LLC
1049 W. Fifth Avenue
Anchorage, Alaska 99501
Telephone: (907) 263-5611
Facsimile: (907) 263-5620
Web Site Address:
Alaska_Sales@sealand.com
Page 240

SPACE MARK, INC.
5520 Tech Center Drive
Colorado Springs, Colorado
80919-2308
Telephone: (719) 531-9090
Facsimile: (719) 536-3560
Web Site: www.space-mark.com
Page 286

TANANA CHIEFS CONFERENCE
122 First Avenue, Suite 600
Fairbanks, Alaska 99701
Telephone: (907) 452-8251,
ext. 3268
Facsimile: (907) 459-3850
Page 200

TESORO ALASKA COMPANY
3230 "C" Street
P.O. Box 196272
Anchorage, Alaska 99519
Telephone: (907) 561-5521
Facsimile: (907) 561-6085/5047
Web Site:
www.tesoropetroleum.com
Page 248

TOTEM OCEAN TRAILER
EXPRESS, INC.
P.O. Box 24908
Seattle, Washington 98124
Telephone: (206) 628-4343
Facsimile: (206) 628-9245
Web Site: www.totemocean.com
Page 244

TRIDENT SEAFOOD CORPORATION
5303 Shilshole Avenue N.W.
Seattle, Washington 98107
Telephone: (206) 783-3818
Facsimile: (206) 782-7195
Web Site: www.tridentseafoods.com
Page 272

UDELHOVEN OILFIELD SYSTEM
SERVICES, INC.
184 East 53rd Avenue
Anchorage, Alaska 99518-1222
Telephone: (907) 344-1577
Facsimile: (907) 522-2541
Web Site: udelhoven.com
Page 252

UNIVERSITY OF ALASKA ANCHORAGE
3211 Providence Drive
Anchorage, Alaska 99508
Telephone: (907) 786-1800
Facsimile: (907) 786-6123
Web Site: www.uaa.alaska.edu
Page 296

WGM INC.
P.O. Box 100059
Anchorage, Alaska 99510
Telephone: (907) 276-5004
Facsimile: (907) 276-1629
Web Site: wgm.com
Page 264

WILDER CONSTRUCTION COMPANY
11301 Lang Street
Anchorage, Alaska 99515-3063
Telephone: (907) 344-2593
Facsimile: (907) 344-1562
Web Site:
bardiesc@wilderconstruction.com
Page 320

WORLD TRADE CENTER
ALASKA INC.
421 W. 1st Avenue, Suite 300
Anchorage, Alaska 99501
Telephone: (907) 278-7233
Facsimile: (907) 278-2982
Web Site: www.wtca.org
Page 203

PROJECT SUPPORTERS:
ARCO Alaska, Inc.
BP Exploration (Alaska) Inc.

BIBLIOGRAPHY

BOOKS:

Alaska: A Golden Past,
A Rich Future;
Wyndham Publications, Inc.,
Kirkland, WA, 1995.

BECKEY, FRED W.
Mt. McKinley, Icy Crown
Of North America,
The Mountaineers, Seattle, 1993.

DEARMOND, ROBERT N.
Alaska 1867-1959,
Alaska Historical Commission,
Anchorage, 1981.

DRUCKER, PHILIP
Cultures Of The North Pacific Coast,
Harper, Rowe, New York, 1965.

Facts About Alaska:
The Alaska Almanac,
Alaska Northwest Books,
Seattle, 1998.

FREDERICK, ROBERT A.
Alaska's Quest For Statehood
1867-1959,
Municipality of Anchorage, 1985.

GARFIELD, BRIAN
The Thousand-Mile War: World War
II In Alaska And The Aleutians;
Doubleday, New York, 1969.

HALLIDAY, JAN
Native Peoples Of Alaska;
Sasquatch Books, Seattle, 1998.

HINCKLEY, TED C.
The Americanization Of Alaska
1867-1897,
Pacific Books, Palo Alto, 1972.

HUNT, WILLIAM R.
North Of 53 pOs, The Wild Days
Of The Alaska-Yukon Mining
Frontier 1870-1914,
MacMillan, New York, 1974.

McCune, Don
Trail To The Klondike,
WSU Press, Pullman, WA, 1997.

MCFEAT, TOM
Indians Of The North Pacific Coast,
University of Washington Press,
Seattle, 1967.

MOORE, FERRIS
Mt. McKinley, The Pioneer Climbs,
The Mountaineers, Seattle, 1981.

MURPHY, CLAIRE RUDOLF
Gold Rush Women,
Alaska Northwest Books,
Seattle, 1997.

ROSCOW, JAMES P.
800 Miles To Valdez;
Prentice Hall, Englewood Cliffs,
NJ, 1977.

SATTERFIELD, ARCHIE
Klondike Park: From Seattle To
Dawson City, Fulcrum, Golden,
CO, 1993.

WATERMAN, JONATHAN
In The Shadow Of Denali,
Dell, New York, 1994.

WOODCOCK, GEORGE
The Hudson's Bay Company,
The MacMillan Co.,
New York, 1970.

THE WEB:

1997-98 information and statistics
were obtained via the World Wide
Web from the following governmental and private *Websites:*

Alaska Anthropological Association
www.alaska.net/~oha/aaa/index.htm

Alaska Demographic Information
www.labor.state.ak.us

Alaska Department of Commerce
and Economic Development
www.commerce.state.ak.us
Includes:
Alaska Department of Community
 and Regional Affairs (DCRA)
Alaska Department of Education
Alaska Department of Fish & Game
Alaska Department of Natural
 Resources
Alaska Department of
 Transportation

Alaska Forest Association
www.akforest.org

Alcanseek.com

Anchorage Telephone Utility
www.atu.com

Arctic Region Supercomputing
Center *www.asrc.edu/*

Arctic Slope Regional Corporation
(ASRC) *www.asrc.com*

Center for Global Change
www.chc.uaf.edu/

Cook Inlet Region, Inc (CIRI)
www.ciri.com

Doyon Ltd. *www.doyon.com*

Elmendorf Air Force Base
www.hqpacaf.af.mil

FAQALASKA *http://sled.alaska.edu/*

General Communications, Inc.
(GCI) *www.gci.com*

Mountaineering Club of Alaska
www.alaska.net/~mca/

National Park Service *www.nps.gov*

PMC Telecommunications
(Piquniq Management
Corporation) *www.alaska.net/~pmc/*

Public Technology, Inc (PTI)
http://pti.org

Sea-Land Service, Inc.
www.sealand.com

Ski Resorts Guide
www.skiresortguide.com

State of Alaska Home Page
www.state.ak.us

Telecommunications Information
Council *www.gov.state.ak.us/ltgov/*
TIC/tichome.html

The Great Alaskan Mall
(Alaskan.com) *www.alaskan.com*

Totem Ocean Trailer Express, Inc.
www.totemocean.com

U.S. Army Alaska (USARAK)
http://143.213.12.254/
HOME.HTM

University of Alaska Fairbanks
www.uaf.edu

INDEX

Page numbers in italics for photos

A

Abalone, 95

Accommodations, 324-326, 327, 330-331

Adak, 14, 28, 311

AFL-CIO, 201

Afognak, 112

Agriculture, 19, 28, 99-101, 157, 227

Agricultural and Forestry Experiment Station (AFES), 157

Air-ambulance service, 161, *301, 307*

Air cargo, 52, 214-215, 218-219, 241

Air Crossroads of the World, 16, 39, 52

Air freight, 52, 214-215, 218-219, 241

Airlines, 52, 216-217, 220-221, 241

Airplanes, small, 52, *54,* 106, 116, *219*

Airports, 16, 52, 185, 214-215, 218-219, 221

Air travel, 39, 52, 214-215, 216-217, 218-219

Alagnak Wild River, 120

Alascom, 67, 68

Alaska Aerospace Development Corporation, 67, *71,* 158, 202

Alaska Agricultural College and School of Mines, 154

Alaska Airlines, 52, *214,* 216-217, *216-217, 218,* 219, 221, 237

Alaska/Canada Highway, see Alaska Highway

Alaska Communications System, 64

Alaska Department of Community and Economic Development, 202

Alaska Department of Fish and Game, 112

Alaska Department of Military and Veterans Affairs-Alaska National Guard, 196-197

Alaska Department of Natural Resources, 86

Alaska Division of Oil and Gas, 78

Alaska Division of Tourism, 39

Alaska Film Office, 204

Alaska Fiber Star, *69,* 232-233, *232-233*

Alaska Forest Association, *21, 84, 86, 88, 89,* 255, *255*

Alaska Gold Company, 77

Alaska Highway, 29, 58-59, *59,* 61

Alaska Home Mortgage, 282, 290, *290*

Alaska Industrial Development and Export Authority (AIDEA), 263, 293, *293*

Alaska Interstate Construction, *76, 80, 163,* 318-319, *318-319*

Alaska Instrument Company, 292, *292*

Alaskaland, *21, 77*

Alaska Loggers Association, *88*

Alaska Marine Highway System, 36, 55, 185, 186, 192, *193,* 243, *243*

Alaska Magazine, 71

Alaska National Guard, 196-197

Alaska National Guard Youth Corp ChalleNGe, 197

Alaska Native Arts and Crafts (ANAC), 146

Alaska Native Enrollment Program, 145

Alaska Native Land Claims Settlement Act of 1971, 30, 132, 139, 198, 200, 256, 262, 281, 310

Alaskan brown bear, 39

Alaskan United Fiber Optic Cable System, 68

Alaska Option, 282, 289, *289*

Alaska Panhandle, 10, 61

Alaska Peninsula, 13, 14, 30, 120

Alaska Permanent Fund, 30, 165-166

Alaska Public Radio Network, 70, 254, *254*

Alaska Railroad Corporation, 19, 36, *38, 54,* 56, 110, 208-211, *208-211,* 214, *223, 233,* 234, 321

Alaska Range, 210

Alaska Regional Hospital, 162, 307, *307*

Alaska's Flag (state song), 49

Alaska Science and Technology Foundation, see ASTF

Alaska Seafood Marketing Institute, 95

Alaska's Fishing Unlimited Lodge, 327, *327*

Alaska State Chamber of Commerce, 205

Alaska State Defense Force, 196, *196*

Alaska State Fair, 19, 100, 103

Alaska State Joint House and Senate Office of International Trade Policy, 199

Alaska State Legislature, 153, 198, *198,* 199, *205*

Alaska, State of, 29, 56, *111,* 161, *162*

Alaska, Territory of, 28, 29, 58

Alaska Tourism Marketing Council, 39

Alaska Tsunami Warning Center, 33

Alaska USA Federal Credit Union, 280-282, *280-282,* 283, 288, 289, 290

Alaska USA Insurance, Inc., 282, 288, *288*

Alaska USA Trust Company, 282, 283, *283*

Alaska Visitors Association, 39

Alaska-Washington Airways, *31*

Alaska World Trade Center, 203, *203*

Alcan, see Alaska Highway

Alpine skiing, 39

Aleut Corporation, 14, 286, 310-311, *310-311*

Aleuts, 14, 135, 310-311

Aleutian Islands, 13, 14, 28, 56, *98,* 100, 135

Aleutian Range, 14

Aleutian Trench, 14

Alexander Archipelago, 10

Alpenglow Resort, 129

Alutiiq, 14, 135

Alyeska Marine Terminal, *181*

Alyeska Pipeline, *74-75, 258,*

Alyeska Pipeline Service Company, 74, *79,* 81, 85, 235, 292, 298

Alyeska Resort, 45, 126, *128, 316*

Amaknak Island, 14

American Federation of Labor and Congress of Industrial Organizations, see AFL/CIO

American fur trade, see Fur trade

American Seafoods Company, 268-271, *268-271*

Amoco, 78

ANAC, see Alaska Native Arts and Crafts

Anaktuvak, 24

Anan Bear and Wildlife Observatory, 186

Anchorage, *10,* 16, 19, 28, 33, 40, *44,* 45, 46, 49, 52, 56, *60,* 68, 71, *117,* 125, *128,* 135, 154, 162, 166, 170, 174-177, *174-177,* 180, 186, 209, 214-215, 250

Anchorage Chrysler Dodge, 328-329, *328-329*

Anchorage International Airport, 52, 174-175, *175,* 210, 214-215, *214-215,* 221, 241, 249, 320

Anchorage Museum of History and Art, *175*

Anchorage Telephone Utility, see ATU

Angoon, 24

Aniakchak National Monument, 123

Annette Island, 132

Anvik, 61

Anvil Creek, 26

Archipelago, 10, 14

Architectural services, 257

ARCO, 78, 253, 258, 292, 319

Arctic, 20, 33, 43, 56, 61, 109, *132-133, 135,* 136, 140, 157, 158, 170

Arctic Care, 196, *196*

Arctic Circle, 20, 86, 170

Arctic Foundations, Inc., 314-315, *314-315*

Arctic National Forest, 86

Arctic National Wildlife Refuge, 135

Arctic Ocean, 78, *140, 141, 257*

Arctic Region Supercomputing Center, 157

Arctic Slope Regional Corporation, (ASRC), 139, 224, 256-257, *256-257,* 260

Arctic Winter Games, 46

Artist communities, 19, 185

Asia, 20, 29, 132

ASRC, see Arctic Slope Regional Corporation

ASRC Communications, 224-225, *224-225*

ASTF, 71, 165

Athabascan, 20, 135, 139, *146*, 200, *200*

Atlanta, Georgia, 68

Atlantic Richfield, see ARCO

Atlas of Cook's Third Voyage, 1780, *139*

Attorneys, 276-279

Attu, 14, 28

ATU, 64

AT&T, 68

Aurora Satellite, 67

Aurora Borealis, 39, *158-159*

Automated teller services, 282, 289

Automobile rental, 236-237

Automobile sales, 328-329

Avalanche, *128*

Avis Rent a Car, 236-237, *236-237*

B

Baldwin Peninsula, 20

Balloon sightseeing, *42*

Bald Mountain communications site, *64-65*

Balto, 43

Bancroft, Sherrie, *292*

Banking industry, 165, 280-282, 283

Baranof, Alexander, 24

Baranof Island, 13

Bardi crab, *92*

Barge transport, 234-235, *234-235*, 239, 240, *240*, 242

Barnes, Ramona, 199

Barrow, 20, *36*, 136, *138*, 139, *140, 256*

Bartlett Regional Hospital, 162, 306, *306*

Baseball, *152*, 166

Basketball, 169, *296*

Basket craft, 135, 136, *144*

Battle of Sitka, see Sitka, Battle of

Bear, 12, 14, 39, 82, *109*, 119, 170, 191

Begich Boggs Visitor Center, *45*

Bellingham, Washington, 55

Beluga Coalfield, 77

Beluga Power Plant, 231

Beluga whales, 115, 140

Bering Sea, 14, 20, 61, *98, 103*

Bering, Vitus, 13, 14, 24, 135

Bethel, 45, 61

Betton Island, *89*

Bicycling, 16, *123*

Big Delta Historical Park, 125

Big Diomede Island, Russia, 20

Big Lake, 33

Biosphere Reserve, 123

Birch Creek, 61

Bird Creek, 117

Bird habitat, 82

Birds, 115

Bison, 112

Bjornstad, Gene, *230*

Black bear, 109, 191

Black gold, 29, 82

Black-tailed Sitka deer, 112

Blanket toss, *134, 147*

Blue Cross Blue Shield of Alaska, 162, 304-305, *304-305*

Boating, *156, 181, 190-191*

Boeing Aircraft, *60*, 216, *216, 220*, 241

Bowhead Transportation Company, 239, *239*

Bowhead whale, 49, 115, 140

Boy Scouts, *31*

BP Exploration (Alaska), 253, 258, 292, 319

Bridal Veil Falls, *181*

Bristol Bay, *92, 93*

Bristol Bay Double-enders, *93*

Bristol Bay fishery, 13

British Colombia, 61

Brooks Range, 78, 123, 125

Building codes, 33

Bulgaria, 199

Buschmann, Peter, 92

Bush, 52, 70, 71, 161

Bush Telegraph, 70

Business, 162-166, 205

Butcher, Susan, 43

C

Cable systems, 64, 71, 212

Caines Head State Recreation Area, 125

Camping, 106, *106-107, 118, 120-121, 123, 193*

Canada, 135, 199, 210

Canneries, fish, 13, 92, 96, 273

Canoeing, *156*

Canoes, birchbark, 125

Cantwell, 119

Cargo lighterage, 239, *242*

Cape Canaveral, 67

Cape Farewell, 26

Cape Krusenstern National Monument, 123

Caribou, 19, 39, 82, *100*, 110, 119, 135, 140

Caribou herding, 100, 140

Carlile Enterprises, Inc., 222-223, *222-223*

Carmack, George, 26

Carnival Cruise Lines, 56

Caterpillar equipment, 312-313

Cellular telephone, 71

Central America, 58

Char, 116

Chena Hot Springs, 19

Chena River, 19

Chena River State Recreation Area, 125

Cher, 145

Chief Shakes Island, 19, 186

Chief Shakes Tribal House, *19, 187*

Chilkat Bald Eagle Reserve, 125

Chilkat River, 61

Chilkat State Park, 125

Chilkoot Pass, *27*

Chilkoot Trail, 13, 26

China, Peoples Republic of, 199

Chinook salmon, see salmon

Chromite, 77

Chugach Electric Association, 230-231, *230-231*

Chugach Mountains, *128, 180*, 191, 210

Chugach Range, 125

Chugach State Park, 125

Chukchi Sea, 20

Churches, 14, 24, 46, 169, *169*

CIRI, see Cook Inlet Region, Inc.

Clams, 95

Clarion Suites, 330-331, *330-331*

Clean-air industry, 162

Clean-coal technology, 77, 238

Clearcutting, 86

Cleveland, 170

Climate, 10, 16, 19

Closed-circuit television, 71

Coal, 26, 77, 260

Coalbed methane, 78

Coastline, miles of, 10, 92

Cod, 95

Cold War, 29

College, 150, 154-161, 296-299

Columbia Glacier, 49

Cominco Alaska Incorporated, 262-263, *262-263*, 265

Communications, 64-71, 170, 224-225, 232-233

Computer, 71

Conrad, Daniel, *292*

Construction, 89, *163*, 253, 257, 260, 314-315, 316-317, 318-319, 320-321

Container ships, 56

Control systems, 258-259

Convention and Visitors Bureaus, 39

Cook, Captain James, 24

Cook Inlet, 16, 26, 30, 33, *52-53*, 78, 210

Cook Inlet oil fields, 78

Cook Inlet Region, Inc. (CIRI), 139

Copper, 26, 74, 77

Copper Days, 46

Copper River, 116

Cordova, 46, 78

Cowder, Representative John, 199

Coyote, 109

Crab, 95, *96-97*, 103

Crabbing/crab fishing, 13, *92, 96-97, 98, 103, 191*

Crab processing, *97*

Credit unions, 165, 280-282, 283

Cross-country skiing, 16, 39

Crowley Marine Services, *79*, 234-235, *234-235*

Cruciform style church, 14

Cruise ships, 14, 36, 39, *39*, 55, *55*, *186*, 188

Cry of the Wild Ram, 46

Curling, 39

Customs house, *27*

D

Dairy farming, 99
Dallas, 170
Dall Sheep, 112, 119
Dawson, 26
Dawson Creek, British Colombia, 59
Deadhorse, 26
Deadhorse Pass, 26
Deep-water port, ice-free, 19
Deer, *21,* 112, 191
Deer Mountain, 183
Delaney, Wiles, Hayes, Gerety, Ellis & Young, Inc., 276-279, *276-279*
Delta, 59
Delta Airlines, 219
Delta Junction Buffalo Wallow Square Dance Jamboree, 46
Denali, 119, 210
Denali National Park and Preserve, *38,* 49, 77, 119, 120, *120-121,* 135, 210
Denali State Park, *121,* 125
DEW stations, see Distant Early Warning stations
Digital technology, 71, 213
Dillingham, 13
Diphtheria, 33, 43
Distant Early Warning stations, 29, 64, 67
Division I Western Collegiate Hockey Association, *153*
Donlin Creek, 77
Donnely Dome, *42-43*
Dowland Bach, 258-259, *258-259*
Drake, Marie, 49
Ducey, Cindy, *276, 278*
Dungeness crab, see crab
Dusenbury, Elinor, 49
Dutch Harbor, 14, 28, *29,* 56
Dyea, 26

E

Eagle, 191
Eagle, bald, 115, *115*
Eagle, (City of), 19
E & S Diversified Services, 291, *291*
Earthquake Park, 33
Earthquakes, 33, *76*
Economy, 10, 13, 14, 202, 205
Eco-tourism, 39
Ecuador, 199
Education, 150, 154-161, *166, 167,* 179, 296-299
Eek, 61
Egan Convention Center, *175*
Egigik, 24
Ellis, Steve, *276*
Electric utilites, 230-231, 238
Elk, 112
Elmendorf Air Force Base, 28, 280, 291, 296
Endicott causeway, *80*
Energy, 165
Engineering, 257, 260, 314-315
England, 24, 52
Environmental cleanup, 321
Environmental impact, 81-82, 85, 86, 284-285
Environmental testing, 284-285
Equipment, heavy, 312-313, 316
Eskimos, 14, *36,* 99, *134,* 136, *137, 138,* 140, *147, 150*
Europe, 24, 64, 199
Evans, Barry, *291*
Evans, Willie Mae, *291*
Evans, Mayfield, *291*
Evergreen Helicopters, *124-125,* 226-227, *226-227*
Exit Glacier, 123
Export trade, 52, 162
EXXON, 78
EXXON *Valdez,* 33, 85

F

Fabrication, 260
Factory trawlers, 96, *269*
Fairbanks, 19, *21,* 26, 28, 33, *36, 38,* 40, 42, 45, 46, 52, 56, 59, 64, 68, 78, 99, *119,* 135, *150-151,* 154, 157, 170, 210, 218-219
Fairbanks Flood of 1967, 33
Fairbanks Ice Alaska, *36-37, 150-151*
Fairbanks Industrial Development Corporation, 219

Fairbanks International Airport, 52, 218-219
Farming, 99-101
Far North/Arctic, 20
Federal Telecommunications Act of 1996, 68
Federally designated wilderness, 10
Ferries, 36, 55, *193, 243, 243*
Festival of Native Arts, 46
Fiber-optic technology, *67,* 68, 71, 213, 232-233
Film Industry, *66,* 204
Financial services, 165, 280-282, 283, 288, 289, 290, 293
Fire Starter, 150
Fireweed, *157*
Fish drying rack, *135*
Fishing, 13, 28, 36, 39, *40-41,* 46, 61, 92-98, *102-103,* 103, 106, *106,* 116, *116, 117,* 123, 132, *135, 164, 180, 187,* 191, 310-311, 327
Fishing boats, *24-25, 92-93, 94, 96, 98, 99, 102-103, 178, 182, 187, 188, 269, 273*
Fishing, commercial, 10, 14, 19, 20, 92-98, 132, *164,* 268-271, 272-273
Fishing, sport, (see also, "Fishing"), 116, 327
Fish habitat, 21, 82
Fishwheel, *95*
Fjords, 10, 36, 191
Flag, Alaska State, 49
Float planes, *40-41,* 52, *56,* 116, *182, 185,* 219
Flounder, 95
Forests, 10, 86-89, 119, 255
Forest management, 21, 255
Forest products industry, 86-89, *89,* 255

Forest regeneration, 21, 255
Forget-me-not, 49, *322-323*
Fork Mine, 77
Fort Knox Mine, 77
Fort Richardson, 280, 296
Fort Wainwright, 28
Foss Maritime Company, 242, *242*
France, 24
Freight, 222-223, 228-229, 234-235, 239, 240, 241, 242, 244
Frey, Mano, *201*
Friderici, Jim, *276*
Fuhs, Paul, *199*
Fur Rendezvous, 19, 40, 46
Fur seal, 92, 115
Fur trade, 13, 14, 24, 61, 92, 198
F/V Bountiful, 98
F/V Oceanic, 98

G

Galena, 61
Galleries, 16
Garnet Ledge, 187
Gateway Alaska, 214-215
Gas, 74, 78-82
Gas industry, 74, 92, 292
Gas reserves, 74
Gates of the Arctic, 123
GCI, 68, 212-213, *212-213*
Geese, 115
General Fund, 92
Geoduck, 95
Geography, 10, 13, 14
Geology, *159*
Geophysical Institute, 157-158, *158-159*
George Inlet, 183
Gerety, Dan, *276, 277*
Gilbert & Sullivan, 169
Gillnetters, *92,* 96
Glacier Bay National Park, 45, 49, *122,* 123
Glaciers, 10, *15, 36,* 45, *47,* 52, *122,* 123, *123, 124-125,* 180, *190-191, 192-193, 204*
Glenn Highway, 56, 180
Global Communications, 29
Global Sentinel, 213
Goat, mountain, 12, *13, 108,* 119
Gold, 10, 19, 24, 26, 49, 77, *83,* 198, 265
Golden Valley Electric Association, 238, *238*

Gold, panning, *83*

Gold rush, 13, 24, 26, *48,* 61, 64, *83*

Gold Rush Stampede, 46

Golf, 46, 74, 156, 166

Good Friday Earthquake of 1964, 33

Gorsuch, Edward Lee, *299*

Government, federal, 16, 28, 56, 64, 67, 99, 139, 145, 192

Government, state, 10, 16, 153, 162

Governor, 153, *196, 205,* 209, *221, 245*

Governor, Lieutenant, 153

Grayling, 116

Gray whales, 39, 115, 143

Gray wolf, 109

Great Alaska Shootout, 169

Great Depression, 99

Great Land, 52-53

Greenland, 112

Green's Creek Mine, 77

Grizzly bear, *12, 64,* 109, 119, 191

Gross State Product, 6

Growing season, *101*

Guidi, Andrew, *276, 278*

Gulf of Alaska, 123

H

Haida, 132, 186, *189*

Haines, 45, 56

Hajdukovich, Jim, *296*

Halibut, 19, *94,* 95, 103, 116, 191

Halloween, 171

Ham radio, 70

Harbor seals, 115

Harding Ice Field, 123

Harding, President Warren G., 56

Hard-rock mining, 26

Hatcher Pass, 45

Hawaii, 115

Headrick, Amy, *276*

Healy, 77, 119

Healy Clean Coal project, 238

Helicopters, *124-125, 196, 226-227, 226-227*

Hematite, 77

Herring, 95, 96

Higher education, 140, 154-161, 296-299

Highways, 29, 56, 58-59

Hiking, 16, 120, *126, 157,* 180, *190*

Hiking, heli-, *124-125*

Hilltop, 129

Hilton Anchorage Hotel, 324-326, *324-326*

Hockey, 39, *153,* 169

Hogback Trail, *127*

Holland America Cruise Lines, 56

Holy Cross, 61

Homer, 19, 45, *47*

Hoonah, 24, 55

Horizon Air, 217

Horse riding, *47*

Hospitals, 160-162, *160, 161,* 185, 300-301, 302-303, 306, 307

Hotels, 16, 324-326, 330-331

House of Representatives, State, 153

Hudson's Bay Company, 26, 135

Hughes Communications, 68

Humpback whales, 39, 115, 143

Hunting, 14, 36, 39, 61, 106, 191

Hurricane Gulch, 36

Huskies, 40

I

Icebergs, *45*

Ice climbing, *127,* 180

Ice fields, 36, *47*

Ice fishing, 39, 46

Ice fog, 39

Ice sculpture, *36-37,* 46, *150-151*

Icy Straits Packing Company, 92

Iditarod National Historic Trail, 43

Iditarod Sled Dog Race, 19, 20, 40, *40,* 43, 45

Igloos, 170

Iliamna, 77

Illinois Creek Mine, 77

Independence Day, *152*

Information Technology, 224-225

Infrastructure, 162, *163*

Inside Passage, 10, *32-33,* 36, 55, 56, 116, 181, 183, 186

Institute of Arctic Biology, 157

Institute of Northern Engineering, 157

Instrumentation, 292

Insurance services, 288

Insurance services, health, 304-305

Interior, 19, 43, 46, *48-49,* 49, 109, 112, 119, 135, *156,* 179, 200, 209

International Arctic Research Center, 157

International Date Line, 20

International business, 16, 199, 205

International trade, 199, 202, 203, 205

Internet, 69, 71, 161

Inupiat Eskimos, 20, 136, 224, 256-257, 260, 262

Investment services, 283

Isaac, Chief Andrew, 200

Ivory, walrus, 140

J

Jack London, 6

Jade, 49, 77

Japan, 14, 28, 46, 52, 58, 86, 96

Japanese plane, *29*

Jefferson, 56-57

Jesse Lee Orphan's Home, 14

Jet America, 217

John, Chief Peter, *200*

Joint House and Senate Office of International Trade Policy, 199

Juneau, 10, 26, 29, 39, 45, 49, 52, 64, 154, 162, 170, 185, 186, 198

Juneau Airport, 52

K

K&W Transportation, 222, *223*

Kachemak Bay, 19, *47,* 116

Kachemak Bay State Park, 125

Kake, 55

Kamchatka Peninsula, Siberia, 14

Kansas, 170

Kasaan, *31*

Katmai National Park and Preserve, 13, 30, 120

Kaltag, 61

Kantishna, 119

Katalla, 78

Kayaks, 135

Kayaking, 119, *122,* 123, 180, 190

Kelly, Mike, *238*

Kenai, 19, 24, 78

Kenai Fjords national Park, 123

Kenai Lake, *87*

Kenai Mountain, *87*

Kenai Range, 125

Kenai Peninsula, 19, 78, 135

Kenai River, 19, 49, 116

Kennecott Copper, 74

Kensington Mine, 77

Ketchikan, 10, *24-25,* 30, *32-33, 56-57,* 64, *99,* 125

Ketchikan Gateway Borough, 182-185

Ketchikan General Hospital, 162, 302-303, *302-303*

Ketchikan Totems, 49

Kiewit Construction Group, Inc., 316-317, *316-317*

Killer whales, 115, 143

King crab, see Crab

King salmon, see Salmon

King Salmon, (City of), 13, 120

Kiska, 14, 28

Klodike gold, 13, 61

Klondike Gold Rush National Historic Park, 123

Klondike Gold Rush of 1898, 24, 26

Knik, 45

Knowles, First Lady Susan, *221*

Knowles, Governor Tony, *196, 205, 221, 245*

Kobuk River, 61, 116

Kobuk Valley National Monument, 123
Kodiak, 14, 24, 45, 46
Kodiak brown bear, 14, 109
Kodiak Island, 13, 67, *71*, 109, 116, *117*, 158, *202*
Kodiak Launch Complex, 67, *71, 158, 202*
Korea, 199, 210
Kostiouchenko, N., *199*
Kotzebue, 20
Kotzebue Sound, 20
Koyukuk River, 61
Kuskokwim River, 61
Kuspuk, *36*
Kuukpik Transportation, 222

L

La Bolle, Pamela, *205*
Ladd Field, 28
Lake Hood, 52
Lamb, Tim, *276*
Law firms, 276-279
Lawyers, see Attorneys
Lazar, Howard, *276, 278*
Lead, 26, 77, 262-263
Leisure and recreation industry, 106
Legislature, state, 153, 198
Libraries, 166
Limbo, 66
Lindh, Hilary, 126
Little Diomede Island, 20
Little Norway Festival, 46
Lockheed Aircraft, *217*
Lodges, 327
Logging, 28, 86, 132, 255
London, 52
Longhouses, 132
Long-liners, 94, 96
Long Tom, *26*
Low bush cranberry, *47*
Lumber mills, 86
Lynden, Inc., 228-229, *228-229*
Lynx, 110

M

Machinery, 312-313
Malemutes, 40
Manhattan, 170
MAPCO Alaska, *211, 292*
Marathons, 45
Marine life, 39, 49, 180, 191
Marine mammals, 96, 115
Marine support services, 242
Marquez, David, *205*
Matanuska/Susitna Valleys, 19, 99, 103
McBride Glacier, *204*
McGrath, 61
Meat processing, 99
Medical care, 160-162, *160, 161,* 185, 300-301, 302-303, 304-305, 306, 307
Mendenhall Glacier, 45, 49
Merrill, Russ, *60*
Methodist Church, 14
Metropolitan Area Network, 68
Mexico, 115
Meyers, Donna, *276, 278*
Microwave broadcast, *70,* 71
Midnight Sun, Land of, 20
Midnight Sun Baseball Game, 19, 46
Midnight Sun Hot Air Balloon Classic, 46
Migration routes, 82
Miller, Senator Mike, *198,* 199, *199*
Mineral and Petroleum Development Laboratories, 157
Mining, 10, *17,* 20, *26,* 28, 77, *82,* 262-263, 264-265, 292, 317
Mining services, 264-265
Mitkof Island, 13
Moe, Tommy, 126
Molybdenum, 77
Moose, *38,* 39, *74,* 82, 110, 119, 135, *171*
Morse, Samuel F., 64
Mortgage services, 290
Mosely, Bill, 276
Mosquitoes, 115
Motto, state, 49
Mountain climbing, 106, 120, 125
Mountaineering, see Mountain climbing
Mountaineering Club of Alaska, Inc., 125

Mountain goat, see Goat
Mountains, 36, *123*
Mountains, nation's highest, 10, *120-121*
Mount Fairweather, 123, 125
Mount Foraker, 125
Mount Hunter, 125
Mount McKinley, 36, 119, 120, *120-121,* 125
Mount Redoubt, 26, 30
Mount Saint Augustine, 30
Mount Saint Elias, 123, 125
Mount Spurr, 30
Mount Wrangell, 125
Mukluks, 43
MultiVisions, 71
Mushing, 39, 40, *40,* 45, 49, *165*
Mushing associations, 40
Mushing World Championship, 40
Museums, 16, 185
Music, 16, 46
Musk ox, 112, 132
Musk oxen herding, 100
M/V Aurora, 55
M/V Bartlett, 55
M/V Colombia, 243
M/V Le Conte, 55
M/V Kennicott, 55, 243, *243*
M/V Malaspina, 55
M/V Matanuska, 55
M/V Tustumena, 55
Mystrom, Mayor Rick, 174, *174*

N

Naa Kahidi Theater, 136
NANA Regional Corporation, 77, 139, 262-263, 264, 265
Nancy Lake State Recreation Area, 125
Nanek, 13, *92*
Nanek River, 61
Narrow Cape, *202*
Natchiq, 260-261, *260-261*
National Historic Park at Sitka, 123, 132
National Park Service, 123
National Petroleum Reserve-Alaska, 78
Native arts/crafts, 112, 132, 135, *136, 144,* 146, 185, 186
Native corporations, 14, 30, 86, 119, 132, 139, 145, 222, 223, 224-225, 239, 256-257, 260-261, 262-263, 264, 265, 277, 281, 286-287, 310-311
Native culture, 49, 115, 132, 135, 136, *136,* 169, *189, 200, 257, 310*
Native peoples, 13, 14, 20, 24, 30, 39, 61, *95,* 96, 99, 110, 119, 132-147, 158, 170, 200, 257, 287, 319
Native Regional Corporations, see Native corporations
Natural gas, 74, 78
Natural resources, 74-89
Navajo, 135
Naval Petroleum Reserve #4, 78
N. C. Machinery Company, 312-313, *312-313*
Nemo Point Campground, *10-11,* 118
Nenana, 19, 56
New Town, *82*
New York, 52
New Zealand, 199
Niblack Mine, 77

Nickel, 77
Nikiski, 78
Nixon Mine, 77
Noatak National Monument, 123
Nome, 19, *20, 26,* 29, 43, 45, 64,
    77, *100,* 162
North American Open, 40
Northern Air Cargo, *60,* 241, *241*
Northern Commercial Company,
    26
Northern Exposure, 153
Northern Lights, 39
Northern Testing Laboratories,
    284-285, *284-285*
North Pole, 78
North Slope, 78, 81, 82, *142-143*
North Slope oil, 29, 179
Northway, Chief Walter, 200
Northwest Airlines, 52, 219,
    220-221, *220-221*
Northwest Alaska Native
    Association, see NANA Regional
    Corporation
Northwest Arctic Borough,
    262, 263
Northwest Arctic Coalfield, 77
Norton Sound, 20
Novarupta Volcanoe, 30, 120
Norwegian Cruise Lines, 56
Nulato, 61
Nunavak Island, 110

O
Oil, 29, 74, 78-82, 198, 260
Oil extraction, 19
Oilfield services, 252-254, 257,
    258-259
Oil industry, 29, 74, 92, 165-166,
    248-251, 252-254, 292, 318
Oil production, 74
Oil reserves, 74
Old-growth preservation, 86
Oonalashka, *139*
Operation Allied Force, 197
Operation Desert Storm, 197
Orca, *144*
Orcas, see killer whales
Outdoor activities, 106-129
Ozerov, Viktor, *199*

P
Pacific Rim, 33, 95, 96
Pacific Northwest, 95, 132, 140
Palmer, 19, 33, 103
Pan-American Highway, 58
Panama City, 58
Parkas, 135
Parks, 13, 16, *38,* 45, 49, 106,
    119-125
Parks Highway, 56
Park Station Hotel, 119
Passage Canal, 191
Paxton Lake, *20-21*
PBS, 71
PeaceHealth, 162, 302-303
Pearce, Senator Drue, 199, *199*
Pearl Harbor, 28, 58
Pebble Copper Mine, 77
Pelican, (City of), 55
Peregrine falcon, 82, 115
Permafrost, 20, 81, 82, 86
Permanent Fund,
    see Alaska Permanent Fund
Petersburg, 13, 46, 55, 92
Petroglyph Beach, 186
Petroleum, 29, 74, 248-251
Petroleum distribution,
    248-251, 257
Petroleum refinery, *80-81*
Petroleum refining, 248-251, 257
Petro Star Refinery, 179, 261
Phillips, Representative Gail,
    198, 199, *199*
Phillips, Senator Randy, 199
Pike, 116
Placer gold, 26
Platinum, 77
Pogo, 77
Point Barrow, 20, *137*

Poker Flat Rocket Range, 158
Polar bear, 39, 109, *109,* 136, 170
Polar routes, 16, 52
Pollock, 95, 96
Polymetallic mines, 77
Ponomarev, Alex, *199*
Population, 10, 13, 14, 16, 19, 20
Porcupine Herd, 110
Porcupine River, 61
Porpoise, 115
Portage, 191, 210
Portage Glacier, 45, *45,* 49
Portage Lake, *45*
Portage Pass, 191
Porter, Representative Brian,
    199, *199*
Port Safety, 64
Potable water testing, 284-285
Potlatch celebration, 132
Power companies, 230-231, 238
Prince of Wales Island, 132
Prince William Sound, 16, 19, 24,
    33, 45, 49, 55, 86, *113,* 116,
    178, 180, *180,* 191, 192, 210
Prince William Sound Community
    College, 179
Prince Rupert, British Colombia,
    55
Princess Cruise Lines, 56
Printers, 64
Providence Health System,
    160, 162, 300-301, *300-301*
Providence of Alaska Foundation,
    162
Prudhoe Bay, 29, 78, 81, 85
Ptarmigan, *114*
Ptarmigan, arctic, *108*
Ptarmigan, Willow, 49, 115
PTI, 64, 68
Public schools, 140
Public Technology Inc., see PTI
Public Broadcasting System,
    see PBS
Publishers/Publishing, 64, 71
Puffins, *1, 114,* 115, *170*
Pulp mills, 86
Purse seiners, 96

Q
Quiviut, 112

R
Racing, 40, 43, 45
Radio, 64, 70, 245
Radio systems, 225
Rafting, 46, 106, *118, 180*
Rainforests, 10, 86
Ranching, 100
Raspberry Island, 112
Raven, 115
RCA Alascom, see Alascom
Real Estate, 89, 310-311
Recreation and leisure industry, 106
Red Dog Mine, *52,* 77, *77,* 242,
    242, 262, 262-263, 264, 265,
    293, *293,* 319
Redington, Joe Sr., 43
Reindeer, 99, 110, 140, 157
Reindeer herding, 99-100, 140, 157
Reindeer sausage industry, 100, 110
Religion, 14
Relia, Scot, 150-151
Remote earth stations, 68
Restaurants, 16, 326
Resource development, 74-89
Resurrection Bay, 19, 116, 210
Revillagigedo Island, 24
Richardson Highway, 180
Richter scale, 33
Riddles, Libby, 43
Riverboats, *21, 48,* 106
Roadhouse, 119
Rock climbing, 106
Rockfish, 95
Rock, Gerard, 226, *227*
Roosevelt Elk, 112
Round-log exports, 86
Royal Caribbean Cruise Lines, 56
Royal Viking Cruise Lines, 56
Ruby, 61
Russia, 24, 26, 28, 136, 199
Russian America, 13, 14
Russian culture, 49
Russian fur trade, see Fur trade
Russian Mission, 61
Russian Orthodox Church,
    14, 24, 46, *311*
Russian Orthodox Church of the
    Holy Ascention of Christ, 14
Revillagigedo Island, 10

S

Sablefish, 95
Safe Harbor Church, *272*
Saint Elias Mountains, 123
Salmon, 19, 49, 61, 92, 95, 96,
  103, 116, *117,* 135, *135, 145,*
  180, 191
Salmon Council, 95
Salmon, Chief David, *200*
Salmon Run Trails, 191
Samoyeds, 40
Satellites, 64, 67, 68, *68,* 71, 158,
  213, 225, 232
Scallops, 95
School of Fisheries and Ocean
  Sciences, 157
Sculpture, *150*
Sculpture, ice, see Ice sculpture
Sea bass, 191
Seafood, 13, 32, 92-98, 189,
  268-271, 272-273
Seafood processing plant, *92, 272*
Seafood production, 92, 189,
  268-271, 272-273
Sea cucumbers, 95
Sea kayaking, *122*
Sea-Land Domestic Shipping, LLC,
  240
Sea lions, *113,* 115
Seals, 92, 115, 135, 191
Sea otter, 24, 92, 115, 135
Sea urchins, 95
Seattle, Washington, 26, 64, 123,
  185, 186
Sedwick, Commissioner
  Deborah B., *202*
Seiners, 96
Senate, State, 153
Seppala, Leonhard, 43, *304*
Seward, 19, 45, 123, 210
Seward Highway, 56
Seward, William, 28
Seward Peninsula, 20, 110
Seward's Folly, 28
Shady Ladies, *188*
Shakes Glacier, 186
Shallow draft landing crafts,
  239, *239*
Shallow Gas Leasing Program, 78

Sheep-raising industry, 14, 100
Sheldon Jackson Junior College,
  150
Shelikof, Grigorii, 24
Shelikof Strait, *117*
Shipping, 52-61, 222-223,
  228-229, 234-235, 239, 240,
  244, 248-251
Shoemaker Bay Harbor, *189*
Shoup Bay Marine Park, 125
Shrimp, 95, 96
Shubina, Lyubov, *199*
Shuyak Island State Park, 125
Siberia, 14
Sightseeing, 36, 39, *42,* 45, 106,
  123, 180
Silver, 26, 74, 77, 265
Silverheels, Jay, 145
Silver salmon, see salmon
Sisters of Providence, 162, 300-301
Sisters of St. Joseph of Peace,
  162, 302-303
Sitka, 13, 24, 45, 46, 49, 64, 123,
  132, 150, 169
Sitka, Battle of, 24, 123, 132
Sitka Spruce, 49
Skagway, 13, 26, 45, 46, 49,
  56, *61,* 123
Skiing, 16, 39, 45, 106, 126,
  129, 180
Skiing, alpine, 126
Skiing, cross-country, 126
Skiing, extreme, 106, *180*
Skiing, heli-, *124-125,* 180
Ski jumping, *124*
Ski resorts, 106
Slavin, Peter, 150-151
Sled dogs, 40, *55,* 109
Smith, Jefferson (Soapy), 26
Sniffen, Ed, *276*
Snowmobiling, 39, 45, *127,* 180
Softball, 46
Soldotna, 45
Sole, 95
Southcentral/Gulf Coast, 13, 16,
  19, 49, 55, 56, 119, 123, 135
Southeastern, 10, 14, 36, 45,
  49, 55, 56, 64, 86, *99,* 109,
  112, 123, 125, 132, 136, *136,*
  143, 186
Southwestern, 13-14, 55, 120, 135
Space Mark,
  286-287, *286-287,* 311
Spain, 24

Stark, Jeff, *276*
Starfish, *113*
Star Trek, *204*
State captial, 10
State High School Basketball
  Championship, 169
Statehood, 29
Sterling Highway, 56
Sternwheeler, *21, 48*
Stikine River, 61, *115,* 186
Submarine Beach, *26*
Subsistence hunting/fishing,
  39, 96, 115, 132, *132-133,*
  135, 136, 140, 143, *257*
Sullivan Sports Arena, *175*
Summer sports/recreation, 36
Support services,
  286-287, 291, 311
Surprise Cove Marine Park, 125
Susitna Valley,
  see Matanuska-Susitna Valleys
Susitna River 116
Swenson, Rick, 43
Symphony, 166, *168*

T

Taiga, 19, 36
Talkeetna Bachelor's Festival, 46
Talkeetna Bluegrass Festiva, 46
Tanana Chiefs Conference, 200
Tanana River, *48,* 61, 125, 200
Tanana River Valley, 26, 99
Tanker, *79*
Tarn Project, *76, 163,* 319
Taiwan, ROC, 199
Tax credits, 165
Tax structure, 74, *163*
Telecommunications, 64, 67,
  68-69, 158, 212-213, 224-225,
  232-233, 286-287, 317
Telecommunications Act of 1996,
  212
Telegraph, 64
Television, 64, *66,* 70-71, 212
Tenakee, 55
Tennis, 166
Tern, Arctic, 115

Tesoro Alaska, 78, *78-79, 80-81,*
  248-251, *248-251,* 292
Texas, 10
Theater, 16
Thirteenth Corporation
  (see also Native corporations),
  139, 145, 256
Thomas, Don, *276, 279*
Thompson Pass, *126*
Timber, 10, 13, 32, *84-84,* 86-88,
  86-87, 88-89, 189, 255
Tlingit, 13, 132, 136, 186, *189*
Tok, 19, 45
Tokyo, 52
Tolkachova, Tania, *199*
Tongass Narrows, 183
Tongass National Forest,
  10, 86, 186
Totem, totem poles, *4,* 10, *18,*
  30-31, 123, 132, *138,* 143, *184,*
  186, *187*
Totem Bight Historical Park, 125
Totem Ocean Trailer Express,
  52-53, 244, *244*
Tourism, 10, 13, 16, 36-49,
  56, 257
TransAlaska Pipeline, 19, 29, 78,
  81-82, 85, 209, 217, 218, 229,
  235, 238, 277, *277,* 281, 313
TransAtlantic cable, 64
Transport, 52-61, 222-223,
  228-229, 234-235, 239, 240,
  241, 242, 243, 244
Transport, marine, 234-235, 239,
  240, 242, 243, 244
Trapping, 61
Trawlers, 96
Treadwell Mines, 74
Trident Seafoods, *92-93, 98,*
  272-273, *272-273*
Trollers, 96
Trout, 116
Trust companies, 165
Tsar of Russia, 24
Tsimshian, 132
Tsunamis, 33
Tug boat, *79,* 234-235, *235,*
  242, *242*
Tundra, 19,20, 36, *47,* 59, 81, *100,*
  112, 119, 136, *142-143, 157*
Turnagain Arm, 26

U

Uchitel, Robert, 71
Udd, Rod, *328, 329*
Udelhoven Oilfield System Services,
  Inc., 252-254, *252-254*
Umiaks, 135
Unalaska, 14
Unalaska Island, 14
Unangan, 14, 135, 136
Union Oil, 78
United Soviet Socialist Republic, 29
United States Army Corps of
  Engineers, 58
United States Army Signal Corps,
  64
United States Bureau of Indian
  Affairs, 145
United States Bureau of Land
  Management, 86
United States Department of
  Defense, 64
United States Military, 14, 28, 29,
  58, 64, 67, 78
Unmiak, 14
Unions, 201
University of Alaska,
  19, 150, 154-161
University of Alaska Anchorage,
  154, *154-155,* 185, 253,
  296-299, *296-299*
University of Alaska Anchorage
  Sinfonia, *168*
University of Alaska Museum, *150*
University of Alaska Fairbanks,
  19, *150,* 154, 157, 232, 257
University of Alaska Seawolves,
  153, 296
Uranium, 77
Usibelli Mines, 77
Utilities, 230-231, 238

V

Valdez, 19, 29, 33, 45, 49, 55, 64,
  79, 81, 82, 85, 106, *126, 127,*
  178-182, *178-182*
Valdez Convention and Civic
  Center, *179*
Valley of 10,000 Smokes,
  13, 30, 120
Value-added business, 162
Vegetables, 99-101, 103
Visions, see MultiVisions
Visitor Industry, see Tourism
Volcanoes, 30

W

Walrus, 115, 140
Washington-Alaska Military Cable
  and Telegraph System, 64
Wasilla, 19
Water and Environmental Research
  Center, 157
Waterfowl, *12, 110-111*
Water quality, 21, 284-285
Webber, John, *139*
Westall, General Tom, *196*
West Coast Tsunami Warning
  Center, 19
Western/Bering Sea Coast, 20, 135
Wetlands, *111,* 115
Wetlands, area, 10
WGM, 264-265, *264-265*
Whales, 39, 49, 115, 140, *140,*
  143, *190,* 191
Whale watching, 39
Whaling/whale hunting,
  136, *137,* 140, 143, *257*
Whitefish, 116
Whitehorse, 40, 59, 61
White Pass & Yukon Route
  Railroad, *61*
White Pass Trail, 13, 26
Whittier, 19, *28, 190-193,* 210
Wilder Construction,
  320-321, *320-321*
Wild fires, 33
Wildlife, 39, 81-82, 85, 109-115,
  123, 191

Wildlife refuges, 39
Willow Ptarmigan, 49
Winter Carnival, 19
Winter sports/recreation, 36
Wireless radio/telegraphy, 64
Wishbone Hill Coalfield, 77
Wolf, 39, 82, 109, 119
Wolverine, 110
Wood-Tikchik State Park, 125
Wooley Mammoth, 49
Work-aid program, 165
World Trade Center Alaska,
  203, 285
World War II, 14, *28,* 191, 209
Workforce, 154
Worthington Glacier State
  Recreation Area, 125
Wrangell, *10-11,* 13, *14,* 19, *118,*
  186-189
Wrangell Island, *85*
Wrangell Mountains, *265*
Wrangell Range, 125
Wrangell/St. Elias, 123

Y

Young, Alex, *276*
Yukon Quest International, 40
Yukon River, 26, 61, 200
Yukon Territory,
  26, 40, 61, 64, 123
Yu'pik Eskimos, 14, 20, 135, 136

Z

Z. J. Loussac Regional Library,
  166, *175*
Zinc, 26, 77, 262-263
Zhikharlsev, Vladimir, 36

PHOTO CREDITS

Index of Credits Not Listed With
Photos

Page 1
Courtesy of Alaska Division of
Tourism.

Pages 2 and 3
Photo by David Stratton

Page 4
Courtesy of Ketchikan Visitors
Bureau

Pages 6 and 7
Photo by Steve Holthaus

Pages 8 and 9
Photo by David Stratton

Pages 22 and 23
Photo by Steve Holthaus

Pages 34 and 35
Photo by David Stratton

Pages 50 and 51
Photo by David Stratton

Pages 62 and 63
Photo by Steve Holthaus

Pages 72 and 73
Photo by David Stratton

Pages 90 and 91
Photo by David Stratton

Pages 104 and 105
Photo by David Stratton

Pages 130 and 131
Courtesy of Wyndham Images

Pages 148 and 149
Photo by David Stratton

Pages 172 and 173
Photo by Steve Holthaus

Pages 194 and 195
Photo by Steve Holthaus

Pages 206 and 207
Courtesy of Ketchikan Visitors
Bureau

Pages 246 and 247
Photo by David Stratton

Pages 266 and 267
Courtesy of Trident Seafoods; Photo
by Bart Eaton

Pages 274 and 275
Photo by David Stratton

Pages 294 and 295
Photo by Steve Holthaus

Pages 308 and 309
Photo by David Stratton

Pages 322 and 323
Courtesy of Wyndham Images

Back Cover Images:
Photo of icicles: Photo by
Steve Holthaus
All other photos on back cover
Courtesy of Wyndham Images

Anchorage

A City Ready For A New Century

By Rick Mystrom, Mayor

Anchorage, Alaska, one of America's most livable cities, prospers and thrives in one of the world's most spectacular settings. Located in the middle of a magnificent wilderness, Anchorage prides itself on being an all-season gateway to adventure and natural beauty. But the city's greatness comes from within. It's found in its quality of life, from clean streets to beautiful facilities to a remarkable "anything-is-possible" attitude among its people.

We who live in Alaska enjoy a reputation as pioneers. This image, earned during the Gold Rush of the late 1890s, still rings true one hundred years later – but in a different sense. We no longer think of ourselves as the last frontier but eagerly look forward to the adventure of crossing the threshold to a new century to the frontier of the future.

A clue to that new frontier is our unique location. As every international pilot knows, Anchorage lies at the hub of the world population centers, closer to Europe, Asia and Russia than any other North American city. That explains why our international airport is number one in North America for air cargo. And that explains why we are becoming the international logistics center for Asia, North America and Europe and the gateway to the Russian Far East.

Welcoming business innovations

Today's Anchorage inspires those with adventure in their blood. For those ready to make business investments, we present opportunities for real financial reward. To those ready to face new challenges, Anchorage offers good wages. Sophisticated satellite and fiber optic telecommunications link us instantly to all corners of the world, and the wealth of natural resources untapped in Alaska, combined with the unrivaled beauty of the natural environment, promise a strong economy for the future.

Exceptional public assets

No other city our size in America has the combination of outstanding, modern facilities that Anchorage has. Nights and weekends are filled with cultural and sporting events in our sports arena, convention center, library, museum and performing arts center. A city of participants, Anchorage has over 30,000 residents who compete in local sports leagues.

Lowest taxes in the nation

We constructed these public buildings in the 1980's with oil revenues from Alaska's North Slope and paid for them with cash, limiting our community tax burden. Even today, we pay neither city sales tax nor state income tax. Not surprisingly, we were ranked in a 1996 survey as the city with the lowest taxes in the US.

Anchorage Museum of History and Art

ZJ Loussac Public Library

Egan Convention Center

The Sullivan Sports Arena

Quiet areas for study are found across the UAA campus.

The University of Alaska Anchorage (UAA) enters the 21st century as an innovative and dynamic metropolitan university. Accredited by the Commission on Colleges of the Northwest Association of Schools and Colleges, many of UAA's professional and technical programs — such as business, nursing, and civil engineering — are accredited by their respective associations. Based in the state's population and service center, UAA is the center of professional and technical higher education, serving over 15,000 traditional and non-traditional students at its four college campuses and extension sites located in the major cities of south-central Alaska and on various military sites.

Through teaching and learning, inquiry and discovery, and service to others, UAA strives to make profound, significant differences in the lives of its students, in the affairs of the communities in which its faculty, staff, and students live and serve, and in the professions and vocations taught. UAA offers academic programs in the liberal arts and sciences as well as in a host of professional and technical fields. Academic specialties include health and biomedical sciences, business and international trade, public policy and administration, and special education. New programs, such as logistics management, are added to the curriculum in response to community needs and opportunities. As an open-enrollment university UAA is committed to helping all students succeed with their educational goals while retaining high academic standards.

UAA's main campus is located in Anchorage with extension sites at Eagle River, Fort Richardson, and Elmendorf Air Force Base. For students residing in the Palmer-Wasilla region, Matanuska-Susitna College offers two-year degrees and certificates as well as access to baccalaureate and some advanced degrees. Students from Kodiak Island and the Kenai Peninsula are similarly served by Kodiak College, Kenai Peninsula College (KPC) and KPC's Kachemak Bay Branch in Homer. Administratively attached to UAA, Prince William Sound Community College (PWSCC) serves students in Valdez, Cordova and Copper Center. The university also serves students across Alaska via various media through the Center for Distributed Learning.

Seawolf Jim Hajdukovich scores in the Carrs Great Alaska Shootout.

Within minutes of the UAA campus, the Chugach Mountains provide year-round outdoor activities.

TEACHING

In today's world, higher education equates to lifelong learning. UAA takes its motto "We Learn for Life" seriously. Whether recently graduated from high school, making a career change, or learning for self-enrichment, UAA students have the opportunity to pursue exciting and challenging opportunities for academic excellence, vocational-technical mastery, or personal fulfillment. In all instances, students have extraordinary opportunities to learn in small classes taught by dedicated faculty. The University of Alaska Anchorage offers certificate, associate, baccalaureate, and master's degree programs and instruction in 115 major study areas. Students have access to scores of tailored short courses,

workshops, and seminars throughout the year with special summer study and conference programs offering students and faculty from around the world the opportunity to study and experience the natural grandeur of Alaska.

UAA's University Honors Program challenges academically advanced and gifted students to expand their intellect in both depth and breadth. Students desiring an international educational experience have a rich diversity of study-abroad opportunities from which to choose. UAA also offers a host of study opportunities at other universities, including, for example, a special agreement with the University of Washington School of Medicine that allows Alaskans to pursue their first year of medical training in Anchorage and their family-practice residency in cities throughout Alaska.

Three academic schools and four colleges form the base of the university's academic mission. The College of Arts and Sciences hosts over 22 academic disciplines in the natural and social sciences, the humanities, and the fine and performing arts. The Community and Technical College houses a full suite of technical, vocational and allied health programs as well as the university's Adult Learning Center which offers adult basic

education programs and the G.E.D. The College of Health, Education and Social Welfare encompasses the School of Education and the School of Nursing, as well as the departments of social work, human services, and justice. The College of Business and Public Policy offers studies in accounting, management, economics and computer information systems. The School of Engineering offers programs in geomatics, civil engineering, environmental quality and engineering management.

RESEARCH

Faculty and student research, scholarship, and creative activity are fostered across the curriculum and throughout the university. An annual Student Showcase emulates professional meetings wherein student

research and creative expressions are reviewed by faculty and culminate in a university publication. Faculty routinely win accolades for their creative works in music, theatre, and creative writing, including *The Alaska Quarterly Review*, cited by Washington Post Book World as one of the nation's top literary magazines. Scores of faculty advance the frontiers of science through their research activities sponsored by the National Institutes of Health and the National Science Foundation.

UAA capitalizes on the unique scientific and cultural opportunities and needs of Alaska through its various centers and institutes. The Environment and Natural Resources Institute; the Center for Alcohol and Addiction Studies; the Center for

The UAA campus comes alive with flowers in the summer.

A state-of-the-art radar control room simulator provides the latest in instruction for aviation students.

UAA has a beautiful new residence hall which was recently constructed to meet the growing demand for on-campus housing.

Economic Education; the Institute for Circumpolar Health Studies; the American Russian Center; the Center for Human Development: University Affiliated Program; the Justice Center; the Institute of Social and Economic Research; and the Center for Economic Development all make significant and sustained contributions to the advancement of their respective disciplines of study and to the welfare of Alaska.

Working with Providence Health System in Alaska, the university operates the Alaska Telemedicine Project that coordinates a consortium of health care providers, telecommunications carriers, and the State of Alaska, all of which are committed to enhancing the delivery of health care and medicine within the state. The School of Engineering works with compa-

nies such as Alyeska Pipeline Service Company to address arctic construction and environmental aspects of development, while UAA's state-of-the-art Aviation Technology Center works with the FAA to improve air transportation safety in Alaska. All advance UAA's mission to be of help to society by applying research knowledge and skills.

SERVICE

Providing service to the communities in which we live and work is an integral part of UAA's mission. More than 400 faculty and staff regularly lend their experience, as a public service, to various public and private groups and organizations. Students also participate in a range of internships and service-learning settings as part of their professional or technical education and training. A number of UAA centers organize formal programs of service. For example, the Small Business Development Center (SBDC) helps budding entrepreneurs create new jobs and garner millions of dollars in loans for their businesses. The BUY ALASKA program, administered by SBDC, provides sourcing services for hundreds of buying needs identified by Alaskan

businesses. The American Russian Center has over a decade of success in operating four business centers in major cities and regions of the Russian Far East, and has trained over 8,000 Russians in the theory and practice of small business enterprise.

STUDENT SERVICES

Helping students achieve their academic goals is the mission of UAA's support service. University students are supported by centers that focus on academic excellence, student health, learning resources, advising and counseling, career development, educational

Surveying students check out the lay of the land on campus.

Mainstage Theatre students prepare for a production.

opportunity, and study abroad. Other services assist students with financial aid, or special needs or interests. The African-American, Hispanic, Asian, International and Native America (AHAINA) office and Native Student Services (NSS) foster an appreciation for cultural diversity and support students of color or diverse ethnic ties. The Union of Students governs vital aspects of student life and fosters student leadership as does Club Council, which represents over 67 student interest clubs. The student-run radio station (KRUA) and newspaper, *The Northern Light*, have both won national and state awards, as has the UAA Speech and Debate team.

The new, $33 million Student Housing project, which opened in 1998, added three state-of-the-art residence halls and a Commons to the existing cluster of condo- and apartment-style student housing facilities. Student housing serves as a

hub for student activities and has enhanced a rich and diverse campus life.

Adding excitement to UAA's campus life are its intercollegiate sports programs. Nicknamed the Seawolves, University of Alaska Anchorage's athletic teams compete as members of the NCAA Division II in basketball, volleyball, gymnastics, and skiing for women, and basketball, swimming, skiing, and cross-country running for men. UAA competes in Division I ice hockey (WCHA). Seawolf teams regularly rank among the nation's best and have produced many All-American and Academic All-American performers.

A COMMUNITY RESOURCE
The University of Alaska Anchorage is a major cultural and social resource for Alaska, hosting activities as diverse as Engineering, Canada, Japan,

and Jazz weeks, the PWSCC Edward Albee Theatre Festival, and the nationally renowned Carrs' Great Alaska Shootout basketball tournament. In return, major state corporations such as Key Bank; Holland American Lines, Westours; ARCO; BP Exploration; the Anchorage Daily News; and others help to fund university programs and scholarships.

Nationally celebrated speakers regularly visit UAA campuses, and have included historian James McPherson; authors Jane Smiley, Michael Ondaatje, Richard Ford, and Tobias Wolff; linguist Noam Chomsky; psychologist Dr.

Ruth Westheimer; comedian Paula Poundstone; and historian Pierre Berton. Recent performers have included Jewel, The Reduced Shakespeare Company, and Rockapella.

Trails winding through the wooded Anchorage campus beckon summer bikers and winter cross-country skiers. With skating rinks, swimming pools, gyms and other athletic facilities around Anchorage, UAA is a rewarding place to both study and experience the Last Frontier year-round. The academic excellence and lifelong learning opportunities it offers students are as great as the state of Alaska.

UAA Chancellor Edward Lee Gorsuch, center, meets with students during the annual fall convocation.

Some people dream of flying halfway round the world to catch a once-in-a-lifetime rainbow trout, king or silver salmon. In Anchorage, that dream can be fulfilled on the way home from work.

Taking pride, taking part

Anchorage is a winning city, receiving national awards for its first class trail system and the best tasting water in America. It is a place where daily life is enriched by a wealth of year-round recreation set in a majestic landscape, and the residents are determined to keep it that way. As Mayor, I admire the pride I find in the people. Literally thousands of individuals, week-in, week-out, plant and tend pocket parks, pick up litter, coach and officiate kids' sports, promote culture and the arts, serve food to the needy, and voluntarily care for the ill and elderly.

"The City of Lights and Flowers"

I see that pride in how the city looks, highlighted in the summer with private and public gardens filled with flowers, and accented in the winter by millions of miniature, white lights, decorating public buildings and private homes throughout the city.

Creating a community of friends

To celebrate the harmony in our community, leaders from twenty-five cultural traditions joined me recently to inaugurate a citywide effort called Bridge Builders. Nearly two hundred members are building "a community of friends" among people of all races, religions and national backgrounds. These new connections among diverse people with multiple talents and perspectives help make Anchorage a friendly, caring and exciting place to live and do business.

A great place to raise a family

Anchorage's outstanding quality of life fills the community with optimism. We're proud of our dramatic drop in crime in all categories, partly the result of community policing and innovative programs such as Parent Networks, which we started here and are now being adopted nationwide.

We applaud our many outstanding teachers with the Mayor's Community Recognition of Educational And Teaching Excellence (CREATE) Awards in which top students pick their most inspirational teachers. Alternative, private and charter schools add to our fine public school system, all reasons why Anchorage was named by *Readers Digest* as one of the best places in America to raise a family.

As you can tell, I am proud of Anchorage, a healthy northern city built in harmony with resource-rich Alaska. We welcome solid investment, creative ideas and those infused with the unlimited potential of the frontier spirit. With that combination, we have not only prospered, we are becoming a model for other cities our size the world around.

With Anchorage's skyline and the Alaska Range beyond, students at the new Tyson Elementary enjoy a break. Ninety percent of our adults have high school diplomas. Sixty-five percent have attended college.